The Modern Nations in
Historical Perspective

R. W. Winks, *General Editor*

The volumes in this series deal with individual nations or groups of closely related nations throughout the world, summarizing the chief historical trends and influences that have contributed to each nation's present-day character, problems, and behavior. Recent data are incorporated with established historical background to achieve a fresh synthesis and original interpretation.

Lewis H. Gann, *the author of this volume, is a Senior Fellow at the Hoover Institution, Stanford University. He is author or coauthor of seven different works dealing respectively with the colonial history of Zambia and Rhodesia, with problems of European imperialism and white settlement in Africa, and with related questions.*

ALSO IN THE AFRICAN SUBSERIES

Egypt & the Sudan *by Robert O. Collins & Robert L. Tignor*
Morocco, Alberia, Tunisia *by Richard M. Brace*
Nigeria & Ghana *by John E. Flint*
Portuguese Africa *by Ronald H. Chilcote*
West Africa: The Former French States *by John D. Hargreaves*

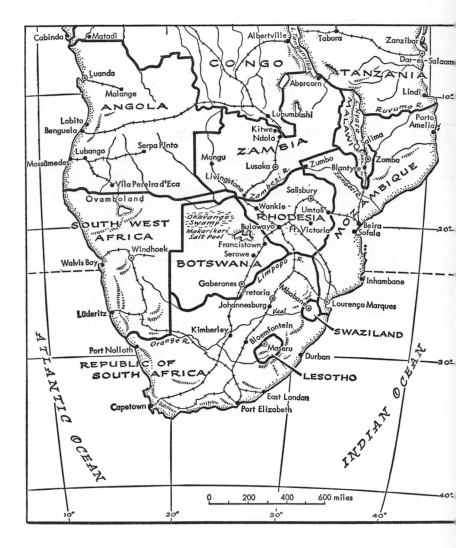

The Modern Nations in Historical Perspective

CENTRAL AFRICA
THE FORMER BRITISH STATES

LEWIS H. GANN

PRENTICE-HALL, INC. A SPECTRUM BOOK Englewood Cliffs, New Jersey

To RITA

PRENTICE-HALL INTERNATIONAL, INC. (*London*)
PRENTICE-HALL OF AUSTRALIA, PTY. LTD. (*Sydney*)
PRENTICE-HALL OF CANADA, LTD. (*Toronto*)
PRENTICE-HALL OF INDIA PRIVATE LIMITED (*New Delhi*)
PRENTICE-HALL OF JAPAN, INC. (*Tokyo*)

Foreword

Since 1965, with its unilateral declaration of independence from Great Britain, Rhodesia has posed a special challenge to those who think all the world's problems should have simple solutions. Ruled by a white minority bent upon preserving its position of economic and political superiority, Rhodesia is anathema to those who oppose racism in its many forms. Attacked by most black African states as one of the remaining strongholds in Africa for colonialism, and yet considering itself no longer to be part of any nation's colonial empire, Rhodesia is hailed by those who fear political and social radicalism more than they fear racial tensions and social inequality as one of the last refuges for sanity on the continent. But the ironies are there for all to see: many observers, normally of liberal persuasion, who would favor independent acts of defiance in the face of imperial authority, find this particular act of defiance unacceptable because it arises from the right rather than the left; many conservatives, who ordinarily might well support the regime in Rhodesia, cannot bring themselves to do so because of the act of rebellion against Britain (and, in 1970, against the Crown), which the unilateral declaration represented. Rhodesia is a special case in African politics and African history, and it requires a rather special book.

Rhodesia was not Britain's only central African colony, however. The present nations of Zambia and Malawi emerged from Northern Rhodesia and Nyasaland. They, and Southern Rhodesia, once were linked in one of Britain's abortive efforts to achieve postwar decolonization through the creation of federations, all of which—Nigeria, Malaysia, the West Indies, Southern Arabia, and the Central African—have either failed or show signs of doing so. Malawi has accommodated itself to the realities of the power centers of southern Africa, while Zambia has aligned itself clearly with the black majority of the west, central, and eastern parts of the continent. The three areas are thus in striking contrast to each other, representing three possible approaches toward viable nationhood in Africa. To find all three examined within a single book is, therefore, particularly rewarding.

This volume forms a part of two subseries within the Modern Nations in Historical Perspective. It may be read together with the other volumes on Africa, five of which have appeared to date (on Nigeria and Ghana, Portuguese Africa, the former French West African states, Egypt and the Sudan, and Morocco, Algeria, and Tunisia), with five more to come; or as a contribution to the subseries on the Commonwealth, in which volumes on Australia, New Zealand, India, Ceylon, Nigeria and Ghana, Egypt and the Sudan, Ireland, and the West Indies have appeared, with six yet to be published. Dr. Gann's work is a contribution of importance to both subjects.

Many readers will take exception to some of the interpretations offered by this study. Indeed, the general editor does so. But they are interpretations which are entitled to be heard, and they are presented with a forthright vigor which should make this short history of former British Central Africa a focus for discussion for some time to come.

Robin W. Winks
Series Editor

Preface

In asking me to write a volume on the former British states of Central Africa, the editor of this series specified a short, readable book that would explain the historical forces responsible for shaping Central Africa. Many scholars have already written on various aspects of this subject. What was required of me was not therefore so much original research as an exercise in compression. The editor asked for a fresh synthesis and an original interpretation. I accepted with alacrity, for I underestimated the difficulties that beset me in my task.

Had this book been written a few years ago, or had it been concerned with some specialized question such as the introduction of the potato into Mashonaland, this preface would have been short. It would have contained little more beyond the customary acknowledgments, and a deserved word of appreciation to my wife for having endured endless historical monologues while this work was in process. However, in the face of postcolonial sensitivities regarding so many facets in the study of Africa, I could no longer stop there. As a teacher I am aware of the demands that are now being made by many students. Existing values are being challenged and accepted credentials rejected. "Historical objectivity" has come under attack for being a scholar's daydream at its best and an ideological weapon for oppression at its worst. Academicians are being rigidly categorized as the product of a particular era and a particular social class. And their research, involving as it does, a process of selection, imposes a bias on the study of history. In an attempt to escape from outdated historical habit, the professor is enjoined to unmask the crimes of imperialism and provide a creed for rebels. Academicians, we are told, must stand in the battle line during the coming struggle for the liberation of mankind; books have a part to play, as much as bombs and bullets.

Central Africa, the argument goes on, is a particularly important field, a region where whites have fought with blacks in the past and where racial clashes will continue in the future. The historiography of South and Central Africa, some believe, should indeed best be left to blacks. Black men have a better understanding of black suffering and black aspirations than whites. Blacks alone are devoid of the ethnocentric bias and the cultural imperialism that invalidates white scholarship.

I do not share any of these assumptions, and in fairness to my readers my own position as an historian should be made perfectly explicit. I am, in certain respects, the product of the colonial era. I have served in a colonial administration, and have done much of my scholarly work in institutions that were founded at the initiative of British imperialists. I reject neither my academic nor my professional past. Far from feeling indicted by the company I have kept, I find much of value in these associations. African studies in general owe an immeasurable debt to the by-products of European conquest. (The scholars who accompanied Napoleon's expedition to Egypt laid the foundations of Egyptology. The "New Imperialism" produced bodies like the Institut Français de l'Afrique Noire, the former Rhodes-Livingstone Institute and the National Museum of Rhodesia, which have played an essential part in the creation of African studies.) Colonial intellectuals like Lord Hailey or Maurice Delafosse can stand comparison with the best minds of the postcolonial era. Their contributions retain its value.

As regards historiography in general, I do not believe that the history of Europeans in Africa can be separated from African history proper. A comparable division would not be acceptable in other historical fields. For instance, the activities of a French prefect in the *département* of Donnersberg (a German Rhineland area temporarily annexed to France during the Napoleonic era) form part of German, as well as French, history. Similarly, the construction of a railway or a mine in Northern Rhodesia belongs to British, as much as to Zambian, economic history. The story of such enterprise is as important to Zambia as the story of, say, a tribal migration.

In debating the record of empires, I am perfectly conscious of the seamy side of colonialism. But the British conquerors of Rhodesia, unlike, for instance, the Ndebele before them, were victors with a difference. Unlike their predecessors, they brought in an entirely new technology, new methods of production that vastly increased the real wealth of the country and its people. Western imperialism as a whole entailed a far-reaching process of cultural transfusion. This is a phenomenon which, on the whole, I welcome. I see no reason to idealize the preindustrial past, in Africa, or anywhere else.

My disinclination to idealize preindustrial societies is matched with an unwillingness to indulge in romanticism when treating historical themes. Revolutionary episodes are peculiarly vulnerable to historical lionization. To my mind, revolutions may be right or wrong, but they are not romantic. The glories, the suffering, the unspeakable boredom of revolutionary wars are qualities common to all wars. To clothe them in colorful trappings is to distort an important aspect of reality. As a historian, I try to understand—among other things—why the British empire fell. As a citizen, I derive no satisfaction from its demise. Parenthetically, I am not surprised that its collapse should have led to bitter conflicts between Hindus and Muslims in India, Turks and Greeks in Cyprus, Jews and Arabs in Palestine, Ibo and Hausa in Nigeria. Their heirs of empire naturally struggle over the colonial legacy, as whites and black nationalists now clash in Central Africa.

In the field of race relations I have attempted to acquire what might be called stereoscopic vision of social relations in a country like Rhodesia which is split by customs, class and color. I do not pretend that I have found this an easy task. Like anyone else, I have approached it with certain preconceptions. I do not find the mere existence of a plural society as shocking as do many of my academic colleagues. Historically speaking, plural societies have been the rule rather than the exception. I do not believe, moreover, in the notion of primitive social equality. Many ancient kingdoms, like those of the Ndebele, the Tutsi or the Langobards were based on extreme distinctions in status.

In treating the history of Central Africa, I am inevitably influenced by social milieu. I understand and appreciate the emergence of black nationalism, and I am conscious of the limitations that beset white Rhodesia. But as a European, I am sympathetic to white Rhodesians and their problems; this attachment has been reinforced by long residence in the country. I see no merit in the view, now widespread in many university departments, that denies the settlers' historical function, and looks upon them as parasites who led lives of lazy lanquor, punctuated only by fits of energetic repression. The earlier encounters between Bantu warriors of the Early Iron Age and British empire builders of the late nineteenth century strike me as essentially tragic events, similar in a sense to confrontations between Agamemnon, Achilles and their lieges on the one hand, and Californian "Forty Niners" on the other. The British won, for fate decreed their victory.

The Europeans created new colonial societies where white and blacks met both in cooperation and conflict.

In planning my book, I have followed the general arrangement used by other writers in this series. I start off with a general section about the country, its problems and its people. I then attempt to trace the history of Central Africa from its beginnings. I pass on to a chapter where I endeavor to deal with the difficulties that face the three states in the present. I conclude my book with a bibliographical note covering works on Central Africa in the English language which the librarian of a smaller college might reasonably be asked to buy. Elsewhere I provide reference sources only where I cite at length from other works, or where a specific statement might appear peculiar or challenging.

Finally, I should like to express my appreciation to Professor Peter Duignan, Clyde Mitchell and George Shepperson, who have read drafts of this work. All opinions expressed, and any mistakes that have occurred, are of course purely my own. I am likewise greatly obliged to Miss Mildred Teruya, who typed my manuscript, assisted with editorial changes and advice—always with unfailing good sense and good humor.

                                                    Lewis H. Gann

Contents

1

The Land

Few geographical designations have been used as indiscriminately as the term "Central Africa." Early mapmakers used to cover the blank spaces of the "Dark Continent" with mysterious kingdoms, strange animals, and exotic mountains situated somewhere in "Central Africa." Later the name did duty for a variety of more specifically designed regions. Today there is a Central African Republic situated north of the Ubangi River and west of Cameroun. Its official language is French. In the past, geographers have also referred to British Central Africa. The term is unfortunate, for the countries that used to make up British Central Africa do not lie in the center but in the south east central portion of the continent.

The boundaries of British Central Africa have expanded and contracted with the varying fortunes of politics. At the end of the last century, cartographers designated the regions now included within the Republic of Zambia (formerly the British Protectorate of Northern Rhodesia) and within the Republic of Malawi (formerly the British Protectorate of Nyasaland) as British Central Africa. Later, Nyasaland for a time became known as the British Central Africa Protectorate. During the last stages of British rule in Africa, from 1953 to 1963, there was an ill-fated association of states officially known as the Federation of Rhodesia and Nyasaland. It included Zambia, Malawi, and Rhodesia (formerly known as Southern Rhodesia). This hybrid state was often

1

referred to as the British Central African Federation, but none of its people ever referred to themselves as Central Africans, as people south of the Limpopo River style themselves South Africans. Herein lay one of its inescapable weaknesses and the federation only lasted for a single decade. Today the term "British Central Africa" is only of historical interest.

Rhodesia, Malawi, and Zambia cover a huge geographic area. Zambia extends over 290,587 square miles; it is somewhat larger than Texas and three times the size of Great Britain. Rhodesia has 150,820 square miles; it is slightly smaller than California, and bigger than both West and East Germany. Malawi spreads over 49,177 square miles and is comparable in extent with Pennsylvania or, to use an example drawn from Europe, with Czechoslovakia. The small inset maps used by newspaper editors do not give foreign readers any idea of the distances in Central Africa. A tourist who takes a train from Cape Town on the southern tip of South Africa to Lusaka, the capital of Zambia, has a long, weary journey before him. He will have to travel almost 1,400 miles. His trip will take him as far as from London to Libya in North Africa or from New York to South Dakota. Yet this is nothing compared with the route from Zambia to the northern coast of Africa, which is the distance from Canada to England.

The climate, vegetation, and scenery of Central Africa bear little resemblance to the Africa of fiction—the imagined land of giant jungles overhung with huge creepers, where Tarzan performed his improbable feats. There is not a great deal of tropical rain forest in Southern Africa; indeed, less than one-tenth of the entire continent is covered by jungle. The "great grey-green Limpopo," the river separating the Republic of South Africa and Rhodesia, is not "greasy," as Kipling's poetry would have it.

Central and Southern Africa, on the contrary, consist of a series of vast tablelands. A resident of Salisbury, capital of Rhodesia, lives at an elevation of more than 5,000 feet. But he dwells on top of a plateau, and has no more of an impression of height than a farmer plowing a Dakota wheatfield. Much of the Rhodesian landscape consists of undulating bush, which ranges from open parkland to arid steppe. The veld is broken by rivers which for the most part flow in an irregular fashion, depending on the rains. The downpours usually start in November and continue until about March. They transform the parched veld into a sea of green, which seems to stretch on without end to the burnished blue horizons beyond.

The Central African landscape varies a great deal. A visitor who motors from Salisbury towards Inyanga in the so-called Eastern Highlands comes to a country that will remind him more of Scotland than Africa. There are rolling plateaus covered with short grass and ferns, and broken by cliffs and waterfalls. The rivers and streams are stocked with rainbow trout. Much of the region is clothed in man-made forests whose trees are almost as cosmopolitan in their origin as the people; there are pines from Mexico and the Himalayas, and wattle from Australia, whose dark green foliage and golden flowers give a characteristic touch to many a hillside. And over the scene splendidly looms Inyangani, Rhodesia's highest mountain, over 8,500 feet above sea level.

A traveler who makes his way northward from Salisbury to the Zambezi will see scenery of a very different kind. When he descends from the plateau into the lowveld (lowlands), he enters a harsh land where malaria is rife and where the bush is studded with sinister-looking "fever trees," their bark a pale greenish-white. Even more extraordinary are the baobabs—tough, gnarled, massive trees that can withstand dust and droughts, heat and cold. Their trunks look enormous; their branches reach toward the sky like twisted pieces of surrealist iron work. Africans say that God, in a fit of anger, stuck them upside down in the soil, their roots sticking up, because he did not like his own handiwork.

Further north lies the Zambezi River, which flows from northwestern Zambia to the Indian Ocean and is one of Africa's greatest water courses. The Zambezi is about 1,600 miles long, eight times as long as the River Thames. It rises in a grove on the watershed that lies along the boundary between Zambia and the Democratic Republic of the Congo (formerly the Belgian Congo). Twisting and turning, the river reaches the torrid Barotse flood plain and then continues on its way to the sea, checked by narrows and rapids that prevent navigation over most of its course. (The most spectacular of these breaks is formed by Victoria Falls, one of the natural wonders of the world.) The Zambezi flows through an apparently limitless plain covered by bush where there is no hint of a cleft. But in its course it meets a number of deep, narrow cracks. After countless millennia, the river has scoured out a deep gorge, and it rushes down in giant waterfalls. Statisticians calculate that their total width is about 1,900 yards; their greatest height, 355 feet; and that during the flood season, an average of 120,000,000 gallons of water crash down every minute. These figures, however, give no impression of the immensity of the falls, the mist of spray, the roar of the rainbow splendor, and the sense of limitless power conveyed by the great crashing wall of white water.

Further downstream the strength of the Zambezi has been harnessed by the Kariba Dam. Four hundred twenty feet high and 2,000 feet long, it has changed the face of nature and even the very climate, by creating

a man-made lake, some 175 miles long, with a water-holding capacity
four times that of Lake Mead at the Hoover Dam in the United States.
The Kariba hydroelectric turbines now supply Rhodesia and Zambia
with cheap power on a large scale. The "white gold" provided by the
Zambezi is one of Central Africa's greatest modern assets.

To the north of the Zambezi, the greater part of Zambia is a plateau,
some 3,000 to 5,000 feet above sea level. Its flat surface is broken by
small hills. The scenery results from countless ages of erosion which
have worn away the underlying crystalline rock containing the bulk of
the country's immense wealth in copper and other metals. The moun-
tainous northeastern corner of the land rises in places to over 7,000
feet, overlooking the western edge of the Great Rift Valley. But these
highlands are isolated by the low-lying, hot, and unhealthy Luangwa
Valley.

Zambia has a great variety of vegetation. A large proportion of
the country's surface does not support tree growth, and perhaps something like 40 percent of the country consists of grassland or swamp.
But there is also a great deal of open parkland, with trees of many
kinds. In the drier regions of the south, vegetation is more stunted.
Thick thorn bushes and sparse, coarse grass cover the veld, except in
the valleys and river depressions where there is sufficient water to permit denser woodland. In the north and east, the rains become heavier,
and parkland merges into forest.

Northeastern Zambia gives rise to the Congo River. Its headwaters
issue from the hills north of Isoka and run southwest under the name
of Chambezi to the vast Bangweulu swamps and lake, where tall reeds
grow in profusion. The effluent from this great watery expanse is called
the Luapula, which runs in a wide semicircle, forming part of the
boundary of the Congo Republic, where it joins Lake Mweru of the
Zambian boundary. The lake is drained by the Luvua River, which
eventually becomes the Congo, one of the greatest rivers in the world.

Malawi, to the east of Zambia, is dominated by Lake Malawi, a
great expanse of water about 350 miles long. A ship that steams from
its extreme north to its farthest south travels about as far as a vessel
that goes from London to the northern shore of Germany or from
Chicago, at the southern end of Lake Michigan, to the Canadian
border. The lake can be treacherous, with fierce storms and heavy
rollers. It can also be indescribably beautiful, as the changing color of
the sunlight tints the surface with blue and silver. Everywhere, great
mountains overhang the lake; indeed much of Malawi consists of plateaus and highlands that range from 3,000 to 10,000 feet. Malawi's

main river is the Shire, which flows southward and later joins the Zambezi.

Public relations men call Malawi "Central Africa's Switzerland," and parts of the country are indeed a tourist's paradise. Lake Malawi itself is almost an inland ocean. And on the Mlanje Mountains, and in parts of the northern highlands, hikers can make their way through splendid cedar forests. The rains are plentiful and the ground is covered with moss where anemones and primulas burst out in color. The trees are tall and straight. The air is cool and bracing. There is a fresh smell of resin in the atmosphere. Big boulders cover the mountainsides, interspersed with Alpine flowers. Streams and rivulets run down the hillsides, and a man might imagine himself a thousand miles away from Africa.

The lower-lying parts of Malawi look very different; here as elsewhere, the type of vegetation is largely determined by the amount of rainfall. Much of the country is covered by open woodland. We are back in the characteristic African bush, which looks grim and forbidding in the midday glare but may glow in varying tints of gold and purple at the rising and setting of the sun. The more arid plains are covered with knobthorns, acacias, and baobab trees. Going to the Shire River, tourists will see some typical vegetation—great groves of borassus palms that rise above banks fringed with reeds and papyrus, clumps of tropical forest clothed in richest greens. At a distance, hazy blue mountains stand out against a translucent sky that seems to stretch onwards to the ends of the earth.

Central Africa then is a land of infinite variety. There are pine-covered mountains where mists hide the peaks and where a camper feels chilled to the bones when he scrambles out of his sleeping bag in the morning. There are immense river plains where periodic floods dominate the farmer's life and crops grow in profusion. There are arid steppes where the scenery conveys a sense of hopeless melancholy and only the toughest plants survive.

But all the states of Central Africa have certain features in common. Like most other parts of the continent, the area is poorly served with natural communications. The rivers are navigable only in part, or not at all. In the nineteenth century some Europeans dreamed of using the Zambezi as a great natural waterway into the interior, but they were sorely disappointed, for the seasonal flow of the Zambezi varies. Its upper basin is subject to floods. Where it empties into the Mozambique Channel the river forms a delta, and its mouths are obstructed by sand bars. The Kebrabasa Falls prevent steamers from traveling upstream, and though some portions of the river can be used for internal transportation, these stretches are short.

Central Africa moreover, is landlocked. Rhodesian exporters have to send their goods to the ports of Beira and Lourenço Marques on the coast of Mozambique, a Portuguese colony flanking the Indian Ocean, or alternately, all the way down to South Africa. Zambians likewise make use of Beira and the southern route. If they wish to avoid these outlets, they must send their exports to Lobito Bay, a harbor on the coast of Angola, a thousand miles from the Copper Belt, the heart of Zambia's mining country. Zambia is now constructing a railway from the Copper Belt to the shore of Tanzania on the Indian Ocean. But this project (which is being carried out with Chinese help) is a tremendously difficult undertaking, and the line will have to go more than 900 miles before it reaches the sea.

Much, though by no means all, of Central Africa suffers from scanty or irregular rainfall; hence the uncertainty of precipitation adds to the farmer's manifold worries. Sometimes there is too little rain, sometimes too much. Then the dry river beds turn into raging torrents; rich soil may be swept away, and in many parts of Africa the fertility of the soil is diminished by leaching.

A large part of Central Africa is also beset by tropical diseases. In the past there was no defense against plagues like malaria or bilharzia. Indigenous mortality was high, and in many areas it remains so. And plague survivors often suffered from endemic sicknesses that reduce their natural vitality. Sickness is also apt to strike at cattle, and only in the present century have veterinarians discovered means of coping with such diseases. The dreaded tsetse fly still abounds; fly belts often formed formidable barriers to invading pastoralists who probably traveled along well-defined routes, which varied as the fly belts shifted. Much of Central Africa once teemed with game. Elephants, giraffes, zebras, antelopes, and many other species offered a livelihood to hunters. But when Arab merchants and European hunters introduced guns to Africa, the balance of nature was upset; moreover, game cannot roam where farmers fence their land. In Rhodesia, one might add, an ill-conceived campaign to eradicate the tsetse fly by killing off game has added to the destruction of wild life, and visitors today rarerly see any of the great beasts outside a nature reserve.

Experts worry about the population explosion and fear that one day there may not be enough land for all the people in the world. In Central Africa, at first sight, such fears look unfounded. In 1969 the total population of the region, which is comparable in size to Western

Europe, was slightly less than that of Czechoslovakia. (Czechoslovakia has an area of 49,371 square miles, slightly larger than Malawi's; its population in 1968 was 14,500,000.) But much of Central Africa's soils lack fertility; the rains may be insufficiently plentiful or too irregular. But above all, there is the problem of land. Land shortage is a relative matter that depends on a great number of factors. A community may be short of land if the balance between traditional methods of agriculture and traditional ratios between soil and population is upset; if there is not enough capital; if there is not enough skilled labor to improve farming methods; if enterprise is discouraged by archaic modes of land ownership or by inept government policies; or if markets and communications are insufficient to provide incentives for more intensive methods of cultivating the land. A region that may seem almost empty to a European, used to the farming practices of England or Holland, may in fact, in relative terms, be overpopulated. The population may have become too large in relation to the available acreage so that fallow lands no longer have sufficient time to recuperate before they once more come under the plow. According to some experts, Central Africa is already overpopulated, and a new agricultural revolution or indeed several revolutions will be required if future generations of Africans are to feed themselves.

Much of the foregoing is perhaps somewhat speculative, but one thing is certain: all three Central African governments have to cope with a steep rate of population increase. Statistics, especially those of earlier periods, are admittedly most unreliable. But it seems likely that, since the beginning of the present century, the indigenous peoples have kept doubling their numbers about every generation. Rhodesia today contains more than 5,000,000 people. Zambia's and Malawi's populations amount to just over 4,000,000 each. Central Africa's economic potential remains very promising. Great changes, however, will be required to feed future generations. At present it seems impossible that —even in the remote future—the apparently limitless acres of Central Africa could ever support a population the size of that of Western Europe today.

The picture, however, is by no means completely bleak. The Central African countries have a good many natural advantages. There is a great deal of hydroelectric power, both used and unused. Central Africa moreover has enormous mineral riches. The deposits of Malawi comprise bauxite, coal, limestone, and graphite—all of which have hardly been touched. Zambia is one of the world's greatest copper producers. Though mining costs have vastly risen, the country continues to occupy an enviable position, for the world's automobile and electrical industries, as well as related enterprises, require enormous amounts of the red metal. Zambia also has lead, zinc, and other base metals. Rhodesia boasts of the greatest Central African coal deposit (situated at Wankie); it also mines copper, gold, asbestos, chrome, nickel, and other valuable raw materials.

2

The People

The Background

When the Second World War ended, the British Empire in Africa seemed more entrenched than ever. In the existing British colonies, British power seemed unchallenged; in addition, British troops as well as units drawn from the Empire had conquered Ethiopia and Libya from the Italians. Most colonial statesmen believed that untold years would pass before the sun of empire would set in Africa. Yet less than twenty years after the end of the war, the British Empire had become an anachronism. Most African colonies had gained independence, and Central Africa had also been partially engulfed by the anticolonial tide.

In 1964 Malawi (formerly Nyasaland) and Zambia (previously Northern Rhodesia) became sovereign states and members of the United Nations. Rhodesia (previously Southern Rhodesia) continued to occupy a constitutionally unusual position as a "self-governing colony," and remained subject to the rule of its local white electorate. Zambians began proudly to display their new banner—green, inset with red, black and gold, with a majestic fish eagle. The Malawi colors fluttered from party and government buildings—black, red, and green, with a rising sun in the middle.

But neither Zambia nor Malawi, much less Rhodesia, as yet constituted united or homogeneous nations. Some of the indigenous people would not have recognized their own flags at the time of independence.

Zambians and Malawians continued to speak a great variety of African tongues; while English, perhaps the main cultural legacy from the colonial era, remained the official language, the idiom of higher education, science, and government. Zambia and Malawi only gradually began to acquire a sense of territorial identity, but the older social divisions remain important. Banda's opponents from Malawi accuse the president of pandering to Chewa nationalism. In Zambia the Bemba now occupy a stronger position than they did at any other time in their modern history, and conceivably, the forces of ethnic rivalry in the country might well become even stronger as time goes on.

As a result of independence, Zambia and Malawi have become subject to African governance. The new ruling stratum is made up of politicians, senior civil servants, high party functionaries, and other members of the so-called "administrative bourgeoisie." The gap between the living standards enjoyed respectively by the new leaders, civil and military, remains as great as in the days of colonial rule. Indeed within the white community, the settler society of Rhodesia, is in certain respects more egalitarian than the emergent postcolonial society of independent Africa.[1]

In Malawi, the new political "salariat" came to rule through a one party system; all power now rests with the dominant Malawi Congress Party. The army remains small and the soldiers are kept in check by political commissars. For its internal security, the country depends above all on the Youth Wing of the ruling party, and on the police. The cautiously liberal impulses at work immediately before and after independence was gained has provided opportunities for some degree of legitimate political controversy. There were various trade unions and political groups; most of these produced their own mimeographed or printed magazines. In 1964, however, Malawi went through a political crisis. A group of ministers became disenchanted with the existing system of personal rule, with the manner in which government patronage was being exercised, and with the slow pace of Africanization. The army and the bulk of the ruling party remained loyal to the government. The principal dissidents fled from the country. But open political debate was muted. By 1970 most of the former political publications had become defunct. Even the Malawi Congress Party turned out little except a constitution and a newspaper. Overt political controversy had largely

---

[1] To give an example, in 1967, the ratio between the salary received respectively by a black private and a colonel in Malawi was roughly one to twenty-three; the equivalent ratio in Zambia was one to fifteen. The ratio between a *white* private and colonel in Rhodesia was roughly one to six. (The figures of course are not strictly comparable, because of differences in allowances, "perks," and other factors.)

disappeared. Dr. Hastings Kamuzu Banda, a physician turned states-man, had in many ways become like an old-fashioned monarch. His birthday, Kamuzu Day, had become an occasion for obligatory public rejoicing; and his personal predilections had come to count at every level of government.

Malawi continues to rely largely on agriculture. The indigenous economy cannot provide enough jobs for all the villagers; hence Mala-wian workmen still travel south to Rhodesia and South Africa in search of higher wages. Being a landlocked country, Malawi also remains de-pendent on the port of Beira in Portuguese East Africa; the country therefore cooperates with the white governments of Portugal, Rhodesia, and South Africa in a manner hateful to most other African govern-ments. Malawi also has put forward demands for Zambian and Tan-zanian territory, an offensive claim in a postcolonial Africa that insists on the sanctity of the colonial frontiers. Banda moreover made himself bitterly unpopular among many African statesmen by frankly insisting that African armies could not fight the Rhodesians; where essentials were concerned, he preferred *realpolitik* to rhetoric.

Banda also alienated many Africans by frankly rejecting all forms of African socialism and by extolling the advantages of free enterprise. Socialism, according to Banda, was a way of ordering society which only rich countries with highly sophisticated economies, or states subject to absolute dictatorships might afford. But black capitalism of the Malawi variety would not have appealed to conventional free traders such as Adam Smith. Banda was determined to defend the interests of the African petty bourgeoisie by eliminating white, and above all, Indian traders from rural commerce—acting on the old assumption that the loss sustained by one ethnic group must be the gain of another.

By 1970 Zambia was in an infinitely stronger position than Malawi. With its huge mineral resources, especially copper, it was one of the wealthiest states in Sub-Saharan Africa.[2] At the end of the 1960s Zambia still maintained a multiparty system. The African National Congress (which drew much of its strength from the Tonga people along the central rail line) was permitted to function as a legal, albeit ineffective, opposition. But in actual practice the governing United National Inde-pendence Party (UNIP) exercised a monopoly of power. Faced with regional and ethnic opposition in Barotseland (in western Zambia), the government banned the United Party, which tried to express Lozi op-position to governance from Lusaka.

[2] Zambia is the world's third largest copper producer, coming after the United States and the Soviet Union.

The Lozi (Barotse) of the Western Province and the Tonga of the Central Province also had other grievances. Zambia sought to disengage herself from the "white" south. Lozi labor migrants were prohibited from seeking work in South Africa on the grounds that Zambians were subjected to inhuman treatment in the land of apartheid. However, since there was little alternative employment for them in Zambia, Lusaka's policy occasioned much discontent, especially at a period when the natural fertility of the Upper Zambezi Valley seemed to decline.

At the same time Zambia tried to redirect its trade to the shores of East Africa. Italian engineers built an oil pipeline from the copper belt to Dar es Salaam, and Italian entrepreneurs received favorable civil and military contracts at the expense of Zambia's British suppliers. In 1969 Communist China arranged with Zambia for the construction of a railway line from the copper belt to the Indian Ocean, so that Zambia would no longer have to depend on the Rhodesian system. The realignment of trade and communications, however, seemed to favor the Bemba of the northeast at the expense of the western communities. Hence Zambia faced severe internal tensions. (Before 1911, Northern Rhodesia had in fact consisted of two territories, North Eastern Rhodesia and North Western Rhodesia, which the British administered independently of each other.) Since Zambian politicians had to cope with a good deal of discontent, many UNIP supporters began to argue that Zambia could not afford the luxury of parliamentary opposition and that Zambia should become a one-party state like Malawi.

Despite all these difficulties, Zambians also had solid ground for a sense of achievement. There was an incipient growth of national pride. Education and many other public services had expanded since independence. Secondary industry turned out all manner of new manufactured goods. Between 1965 and 1967 Zambia's gross national product had grown in an impressive fashion. (The annual growth rate amounted to 9.5 percent, one of the highest in Africa and in the world at large.) Regional separatism was held in check by the desire of all provinces to share in the wealth of the Copper Belt. The multiplicity of ethnic communities itself stood in the way of effective tribal independence movements. Politicians were forced to form intertribal alliances of a nontraditional kind. The Lozi thus sought cooperation with the Ila and the Tonga of central Zambia, and with the Ngoni of the east. The Bemba in turn looked for agreements with other groups. Zambia as a whole faced Rhodesia on the other side of the Zambezi, and had to meet the challenge of making itself less dependent on the former Rhodesian connection. Despite some bitter political struggles, despite a good deal of inefficiency in high and low places alike, the machinery of administration created by the British continued to function fairly effectively. Above all, the army (numbering just over 4,000 men in 1970) had not as yet become sufficiently strong or politically effective to stage a *coup* of the kind familiar in West Africa. During the heyday of the colonial era, major political decisions had hinged to a considerable extent on the top layer of the British colonial bureaucracy and on the personality of the Governor, while local affairs were affected to a considerable extent by the doings of the local district commissioner, "the man on the spot." Postcolonial politics in Zambia and Malawi to some extent reverted to the politics of bureaucracy, with the difference that decisions no longer depended on a civil service headed by British expatriates, but on internal struggles within the respective ruling parties. The new elite depended heavily on political and party patronage for advancement. At the same time, the governments faced serious economic problems. Villagers continued to drift into the towns, and there was growing urban unemployment. Standards of efficiency in many public services had declined. Kenneth Kaunda, the Zambian president, bitterly complained that since independence the country had been forced to cope both with a sharp drop in labor productivity and a serious increase in prices and wages. According to Kaunda, absenteeism in industry, drunkenness, and nepotism had all grown apace, and investment had suffered.[3] Nevertheless, economic progress in Zambia continued. The country's secondary industries kept advancing. By 1970 few could doubt that provided the country retained its political cohesion, it would have a bright economic future.

Rhodesia remained under the governance of its local European population. Indeed the very name of the country had become a subject of political controversy. The whites had called their territory Rhodesia to commemorate the name of Cecil John Rhodes, the man who had added the country to the British Empire. Black nationalists, on the other hand, preferred to recall Zimbabwe, harking back to the splendor of an ancient African Iron Age kingdom. The quarrel about names was actually symptomatic of a much deeper rift. Since 1890 whites had settled in Rhodesia as permanent colonists. In 1923 the Europeans attained almost unfettered internal autonomy, and Rhodesia became —in the strange language of the day—a self-governing colony. White rule depended on a political partnership between Great Britain, the imperial suzerain, and the local Europeans who dominated the voter rolls.

In the late 1950s the Anglo-Rhodesian partnership collapsed. In

[3] *New York Times*, January 30, 1970.

1962 the old Rhodesian establishment lost power. The Rhodesian right wing, reorganized as the Rhodesian Front, gained an electoral victory so stunning that even the most ardent Rhodesian Front supporters stood agape. In 1965 a Rhodesian government headed by Ian Smith proclaimed the country's unilateral independence from Great Britain. White Rhodesians, supposedly the staunchest of British royalists, bade good-bye to the Queen, hauled down the Union Jack, and raised their own banner of green, white, and green—colors strangely chosen on the grounds that they were light resistant and would not fade in Rhodesia's sunny clime.[4] In 1970 the Rhodesian settlers turned their country into a republic, left the Commonwealth, and firmly aligned themselves with South Africa.

We shall return to these issues in a subsequent section of the book; at this point it is sufficient to say that an oligarchy continues to function in an effective manner and that the parliamentary system survives in Rhodesia. Also the Europeans conceded some degree of minority representation to those blacks who were willing to cooperate in the system. African demands for political advancement hinged on extending the franchise. The franchise retained its importance because the electoral system continued to operate and was not replaced by the single-party system of a "national unity" bloc, whereby the people had suffrage but no choice. The Europeans said they would ultimately permit Africans to gain parity in Parliament, but at the same time, Smith insisted that increased parliamentary representation would be linked to the Africans' contribution as taxpayers. Europeans, however, paid the bulk of the country's imposts. Hence political advancement for Africans would be an exceedingly slow process.[5]

In resisting sanctions and diplomatic pressure from abroad, Rhodesia enjoyed various unforeseen advantages. The Rhodesians had never yielded to the temptation of using the civil service as a means of exercising political patronage. The quality of the Rhodesian civil service remained high. Rhodesia did not suffer from widespread graft, which interfered with governmental efficiency in so many African countries. Rhodesia also enjoyed the benefit of having a small and cohesive bureaucracy.

[4] *Rhodesian Commentary*, Vol. 2, November 11, 1968 (Salisbury: Government Printer).

[5] In 1969 the Rhodesian Front accepted a new set of constitutional proposals. It provided for a national Parliament consisting of fifty members elected by a mainly European electorate, and sixteen African members. Of the latter, eight would be elected; eight would be nominated by chiefs and headmen. African membership in the House would gradually rise in proportion to the amount of income tax paid by Africans. In addition, the constitution provided for a Senate of ten whites, ten blacks, and three persons of either color nominated by the head of state.

Decisions could be taken quickly; communications did not clog up in a complex bureaucratic jungle, as they so often did in Great Britain. The army and the police retained an unusual degree of efficiency. The Rhodesian army, when mobilized, mainly represented the white electorate in arms. The Rhodesian, like the South African army, thus turned out to be one of the few military forces on the African continent that were never likely to stage a *coup d'état*. By 1970 disrupting the Rhodesian army represented an apparently insoluble military problem to its opponents. The European's morale moreover stood high. They did not suffer from a crisis of conscience. When attacked for their privileges, the Europeans retorted that they paid the bulk of the country's taxes and supplied most of its capital and technical skill. When censured for their political methods, the Europeans pointed to the civil strife that had beset so many African countries. The Zambezi seemed to have become a boundary between two worlds. The so-called tide of history suddenly stood frozen in its course.

On the face of it, Zambia on the one hand and Rhodesia on the other had nothing in common. Zambia, like Malawi, was governed by a black elite of civil servants and party functionaries. The Rhodesian government derived its support from an alliance between the bulk of the white middle class, the white workers, and black chiefs. The Rhodesians put their trust in the free enterprise system and tried to encourage both foreign investment and immigration. The Zambians, on the other hand, tried to find their own form of African socialism (known as "Zambian Humanism"). This rested on an enforced partnership between the government and the foreign investors in the mining industry. In 1969 Kaunda announced that the state would acquire 51 percent of the stock in the two main copper-mining trusts, the Anglo-American Corporation (dominated above all by South African interests) and the Rhodesian Selection Trust (which was principally linked to American capital).

In 1970, the Zambian government established a far-reaching measure of control over banking, insurance, building societies, trade, and various other enterprises. But for all its rhetoric, Zambian Humanism, in practice, implied an alliance between the state and certain specially favored financial groups. This partnership tended to reduce the possibility for successful strikes in mining. It provided the mining companies with extra liquid funds derived from compensation payments, thereby enabling large corporations to broaden their field of operations.* This

* For a statement concerning the advantages obtained by mining investors through Zambianization, see for instance, Zambian Anglo-American Limited: Extract

would turn out to be perhaps a valuable advantage for mining companies whose deposits are naturally a wasting asset. At the same time the number of positions available for political patronage increased. For the consumer at large, as against the newly privileged stratum of party and state officials, Zambian Humanism was not likely to have much relevance. State control, moreover, was likely to increase costs in fields such as the marketing of crops and fertilizers, and apt to put an extra burden on the shoulders of the peasants, while providing more opportunities for political intimidation and favoritism.

But despite these differences in outlook and policy among the three territories, they had much in common. As we have seen before, all of them were imperial creations. The new rulers continue to use the English language. Their governments depend on select elites; a political scientist might almost speak in terms of "auto-colonization." All three Central African territories also have to cope with the problems of what has been called the dual economy, which is deeply rooted in African history.

In the precolonial era less than a century ago, the indigenous peoples of Central Africa lived in the early Iron Age. Existing methods of production depended on the power of human brawn. The tribesmen did not know how to harness oxen to the plow; they had neither wheel nor wagon; they could employ neither the force of wind nor of water. Men's muscles were used for every conceivable purpose: for hoeing the soil in times of peace, for hurling spears in times of war, for paddling canoes, for mining metal, for transporting merchandise. To such a setting, European conquest brought about an economic revolution, a vast transformation of society made possible not only by the Maxim gun but even more so, by the steam engine, the internal combustion motor, and the hydroelectric turbine. The impact of these forces was stupendous. Within the lifetime of one grandmother, Central Africa was hurled from the Homeric age to the era of modern industry. But the effects of this change were exceedingly uneven. A Zambian government report describes the prevailing dual economy as one in which economic activity centers in a small minority, while the mass of the people depends on semisubsistence agriculture. They provide a reserve of unskilled manpower and a limited market for consumer goods. They have a foot in the country and a foot in the town. But the people are neither fully proletarians nor fully peasants in the European sense. The

from a Statement by the President, Mr. H. F. Oppenheimer, *African Development*, November, 1970, p. 16. The policy is defended by President K. D. Kaunda, *Humanism in Zambia and a Guide to Its Implementation*, Government Printer, Lusaka, 1969.

imbalance between rural and urban enterprise is aggravated by the concentration of economic activity along the rail line and in the Copper Belt. Also there is a great cleavage within the rural sector itself. The European farmers—there are about 700 of them—work with a great deal of capital and with considerable expertise. But the mass of the rural population, about 450,000 families, are spread all over Zambia, and their level of production is not even remotely comparable with that attained by the whites.[6]

Despite this somewhat grim assessment, all three Central African territories experienced economic growth of astonishing dimensions during the last half century. In demographic terms alone, every twenty-five years or so since the turn of the century, the population of the region has probably kept doubling. Central Africa has thereby greatly increased its command over one of the world's valuable economic resources—manpower. Production, too, has grown tremendously over the last two generations. And increasing national wealth has enabled the various governments to raise more money for public purposes. To give just one example, the annual Rhodesian revenue has increased nearly tenfold during the last twenty-five years, from just under £8,000,000 between 1942 and 1943 to about £78,000,000 in 1968. During the same period the yearly income of Malawi, the most backward state of Central Africa, has gone up in an even more dramatic fashion, from £1,000,000 to just over £17,000,000.

By the standards of the larger industrialized countries, the Central African states nevertheless remain weak and their political influence minimal. Admittedly, the revenue which a government collects from its citizens does not alone determine the influence which it can command abroad. But there is a clear relationship between wealth and power. Measured on the monetary scale, the Central African states, like most new members of the United Nations, count for little. In 1968, for instance, the entire revenue collected by the Republic of Malawi hardly exceeded the amount spent by Great Britain on museums, art galleries, and similar institutions during the same year.

Malawi, of course, was almost entirely an agricultural country. Rhodesia and Zambia are a good deal wealthier; Zambia is one of the world's great copper exporters (mining accounted for nearly half of its gross national product). Rhodesia had a more balanced economy, with developed secondary industries as well as mines and farms. In 1967 the Rhodesian revenues were four times as large as those of Malawi.

---

[6] Republic of Zambia, *First National Development Plan 1966–1970*, July 1966 (Lusaka: Office of National Development and Planning, 1966), p. 2.

Yet even so, Rhodesia's budget remained insignificant when compared with the budgets of larger countries. In 1967 the revenue of South Africa, the industrial giant of the continent, exceeded Rhodesia's by more than nine times.[7] Rhodesia's financial strength appears even punier by comparison with European examples. In 1968 the British Overseas Airways Corporation (BOAC) earned nearly twice as much as the revenue of the Rhodesian state. At the time of writing, the University of California spent something like $1,000,000,000 a year on its operations. For less than one-third of this amount Rhodesia effectively administered a region as large as California; ran schools and hospitals; maintained prisons, an army, an air force, and other amenities of modern civilization—and also defied the United Nations in the bargain. Central Africa is indeed a land of paradoxes, where the untoward seems normal and the unexpected always happens.

White and Brown People

Central Africa is, above all, a land of ethnic minorities. The largest non-African group is the whites. Most of them live in Rhodesia, where in 1969 they numbered about 230,000. The majority are of British or British South African origin. They often speak English with that peculiar South African accent that turns "car" into "cor," and clips certain vowels in the fashion of Afrikaners (South Africans of Dutch descent who speak a derivate of the Holland tongue). About one in every seven Europeans is an Afrikaner, but there are also newcomers from many parts of the European continent and North America. The whites are a relatively youthful group and have a high rate of natural increase; their number continues to be supplemented by immigration

[7] In world terms even South Africa occupied a modest position, reflecting the enormous gap between the older industrial countries and those of Africa. According to the *Encyclopædia Britannica Yearbook*, 1970, p. 407, the national income in these selected countries stood as follows in 1968 (in U.S. $100,000,000).

Congo (Kinsasha)	0.9
Zambia (1967)	0.9
Rhodesia	1.0
Ghana	1.8
South Africa	11.8
Switzerland	14.0
Federal Republic of Germany	100.6
U.S.A.	720.0

from South Africa and farther away.[8] Rhodesia is still to some extent
a man's country, though the proportion of men to women has declined
since frontier days.[9]

White Rhodesians used to be a mixed bunch; in a way they still
are. The pioneers included soldiers of fortune and also blue-blooded
aristocrats such as the Viscomte de la Panouse, a *grand seigneur* who
married a London chambermaid, and settled in Mashonaland to breed
cows. There were hard-working artisans wont to pray in chapel. There
were remittance-men, gay sprigs whose wealthy fathers sent monthly
checks from England, so that the black sheep would stay in the colonies
and not disgrace the family's name at home. (This particular breed
decayed in the Great Slump of the early 1930s when remittances dried
up.) There were professional men with degrees from good universities
and high ambitions. There were whores from the backstreets of Kimberley, who went north in search of clients or a husband. They had no
trouble in their quest in frontier towns where women were scarce and
the settlers asked few questions. Today, white Rhodesians are a more
homogeneous and better-educated group, at least in the formal sense.
The excitement of frontier days has given way to a regime of respectability,[10] and the streets of Salisbury are considerably safer than those of
New York. A strong feeling of white solidarity persists. A Rhodesian
could not conceive of a girl's being stabbed to death in full view of
gaping onlookers, for settlers—unlike so many New Yorkers—are in
some ways like Africans; they are quite willing to "get involved."

The shift in the makeup of the European population was accompanied by a profound change in the country's economy. The first

[8] In 1901 there were about 11,000 whites in Rhodesia. Forty years later their
number had increased something like twelve times, to 136,000; by 1969 their number
had risen by more than twenty times. Comparative statistics for Africans are difficult
to assemble. According to official figures, there were about 500,000 in Rhodesia in
1901. In reality the number was probably nearer to 1,000,000. By 1969 the Africans
numbered about 4,840,000; that is to say, they had a fivefold increase over seventy-
five years.

[9] Between 1926 and 1969 the ratio of females to males rose from 80:100 to
97:100 among the European population. The Asian ratio rose from 31:100 in 1931
to 93:100 in 1969. The Colored people (that is to say, people of mixed origin) had
the highest proportion of women. The ratio of 95:100 in 1926 rose to 103:100 in
1961.

[10] Between 1911 and 1915 and 1959 and 1963, the rate of persons accused of
serious crime in the High Court diminished as follows: Europeans from 119.2 to
13.4; Coloreds from 224.4 to 32.5; Africans from 23.7 to 16.0. See F. Y. St. Leger,
"Crime in Southern Rhodesia," *Rhodes-Livingstone Journal*, No. 38 (1966), pp.
11–4.

colonists came to look for gold. They raised beef; they grew mealies (corn); they gradually developed tobacco as a valuable article of export. As time went on, the whites improved their farming methods, pioneered new crops, and set up agricultural processing plants. From the Second World War, the Rhodesian economy experienced an even more dramatic change. The Rhodesians began to make iron and steel and started to turn out a great variety of manufactured goods. Outside of South Africa, Rhodesia today is the most industrialized part of Sub-Saharan Africa. The country's economy continues to expand at a considerable rate. (Between 1958 and 1968 alone, the gross national product went up from £301,000,000 to £385,500,000.) The average white Rhodesian no longer lives in the country or in a small town, but in a big city. The majority of Europeans reside either in Salisbury, the capital (93,000 whites in 1967), or in Bulawayo, a major industrial center (53,000 whites in 1967). Unlike the average African who moves to the urban areas, the European immigrant is no longer a countryman who drifts to the town, but a townsman who moves from one city to another.

Much of the money invested in Central Africa is still owned by shareholders living in South Africa, Great Britain, and the United States. But already during the 1950s, local capital had become a factor of major importance in the economic development of the region. (During the period from 1954 to 1959, for example, gross domestic capital formation amounted to over £805,000,000. Of this, nearly £581,000,000 derived from domestic saving and less than £225,000,000 from borrowing abroad.) The European population contains a substantial bourgeoisie, which supplies most of Rhodesia's and much of Zambia's scarce technical and administrative skills. The average European is not, however, a rich man. He probably owns a car; he is paying off a mortgage on his house; he holds an insurance policy; but he depends for his living on salaries or wages. Europeans work as managers, technicians, and industrial supervisors and they practice various professions. They form an aristocracy of skilled labor.

Fewer than one in ten of all whites are now employed in agriculture. Nowadays the white farmers too are very different from the frontiersmen of old. They usually have a diploma in agriculture or its equivalent; they may even have a degree in engineering or some similar qualification. Their enterprise requires a good deal of capital and of agronomical expertise. The palmy days of a "tickey an acre" (three pennies for an acre of land) have gone forever; land prices have risen enormously over the last generation, and farming has become a job for experts rather than pioneering amateurs.

North of the Zambezi, the Europeans occupy a more ambiguous situation. They no longer exercise political power. Nor are they a permanent element of the population as in Rhodesia. The great majority of whites come as labor migrants who work for limited periods and then retire to Great Britain, South Africa, and other countries when their contracts expire. They still form a social and economic elite, albeit an elite placed in an uncertain position. In Malawi there are just over 6,000 whites—planters, missionaries, teachers, and technicians. While Africans hold all ministerial posts and the directorships of most government departments, many specialist and senior executive positions in the civil service continue to be held by white expatriates at the time of this writing. Many of these men were former colonial officials, who signed on for limited periods under the new regime.

In Zambia the white minority is much more numerous. By the end of the 1960s there were something like 65,000 whites in the country. Zambia's industrial and mining production still depends—to a considerable extent—on the skill of expatriates, and Zambia would have suffered a disastrous economic blow had all the whites suddenly decided to pack up and leave. The Europeans work as managers, mining engineers, and technicians; they are active in business and in the professions. European farmers continue to farm along the line of the railway; throughout the 1960s they still accounted for a major proportion of Zambia's maize and tobacco exports.

Throughout Central Africa skills remain scarce. As in all underdeveloped countries of the world, there is a great differential between skilled and managerial work, on the one hand, and unskilled on the other. During the late 1960s non-Africans in fact earned higher salaries on an average, in black-ruled Zambia than in white-ruled Rhodesia.[11] In Zambia the whites are still needed, but their tenure is insecure, and their presence is resented by many black nationalists. The whites usually have little confidence in the permanence of their position; by the late 1960s only a few hundred Europeans had taken out Zambian citizenship; they realize, for the most part, that they are in Zambia on sufferance. All Zambian nationalists wish to Africanize the major positions now held by Europeans. They argue that true independence cannot be achieved unless the "commanding heights" of the economy and the administration are controlled by nationals. Zambian nationalists may

[11] In 1966 the average real wage rate of non-Africans in Zambia amounted to £2,045. In 1968 the average real wage rate of non-Africans in Rhodesia stood at £1,313.

disagree regarding the timespan that will be required for this change in personnel, but they rarely question the intrinsic desirability of such a course. Political idealism and self-interest alike call for the removal of whites from the best jobs. The nationalists subscribe to "African socialism," a widely discussed and ill-defined ideology, which might in certain respects be defined as a movement aiming for the Africanization of the means of production, distribution, and exchange.

In Rhodesia, however, the Europeans mean to stay. They intend to hold what they have. They form a cohesive and self-conscious "proto-nationality" of their own that has ceased to be British in name, though not by tradition. The Europeans differ a great deal among themselves. Some believe in the virtues of private enterprise; others may call for the nationalization of the means of production. But whatever their profession or political background, the great majority of whites think of themselves as an "in group." Differences in national origin, for instance, count for much less in Rhodesia than, say, in Canada. For the whites, it is a matter of "we" against "them"—the blacks. Most Europeans feel that their entrepreneurial ability, administrative experience, and technical know-how are essential to the country's prosperity, and that possessing these qualities morally entitles the whites to rule. There is a small self-critical intelligentsia, but this consists largely of labor migrants without roots or influence within the European community at large.

The political and social convictions held by Europeans have many sources. They may spring from economic rivalry, from race prejudice, from political fears, or from apprehension about events in independent black Africa, where wealthy minority groups of differing colors have at times been robbed, thrust out, or slain.

But the split between the average settler and the average African (if there are such people) goes a great deal further. Europeans and Africans in Rhodesia are not like whites and blacks in the United States, who, for all their differences, speak the same tongue and sing the same songs. Europeans and Africans are more like distinct nationalities, differing more from one another than Turks from Greeks in Cyprus, Walloons and Flemings in Belgium, and Ibo and Hausa in Nigeria. Europeans differ widely from Africans in speech, customs, political aspirations, and in their views concerning kinship etiquette, marriage, and magic.

There are, of course, cultural bridges, and a few manage to cross them. But by and large, Rhodesian Africans who have adopted European ways are not socially accepted by the vast majority of whites. Intermarriage, though legal, is held in contempt. Conversely, the handful of Europeans who have joined Zambia's black ruling party and have made all kinds of cultural concessions find themselves between two stools.

For the clashes of caste and color are many, and these are rarely removed by education.

Europeans and Americans are apt to regard their own customs as superior, and this is true whatever their life-style or their formal professions may be. Black men often reciprocate these sentiments. A black Cabinet minister in Zambia may berate what he calls the gluttony of white men who "eat and drink tea all day, like locusts." He may remark with contempt at the seemingly brazen ways of their children, who pay no respect to their parents and "bark at their elders without the courtesy of looking down and sitting down." (White boys stand up in the presence of their elders; black children sit down when addressed by their superiors. White children are made to say "thank you" when they get a present. Black youngsters remain politely silent and cup their hands in gratitude.) Differences in etiquette and the psychological importance of these differences are considerable.

Cultural nationalism may also assume other unexpected forms. In 1969, for instance, Tanzania's ruling party declared "cultural war" on American imports such as "soul music." Militants complained that soul music and "soul digging" were contrary to the precepts of African socialist morality. Or they argued that soul music and as such transatlantic products as "Afro-clothes," "Afro food," and "Afro wigs" were used as a means of cultural penetration to further the interests of American imperialism.[12] The miniskirts worn by African fashion fans likewise proved offensive to the new political puritans in East and Central Africa, on the grounds that such outlandish garments of Western provenance sullied the dignity of black womanhood.

To complicate the ethnic situation even further, African and white politicians have to contend with other minorities. For instance, small groups of East Indians (many of them Gujurati-speaking) now live in Central Africa. Usually residing in the cities, they make their living mainly from trade and service occupations. Some also engage in market gardening and various crafts, or they work in the professions and in industry. The East Indians, who are further divided into Muslims and Hindus, are a group apart. They hardly ever marry Europeans or Africans. Some of them are fairly anglicized; others prefer more traditional ways. The Indians' rise from poverty to relative affluence, from bush-trading to shopkeeping, has had nothing to do with governmental favor, social privilege, or hereditary wealth. Rather it has been the result of their entrepreneurial skill, and their capacity for saving and for taking

---

[12] See, for instance, J. K. Obalata, "U.S. 'Soul' Music in Africa," *The African Communist*, No. 41 (1970), pp. 80–89.

risks. But it was these, precisely these, qualities that created enemies for the Indian community: many Europeans resented Asian competition and nowadays the African petty bourgeoisie tends to be even more hostile to the Indians than the whites. Indians are often (though by no means invariably) accused of exploiting Africans or of secretly holding black men in contempt. Judging from the experiences of a country such as Kenya, where the Indians are being squeezed out, the Indians' future economic position will now certainly be more secure under European than African rule.

Perhaps the most marginal of minority groups are the people of mixed European and African or mixed Indian and African descent. (In Rhodesia there were about 15,000 persons of composite ancestry in 1968.) Unlike the Africans, these so-called Coloreds nearly always speak English at home, yet they are not accepted by the whites. Also, they suffer from considerable internal dissension. There are great variations of culture between, say, a well-to-do Colored transport contractor —who lives like a European and almost looks like one—and the Colored child of an African mother, who is brought up in a village together with other Africans. The better-off Coloreds are schoolteachers, foremen, supervisors, or contractors; the poorer people make their living as skilled or semiskilled workmen, but there are few Colored capitalists. The Coloreds face serious economic problems; some are also stricken by a problem of identity, which makes them comparable, in certain respects, with Afro-Americans rather than Africans or whites. The Asians and Coloreds have little in common; both are minorities which in turn comprise a multiplicity of minor minorities. No common national feeling, no common political or religious ideology transcends the "union of color."

The Africans

The overwhelming majority of Central Africa's population are Africans who belong to the Bantu-speaking group. The term "Bantu" does not refer to race, but to a group of related languages. The Bantu-speakers, a Negroid people, are made up of many ethnic stocks. Their skin color varies from ebony black to light brown. The shape of their skulls, their physical size, and their type of blood may differ a great deal even among members of the same village, but they all speak a group of related languages. There are, however, a great many of these tongues: a provisional list compiled in 1960 shows more than 160 in Central Africa. Indeed a detailed ethnolinguistic map of Central Africa would eveal a patchwork of a great variety of speech forms and dialects, only ome of which have been reduced to writing by missionaries and ethno-,raphers.[13]

No single indigenous tongue is understood throughout Africa as a vhole. And in the past no single tribe ever managed to assert its upremacy over even one of the three Central African territories. Fana-alo, a kind of basic Bantu enriched by European loanwords, serves as ingua franca in parts of Central Africa, but Fanakalo and related idioms developed in workshops and mining compounds) are not likely to :volve into a literary language like Swahili. Today Nyanja (officially :nown as Cewa, pronounced Chewa) is widely understood in Malawi nd beyond, but it is not a universal language and cannot easily rival Cnglish for the purposes of trade or scholarship. In Copper Belt towns 3emba is spoken more widely than any other native tongue because the 3emba, once a nation of warriors, sought employment in the mines here. Lozi is the dominant language of Barotseland, formerly a great ndependent kingdom which dominated the valley of the upper Zam->ezi. Shona and Ndebele are spoken south of the Zambezi. But in Rhodesia, Zambia, and Malawi alike—however much these countries nay differ in their political complexion—English serves as the official anguage. Educated Africans speak English with great proficiency, and :ven in the remoter Rhodesian reserves, a European visitor can get .long with the local African postmaster, the constable, or teacher. Many •rdinary villagers also have worked for a spell in Salisbury, and some of hem can carry on an English conversation with a degree of fluency. 3ut the indigenous people of Central Africa—unlike the transplanted \fro-Americans, Afro-Britons, or West Indians—were never in any ense anglicized. Neither is there much prospect of linguistic assimila-ion in the future. English will continue as the language of diplomacy, cience, university education, and higher administration, but the vast najority of Central Africans will hardly ever use it to express their most ntimate thoughts, and there is a great future for new literature in \frican vernaculars.

The African, unlike the average European, Indian, or Colored per-:on in Central Africa, remains essentially a countryman. By the late 1960s, only one out of every five black Zambians, one out of every six)lack Rhodesians, and one out of every twenty black Malawians lived n one of the larger cities. Even so, from the turn of the century, black

[13] Clyde Mitchell, "The African Peoples," in *Handbook to the Federation of Rhodesia and Nyasaland*, ed. W. V. Brelsford (London: Cassell & Co., Ltd., 1960), •p. 179–81.

Central Africans have experienced changes on a scale hard to imagine. European governance north of the Zambezi began in the 1890s and ended in 1964. British rule in Zambia and Malawi did not exceed the lifespan of a village elder. A hypothetical Ngoni born in 1880 would have been brought up under conditions comparable in certain respects to those of the Teutons in Roman times, as described by Tacitus. He would have marched to war against the British in 1898, with his spear, his knobkerrie and his great oxhide shield. He would have experienced defeat at the hands of the invaders; he would have witnessed the appearance of new industrial marvels—steam engines, motor trucks, and jet planes. One of his sons might have become a factory worker in Bulawayo; a second, a welfare officer in Mufulira; a third, a secondary school-master in Ndola; and a fourth, a prominent politician. As an octogenarian, the Ngoni veteran might still have been sufficiently hale and healthy to attend his country's independence celebration in 1964.

Generalizations with regard to the so-called traditional villagers, however, are hard to make, since their conditions of life differed a good deal in precolonial days, and are changing greatly under the impact of a modern economy. By the 1930s, observers of rural life in Northern Rhodesia were struck by the way in which village life was altering under the impact of a cash economy. A few cultivators were beginning to rotate their crop of kafir, corn, maize, and beans. Plows and wagons were coming into use along the railway line. Mambwe cultivators near Abercorn, in what is now northeastern Zambia, were using a fairly stable system of mound cultivation, well adapted to the conditions of a treeless country, though other Mambwe still adhered to the traditional ways of tree-loping and burning.

Today the differences in the countrymen's ways of life have grown even more distinct. In Rhodesia, for instance, there are more than 25,000 "master farmers" (trained agriculturists who must abide by certain government-approved rules of tilling the soil and who own their own land on an individual—not a tribal—basis). Some of these men achieve even better results than whites (record maize yields of over thirty bags an acre are not exceptional in good seasons). Master farmers normally work their land with the help of their families; they also employ a few hired hands. Many have attained a modest degree of prosperity. Their families probably live in a small square brick house, and they may own some European-made furniture or even a second-hand car.

The great majority of black people in Central Africa, however, still work the soil with a minimum of capital and live on tiny incomes. In 1966 70 percent of Zambia's black population still made their living by subsistence farming; more than nine out of every ten Malawians de-ended on their fields for the sustenance of their families. (During the same year, only 3.4 of Great Britain's, 5.5 percent of America's and 10.8 percent of West Germany's populations were working on the land.) The African villagers' living standards naturally varied in accordance with the fertility of the soil, the regularity of the rainfall, the availability of transport and markets, the amount of good land left for farming, and so on. But, however well-placed a black villager is, he has to exist on a budget infinitely smaller than that of the poorest peasant in Europe. A Zambian is much more dependent on the vagaries of the weather than, say, an English farmer, who has much greater reserves and many more technical and financial facilities to tide his family over a bad season. The black countryman worries far more about possible droughts and failures of the harvest than about the issues of politics and ideology that make the headlines in the daily press and provide material for interviews on TV.

Admittedly, the countryman's real wealth is not easy to calculate, for Western statisticians have great difficulty in measuring income without money. A village in some remote part of Malawi, for instance, will earn only a negligible amount of cash. But he pays no rent for the huts which he occupies with his wives and children. His habitation costs no money to build. He has more living space at his disposal than a town laborer crammed into some tiny apartment. Normally he does not need to purchase his corn or his beer, and his entertainment is cheap. His effective income is surely higher than most statisticians would indicate. Yet the average black villager is poor by many standards. Scarcity is the rule of life. An empty bottle or beer can carelessly thrown away by a Western tourist still serves a useful purpose in many a Bantu hut. There, people don't worry about a tapering waistline, but about an empty stomach.

Moreover, conditions of life are not static. The subsistence farmers of Zambia do not produce food solely for their own households; the great majority sell their surplus for cash. Most able-bodied men in a Central African village have worked for wages in the towns at some stage in their careers, and they have acquired some notion of city life. They are in some ways half-peasant, half-proletarian. Even in the remotest villages moreover, people have become accustomed to all sorts of new products: water pumps, bicycles (an important means of transportation for the poor), plows, sewing machines, and semiluxuries like tea, coffee, and matches. The round, thatched cottages of old have often given way to small square houses built of sun-baked brick with corrugated iron roofs, which look like the houses of poor whites of a generation ago. Village stores, village schools, medical dispensaries are all

helping to change the mores of the people. Khaki shirts and shorts hav
replaced the traditional fashions of the villages, and factory-made guitar
often take the place of more ancient musical instruments. Traditiona
crafts are dying out as manufactured goods become cheaper and mor
easily available.

Nevertheless, many traditional African institutions survive, albei
in a different form. The great majority of Africans continue to mak
their living by fairly simple kinds of farming. They still rely for hel
above all on their kinfolk rather than on more impersonal organization
such as a social insurance agency or a private insurance company. Fo
the most part, Africans recognize family obligations that would hav
been more readily understandable to a Montague or Capulet fron
Shakespeare's Verona, or to a Macdonald or Campbell from eighteenth
century Scotland than to a modern Westerner.

A Western family today is of the "nuclear" kind. Among whit
Rhodesians, as among Americans of all colors, a family consists of :
husband, his wife, and children. There may be aunts, cousins, and othe
relatives. Grandmother often lives at a great distance—in Cape Town
or even in London. Kinship obligations to these more distant relative
are nowhere near as extensive or as well defined among whites as the
are among the majority of Africans. Western marriages moreover ar
monogamous; a white Rhodesian may keep a mistress, but he canno
legally wed a second wife. Among black Africans there is a much greate
variety in the family system. Some Africans will take a spouse accordin
to Christian rites and adhere to Western ways. Polygamy—though no
practised as widely as legend asserts—remains, however, legal; Rho
desian courts will enforce the formal rights of an African's second o
third wife. Indigenous African law also provides its own rules of inheri
tance, which vary a good deal from region to region. The structure o
African family life has created its own form of etiquette, one that i
totally alien to Third-World enthusiasts on college campuses. Th
freedom enjoyed, say, by a settler's wife in Salisbury or a coed in a
American university would appear as strange or as repugnant to a Bemb
villager as it would to an old-fashioned peasant from Europe.

All indigenous kinship systems entailed complex forms of socia
cooperation. A person's relatives were asked for—and widely continue t
be called upon for—assistance in emergencies of many kinds. Amon
most Africans, loyalty to kinsmen and also to members of one particula
ethnic group widely takes precedence over loyalty to impersonal bodie
of more recent origin, such as the state, the civil service, or even th
ruling party. Kinship and ethnic loyalties do not disappear in the cities

on the contrary, the pressures of urban life may place even greater stress on such ties than before.

Already in the 1940s, to give just one example, Bemba workmen in the Copper Belt used to accuse the better-educated Nyanja clerks of reserving the more desirable positions open to blacks for their fellow Nyasalanders. Black politicians today cannot avoid ethnic entanglements, even if they preach against the dangers of tribalism. All African administrative machines moreover are beset by corruption, by practices which offend European notions of self-interest, efficiency, and morality. But corruption is a relative term. Transactions that appear immoral to whites or that whites would practice only in secret may appear perfectly acceptable to many Africans who expect to receive favors from kinsmen in high places.

A minority of Africans nowadays live in cities. Without exception, these urban communities are recent creations that owe their origin to white colonization. The traditional Bantu—like the ancient Teutons, Britons, and Hebrews—were rural people. Even the largest Bantu settlements, including the royal capitals, depended mainly on agriculture for their sustenance. The modern towns are all young, even by American standards. Salisbury, for instance, was founded in 1890—nearly two centuries after French fur traders first set up Detroit as a permanent post. The Zambia Copper Belt, which comprises a cluster of mining towns, only started to grow during the late 1920s.

The cities are not only of recent vintage; they are also few in number. Most African townsmen thus congregate into a relatively small number of urban areas. This is particularly true in Rhodesia, where Salisbury and Bulawayo form the largest towns in Central Africa. Once a city has come into existence, it seems to snowball; factories attract workers, and their presence gives employment in additional service industries, which in turn create new facilities. The town planners thus often complain about the way in which Salisbury, a large city with nearly 400,000 people, continues to grow, supposedly at the expense of its neighbors. In Zambia the towns are much smaller; in 1969, for example, Lusaka contained something like 160,000 people, but the Zambian towns also keep expanding despite government attempts to slow down the influx of country folk into the cities.

The majority of black towndwellers—unlike their white, Indian, or Colored counterparts—generally retain some links with the village, in theory if not in practice. These ties vary a good deal from place to place. Much depends on the amount of land still available in the rural hinterland, on the geographical distance between the city and the citydweller's home village, on the availability of jobs in the towns, and on the African's social status, his personal expectations, and the nature of his kinship ties. The position moreover continues to change. But statistical data collected during the 1950s in Zambia speak eloquently. Among the men interviewed by Professor Clyde Mitchell in Ndola, the chief marketing center in the Copper Belt, for instance, only about 18.9 percent were permanently urbanized, 21.4 percent were temporarily stabilized; and nearly 60 percent were still classed as migrant laborers or peasant visitors. Only 12.5 percent of the people thought they would always remain in the Copper Belt or considered the city "their village."

The general structure of African townships retained many of the characteristics of gold rush settlements. The majority of Africans in the Copper Belt are in their prime of life. Many children play in the streets, but there are few old people about. Standards of education remain low, and there is much poverty and a great deal of marital instability. Cities breed all kinds of crime, though the Rhodesian crime rate remains low by American standards, and visitors from the United States note with surprise that Rhodesian constables do not carry firearms when on ordinary duty.

Urban workers may have a hard time. Yet on the whole the townspeople are better off than their cousins in the countryside, where there are fewer amenities such as schools, hospitals, and stores, and where incomes tend to be lower. Africans flock to the towns from many parts of the adjacent territory and beyond. African city folk are beginning to develop a collective identity and think of themselves as the people of Salisbury or those from the Copper Belt. Yet the process is slow. Urban Africans speak many different languages; they still practice different customs; there is a constant coming and going of people. The rapid growth of towns helps to speed circulation, for as new housing areas are opened up, residents from older parts of a location often move in, and their vacated homes will be taken by people coming from dwellings marked for demolition. The majority of black townsmen are unskilled or semiskilled workmen who tend to change their jobs fairly often, and move from city to city or from the city back to the country. Hence, city life depends on the ability of Africans to adapt traditional tribal and kinship ties to an urban setting or to develop new forms of association —clubs, burial societies, and so on. These enable black people to discover relatives or friends who will help them over an emergency or even put them up for a night.

The African townsman's ambiguous social position produces curious cultural consequences. Among African city folk, European and traditional ways are apt to mingle in a strange fashion. A listener who tunes in on a Lusaka broadcasting station will hear a medley of music which blends traditional African themes with American jazz and strains derived from European hymns or marching tunes. Africans have come to respect modern technology; many appreciate the merits of Western medicine, but at the same time beliefs in magic may continue, albeit in a different context. By the late 1950s for instance, something like one-third of all African patients in Harari Hospital, the greatest in Rhodesia, still attributed their sickness to witchcraft. Africans may consult a white physician, but at the same time may have recourse to a black medicine man. The African healer in turn may prescribe traditional remedies and yet wear a white surgical coat in the manner of Dr. Kildare or Dr. Ben Casey of television fame. Black secondary school students may learn Latin and play soccer in the British way, yet the athletics master may be asked to guard the ball until the game starts, lest some cheat bewitch the ball and win by unsporting means. Traditional Africa, in other words, has not disappeared but manages to adapt its ways and beliefs to changing situations.

The rate of change moreover may well be on the increase. For whatever politicians and demagogues, romantically minded intellectuals, or clergymen may say about the real or assumed vices of city life, the drift to the town continues. The press, newspaper advertisements, television (in Rhodesia), the movies, broadcasts (which can be picked up by cheap, battery-powered radios even in remote villages) continue to spread Western notions of the good life and of social prestige. The traditional lore of village elders no longer provides all the answers. The biggest daily paper in Zambia thus hit on a most popular feature when it started a column in which "Josephine," an anonymous African lady answers pressing questions of an intimate nature in the manner of "Dear Abby," though with greater verve and wit.

City life was apt to have a double-edged and contradictory effect on the immigrants' views concerning a man's station in life. The old hereditary distinctions became less important. A Bemba worker in a copper mine might still, under certain circumstances, derive some advantage from his membership in the aristocratic Crocodile clan. But however famous his ancestors might have been, it is more important to be on good terms with the foreman. Above all, a laborer anxious to advance in the world needed new skills. Traditional differences in status diminished. But wealth and education introduced new criteria into the social pecking order; white-collar jobs became desired above all others, even by those most fervently committed to some form of populism or revolutionary socialism.

In Zambia and Malawi today, the African top stratum does not consist of merchant princes or industrial entrepreneurs. There are no great African capitalists in Central Africa. At the head of society there is a new class of black politicians, state officials, and party functionaries. Their income derives not from commercial profits but from the public purse; their standard of living excites the admiration or the envy of the plebs. Many critics of independent Africa describe the new rulers as yet another privileged caste which has simply stepped into the colonizers' shoes, without, however, possessing their predecessors' technical expertise. African socialism, all too often, has become an ideological tool for school and college graduates in search of more state positions. The "outs" accuse the "ins" of wallowing in ill-merited luxury. But when the "outs" become the "ins," they do not abolish differences of prestige and power.

Beneath this top stratum there is a larger group of middle- and lower-grade civil servants, commercial employees, and so forth. There are also a few professional men and some black entrepreneurs. These African businessmen usually provide services of various kinds; they earn money as bus owners, building contractors, or as traders; they do not own any of the country's great enterprises. The great majority of urban Africans are semiskilled or unskilled workers. Their families usually have a hard time making ends meet, and the breadwinner is likely to change both his job and place of occupation fairly often; much of the highly skilled and supervisory work remains in white hands. Yet townsmen as a group are better off than the great majority of country folk, who often envy the industrial workers' superior standard of living. The cities continue to act as magnets, drawing in numerous labor migrants from the villages, and black as well as white administrators try to stop this influx by various direct and indirect devices. In other words, decolonization has altered the social pyramid without shattering it to pieces. Captains and kings may have departed from the colonial scene. But inequality remains a fact of social life, and in the writer's opinion, will continue to do so under any form of government that the future may bring.

3

The Ancient Past

The Stone Age Hunters

The human race in all likelihood derives from Africa. The eastern and central portions of the continent probably have the oldest history in the world, for men or manlike beings must have lived there for at least a million, perhaps even two million, years. During almost the whole of their existence, men made their living as hunters and food gatherers. Their raw materials were wood, bone, and stone, and their society consisted of bands who moved over great distances in search of wild crops and game. Judged by the standards of present-day archaeology, the three and a half millennia or so occupied by the pioneers of the Iron Age, the heroes of Homer, the emperors of Rome, the popes of medieval Europe, and the captains of modern industry take up but a fleeting moment in the annals of man.

Suppose a scholar decided to write a definitive history of Central Africa, a mammoth work filling a thousand pages. Assume also that he arranged his work in such a manner that the number of pages roughly corresponded to the length of each period described. He would then have to devote something like 999 pages to the various stone ages. A page or two would suffice for the Iron Age which lasted about two thousand years in Central Africa. A few lines in the whole book would cover the era of European exploration, of empire building, of the growth of modern industry, of decolonization and its aftermath.

Such a history, of course, will never be written. The origins of mankind are still shrouded in mystery; archaeologists still do not agree on how our species originated and grew to maturity. History moreover is subject to the law of increasing acceleration. The conditions of life have changed far more rapidly during the last milennium than ever before. Too, archaeologists work under tremendous limitations. They can disinter tools, weapons, and skulls, but they can only speculate concerning the societies that produced the tools and weapons; they can never know what went on within the skulls which they arrange on the shelves of museums. They can generalize about the species, but they can tell us nothing about individuals. To us, our Stone Age and Early Iron Age ancestors must forever remain "faceless" men. Yet we have not the slightest reason to think that their nomadic bands did not contain personalities as powerful and inventive as any to be found in our own age.

For all our ignorance, our Stone Age legacy is, in many ways, man's most important possession. It was during these countless millennia that man assumed his present form and personality, that he learned how to make tools and weapons, to create objects of beauty, to develop language, to create elaborate rituals, to speculate about his destiny, to spread over extensive portions of the globe—in the words of the Bible— to "replenish the earth, and subdue it: and have dominion over the fish of the sea, and the fowl of the air, and over everything that moveth upon the earth." [1]

Among the great technical innovations in the history of mankind was the invention of some type of tool. The manlike beings who roamed across the bush and savanna lands of East and Central Africa gradually learned how to shape pebbles by removing flakes to produce a short, jagged cutting edge. Gradually the early toolmakers became more skilled and turned out a variety of implements designed for particular purposes —for piercing and digging, for cutting and scraping. Pebble tools gradually developed into hand axes, which have been in use for at least half a million years. The hand axe makers probably spread far beyond their African homeland; today remains of their industry are found as far afield as Zambia and France, Morocco and England. Early craftsmen developed another characteristic artifact, the cleaver with a straight, transverse cutting edge which made an excellent butcher's knife. In addition, early Stone Age bands had a great number of smaller tools used for cutting, scraping, and boring. They also used perishable substances like wood, reeds, and other raw materials, though we can only guess at the manner in which these were employed.

[1] Gen. 1:28.

With regard to the social organization that made life possible for our early ancestors scholars can likewise only speculate. No ancient evidence remains to guide our imagination. We may assume, however, that life was strictly organized. Even wild animals do not roam through the countryside at random. They have their own territories, with drinking places, stores of food, and areas set aside for feeding and defecation. Herds are normally patterned according to definite social hierarchies. Monkeys, for example, conform to strict rules of behavior. There is a kind of social ranking, and only the very young are excused from conforming to the behavior pattern of the group. The nimrods of old must have required a similar discipline. The strongest fighter was infinitely weaker than an elephant; the swiftest runner could not overtake an antelope. The requirements of the chase alone must have imposed very definite rules of behavior on early man. As Aristotle once put it, only gods and beasts can live on their own.

In reconstructing the lives of Early Stone Age man, we can probably learn something from the way in which bands of modern Bushmen still manage to function in remote parts of Southern and Central Africa. Admittedly, we cannot simply generalize from one hunting culture to another; modern Bushmen are the product of untold millennia of human evolution. However, the observations made by present-day anthropologists can serve to enrich our imagination. Bushmen bands today have their own territories. They have learned how to use their senses to an extraordinary extent—so much so that to an aboriginal hunter even a modern game ranger would appear half-deaf, half-blind, and largely without a sense of smell. Bushmen search for wild berries, roots, tubers, and nuts; they also look for game, and their migrations depend on a strict pattern. The bands necessarily lead a nomadic existence; hence, their members must carry all their possessions with them through all their wanderings. Bushmen will not therefore accumulate possessions that only burden the band. The logistics of their group depends on a great many factors—changes in the seasons, in the movement of game, in the presence of water.

The margin for survival is small. Elders must be capable of doing elaborate staff work; managerial ability is a matter of life and death. And the imagined social and sexual freedom enjoyed by the "primitive savage" is but a pipe dream used to brighten up television shows. Bushmen bands depend above all on collecting food from the veld. They supplement these supplies with the meat of wild animals. The art of hunting must have helped teach men the art of cooperating in groups. Women and children can easily gather wild food in small parties or on their own, but men armed only with rounded throwing stones, hand axes or primitive spears could not possibly kill great beasts without help from their fellows. Among modern Bushmen (whose technical equipment is much more elaborate than that of Early Stone Age men) whole parties still gather for the chase. The kill is distributed according to a complicated system which depends on participation in any particular hunting group and on ties of kinship. We have no idea how our early ancestors managed to divide their food among the band or how they fared in times when fruit and meat were scarce. But we may be reasonably certain that they must have already evolved strict codes of behavior which permitted the survival of tiny hunting bands in the immensity of the African bush.

Another great step forward in the advance of mankind was the use of fire. The first evidence of a regular employment of fire in Africa dates from the end of the hand-axe culture, about 60,000 years ago. The Kalambo Falls (situated near the present border between Zambia and Tanzania) is the site in Sub-Saharan Africa where investigators have found the earliest traces of campfires. In the remote period when they were first lit, the world probably experienced some major climatic changes. The days and nights turned colder; the rains became more frequent. Plant life altered to correspond with the modifications in precipitation and temperature. Many of the giant animals that used to roam the veld became extinct. It was during this era that aboriginal man hit on the idea of capturing the flames and keeping the blaze alive—mysterious and terrifying though the conflagration might appear at first. Later on, some Paleolithic genius found a way of making fire at will. The controlled use of combustion made an infinitely greater impact on humanity than the discovery of nuclear energy. Bands became less restricted in their movement and less dependent on the vagaries of the weather. Trees could be felled by fire rather than laboriously hacked down with stone axes. Fire enabled men to sharpen their spears and digging sticks; charred pieces of wood could serve for painting on rocks. Fire gave mankind a decisive superiority over the fiercest of beasts; wild animals could be driven away, and game could be driven into prepared ambushes by starting controlled blazes. Hunters carrying torches could occupy caves in which ferocious creatures used to lurk in the dark to pounce on the unwary. The use of semipermanent camps, warmed by fire, may also have given a greater degree of stability to human life. It may likewise have occasioned a more exact division of labor between the sexes, creating perhaps the first rudimentary division of labor known to mankind.

Concerning the psychological impact made by the use of fire on man, we can only conjecture. Hunters huddled round a roaring blaze, staring into the flickering flames, may have come to speculate about a strange fire spirit who brought both perils and blessings in his train. They may have evolved legends like those concerning Prometheus, the son of a Titan, who stole fire from heaven as a present for mankind. But we know for certain that when man tamed fire, he accomplished a tremendous technological feat, comparable only to the creation of a tool deliberately designed by a human mind before it actually took shape in wood or stone.

For untold millennia Stone Age craftsmen improved their tools, and more regional specialization came about. The denizens of the Congo forests, for example, developed a culture known to archaeologists as the Lupemban, which was distinguished by the production of magnificent stone tools, particularly large, leaf-shaped points of lances, beautifully flaked over the whole surface. (Lupemban finds at the Kalambo Falls date from about 29,000 to 27,000 B.C.)

In time, the process of change accelerated, and sometime between 12,000 and 10,000 years ago inventors hit on the idea of hafting several small stone blades on wood and stone. This technique permitted craftsmen to use finer and more suitable rocks, for toolmakers now only required small pieces. The employment of rock crystal, agate, and other fine-grained raw material facilitated skillful workmanship and also led to various technical improvements. Aboriginal archers could now use barbed arrows that would stick in the wounds of their prey, allowing poison to take its effect. Hunters were able to shoot more game, and there was more food to go around. The population increased and so probably did the leisure available for artistic pursuits.

Artists in Central Africa developed a whole variety of styles. The rock paintings found in Zambia today can be divided into two main classes—representational and stylized forms. The so-called Wilton people in what is now Rhodesia produced naturalistic rock paintings of great beauty, which may have served magic as well as aesthetic purposes. Whatever the artists' intent, their pictures show us a great deal about the life of the Late Stone Age. They even reveal the individual style of particular draftsmen, whose work apparently can still be identified by experts today. The ancients depicted masked dancers and hunters disguised as animals, and they showed people performing various ceremonies which may have been connected with the worship of spirits, with rain, fertility, and burial cults. Other scenes indicate that friendly meetings must have taken place between different bands. In all likelihood there was already some kind of long-distance barter in commodities like obsidian, ochre, and finished ornaments, goods of small bulk and high value which would stand the high cost of transport. In addition, artists depicted incidents in tribal wars which may have broken out over hunting preserves, the use of wells, or the favors of women.

Central Africa during this era must already have been a racial melting pot. Most of the ancient hunters probably looked something like modern Bushmen; physical anthropologists class them as Bush-Boskopoids. The Bush people probably absorbed more ancient strains such as that of Rhodesian man. (Rhodesian man belonged to a Middle Stone Age stock now extinct; he was similar in appearance to the Neanderthal man in Europe, with massive brows and a flat, sloping forehead.) In all probability, a proto-Caucasoid people, styled Erythriotes by experts, also penetrated into Central Africa, where they mingled with the local people and possibly enriched their culture.

But for a great variety of reasons, however, East and Central Africa —which once had taken the lead in human evolution—gradually fell behind in the development of civilization. While the inhabitants of Central Africa adhered to hunting and gathering wild food, the denizens of more favored areas gradually turned to farming. Archaeologists believe that villagers in Southwest Asia had learned how to cultivate the soil by at least 7800 B.C. The art of growing crops probably reached Egypt and other parts of North Africa some time before 4500 B.C. In Mesopotamia about 4500 B.C. urban civilization had its beginnings. Clearly geography must have played a major part in bringing about this shift in culture. Central Africa lacks fertile river valleys like those of Mesopotamia and Egypt, where all manner of crops could be grown on rich alluvial soil and where boats could ply up and down great natural waterways. The inland people of Central Africa lacked access to the sea. But above all, they presumably had no economic incentive to improve their methods of production. As long as land was abundant, water in good supply, and game plentiful, the technology of the Late Stone Age sufficed for their needs, and Central Africa remained a land of hunters and food gatherers, though some of its communities may have begun to cultivate bush produce in a more systematic fashion.

The First Farmers

For untold millennia Central Africa was inhabited by tiny bands of Bush people who depended for their livelihood on the chase, on the collection of wild food, and possibly on some primitive forms of vege-culture. They lacked contact with more advanced civilizations and had no incentive to improve their methods of production, which presumably sufficed for the needs of an infinitesimally small population.

From about the birth of Christ onward, however, Central Africa began to experience a major change in its culture. Farmers and husbandmen moved southward through the Rift Valley into what is now Malawi. Others pushed into what is now Zambia, probably using "corridors" free of the tsetse fly, a great destroyer of cattle, to move their herds into what is now Zambia. The newcomers knew how to domesticate various animals; they had mastered the arts of making pottery and smelting iron. They cultivated sorghum, millet, and other grains. They also supplemented their diet by gathering edible fruit, roots, and berries, and by hunting game—a comparatively simple task at a time when the country must have been teeming with great herds of wild beasts.

The details of these great migrations as yet require further elaboration, but archaeologists like John Desmond Clark, Brian Fagan, and Roger Summers have already made a remarkable contribution to our knowledge of early Central Africa. By about A.D. 100 Early Iron Age farmers were tilling the soil in what is now western Zambia. The remains of Iron Age villages, dating from perhaps A.D. 320, have been found at Zimbabwe in Rhodesia. By about A.D. 400 Iron Age people were established at Dambwa near what is now Livingstone in Zambia. Others made their way to where Kalomo now stands in the Zambian railway belt. Thus by A.D. 700 or thereabouts, small groups of cultivators were thinly spread over what is now Central Africa. These communities had already elaborated several different though related cultures. These were marked by different styles of pottery and other artifacts, as well as by regional adaptations to local farming requirements.

In all likelihood these various peoples contained many different strains. Some were predominantly Negroid; others contained a strong admixture of the Bush-Boskopoid. They presumably spoke a group of related languages collectively known as Bantu, though no one of course can be certain as to the tongues used by people who did not know the art of writing and left no literary records. Their ancestors probably came from the lands north of the great Central African forest belt, from a region where there was both woodland and savanna, and where the use of iron was already known. Historians as yet do not agree on where the Bantu-speakers originated; one plausible theory, however, places their origin somewhere near the central Benue Valley in what is now Nigeria. Many different factors must have played a part in bringing about these population shifts, but ecological changes seem to have been of particular importance. The great plains now covered by the Sahara used to be better watered than they are now. But gradually the rains grew scarcer, water courses ran dry, and this enormous region began to desiccate. Some of the indigenous people of the Sahara probably had to wander far in search of new pastures and thereby pushed in on their neighbors. Simply to provide more food for an expanding population and growing herds, some communities may have trekked. But whatever the reason for these Völkerwanderungen, they changed the face of Africa.

The newcomers who gradually drifted into Zambia, Malawi, and Rhodesia presumably learned a great deal from the existing Stone Age people concerning the ways of the game and the nature of the wild food to be found in the country. In fact, the contacts between the first Bantu-speakers and the Bush folk were probably peaceful. There was no shortage of hunting grounds and no need to fight. Nevertheless, the immigrants, who did not depend on stone, enjoyed a vast technological superiority over their neighbors. They knew how to make furnaces with artificial draughts. They could fashion tools like hoes and axes, which enabled these Bantu-speakers to clear the soil, to penetrate into more difficult woodland, and to practice primitive forms of slash-and-burn agriculture. Iron-tipped lances and arrows provided the villagers with effective armaments for hunting and war alike. And while the farmers had to move when they exhausted the soil, nevertheless they produced sufficient food to sustain stable communities. Suddenly there was room for a considerably greater population than in the hunting days of old.

The new Iron Age technology was of course still of the simplest kind. Welding and other more advanced forms of metal working characteristic of the later school of iron working in the Congo Basin, not to speak of techniques used in India, China, and the Mediterranean Basin, remained unknown. In all likelihood, the standard of civilization reached by the Bantu-speaking peoples of Central Africa during this early period of settlement was probably similar to that of the Aestii, a Teutonic people living by the Baltic shore in Roman times.[2]

But there is clear evidence of cultural development, and during the first millennium A.D. the rate of technological change greatly accelerated in Central Africa. The Bantu migrations opened up an enormous new frontier to pastoral and arable farming. They also involved contacts with Asian cultures, which must have given some stimulus to development in the interior.

Sometime during the first millennium A.D., Indonesian seafarers from Dutch East Asia colonized Madagascar and subsequently reached the African shore. In addition, from ancient times, Muslim navigators

[2] Julius Caesar wrote of them that: "They worship the Mother of the gods [a custom that may have found parallels among the early Bantu, some of whom may have practiced a fertility cult marked by clay female figures]. . . . They seldom use weapons of iron, but cudgels often." (H. Mattingly, *Tacitus on Britain and Germany: A Translation of the Agricola and the Germania* (Baltimore: Penguin Books, Inc., 1964), p. 138).

had made their way to the East African coast. The banana, the Asian yam, and other tropical crops, as well as various new devices such as the xylophone and the outrigger canoe, were probably brought to Africa by the Indonesians.

Traders from afar were probably interested in ivory, an important raw material for bracelets, carvings, and other ornaments. Ivory was to Central and East Africa what amber was to the Aestii of the Baltic— a valuable luxury export of small bulk and high value, which could be produced without an elaborate technology. But ivory hunters required personal qualities very different from those needed for the collection of amber. Elephant hunting is still a dangerous sport, even for people armed with rifles. The pursuit of these great beasts with lances and arrows entailed skill and valor of Homeric proportions. Hence, the yield could not have been very great. The markets in India, the Near East and, later on, in Medieval Europe must have been enormous, and the demand for ivory presumably exceeded the available supplies.

On a small scale the people in what is now Rhodesia began to engage in gold mining. Rhodesia has many scattered deposits of the yellow metal; some could be worked by miners with simple tools. Thus, in time gold also became a valuable export. Like hunting and trade, gold mining probably also brought a certain degree of differentiation in its train.

Men who engaged in the chase for dangerous beasts, in perilous commerce over great distances through little-known country, or in the chancy search for gold were not all equally successful—perhaps this paved the way for class differences. How they first developed is far from clear; but their existence can be documented by archaeologists. Modern scholars, for instance, have disinterred an ancient village near the confluence of the Lusitu Stream and the Zambezi, downstream from the present-day Kariba Dam. The village must have dated from about the seventh century A.D. By A.D. 850 or so, great dignitaries were buried with objects of gold, and copper crosses, copper wire, cloth, and other luxuries were placed in their graves. The bodies of common people, however, were but poorly decorated. We may assume, therefore, that at least by the latter part of the first millennium, the more important denizens received special privileges in life as well as in death.

The Emergence of Kingship

The background. By the end of the first millennium, Iron Age people, most of them probably Negroid, were widely spread throughout Central Africa. In all likelihood they were also expanding southwards, into the highveld of South Africa, which afforded excellent pastures for cattle. There were regional variations in the cultures of these peoples; some can still be traced through differences in the style of various artifacts, especially pottery. Nevertheless, all these peoples had much in common. They were organized in small communities. They lived in villages consisting of simple round huts made of poles and hardened mud, very much like those still used by traditional African farmers today. The people knew how to smelt iron; in parts of Rhodesia they also produced gold. The miners dug pits deep into the earth—some down to 150 feet—until they reached the water level or the air became too foul to breathe.

The expansion of the economy entailed a certain degree of foreign trade. There was also some social differentiation within the various Iron Age communities. Opportunities for the creation of larger states may have been provided through the economic development. Their origins are still clouded in mystery, but we may at any rate speculate as to how they first came into being.

In all probability the rise of early monarchies was connected with war and conquest. No contemporary Bantu sources remain to enlighten us with regard to this transformation of society. We are reduced, therefore, to the difficult and dangerous expedient of using comparative data. If the value of this method be admitted, a historian might do worse than turn to the Old Testament. The Book of Samuel contains a magnificent account of what may well have been a similar social process. The Bible describes how the ancient Hebrews, a cattle-keeping Early Iron Age people who resembled the Bantu in certain ways, were forced to alter their political institutions under the pressure of war. The Hebrews used to be commanded by Judges, that is, by tribal elders. (Like most primitive peoples, they also consulted spirit mediums whom they believed to be inspired by supernatural forces.) But tribal elders were not fitted to command armies engaged in extensive campaigns. According to the Bible, the Hebrews therefore asked Samuel, their Judge, to anoint for them a king. Samuel warned the people that kingship would lead to the creation of an oppressive state. A monarch would take for his service the sons and daughters of his subjects; he would impose tithes, labor dues, and all manner of hardship.

Nevertheless the people refused to obey the voice of Samuel; and said, Nay; but we will have a king over us; That we also may be like all the nations; and that our king may judge us, and go out before us, and fight our battles.[3]

[3] 1 Sam. 8:19–20.

Kingship may have offered other advantages. Among the Bantu, as among the ancient Teutons and all other primitive peoples, the giving of presents played a major part in life. Judiciously bestowed on friends and neighbors, gifts helped to strengthen the bonds of society; presents might also serve as a kind of insurance, by creating unwritten claims to assistance from the recipient of a present and his kinsmen. Among the Bantu, as among the Teutons of old, generosity was counted a virtue and niggardliness, a vice. In a society that had no means of storing food over long periods, the road to power lay in a man's ability to secure the loyalty of relatives and the allegiance of strangers through gifts. A more powerful ruler would be in a position not merely to extort tribute but also to extend the network of mutual favors. He would be able to levy taxes in kind, which would be redistributed among his dignitaries and their followers. A king would be in a strong position to participate in foreign trade; he might even be able to enforce some compulsory labor dues. These would enable him to build up a small food surplus to entertain his guests and to help his subjects when times were bad.

Admittedly, the power of a Bantu monarch must have remained circumscribed by economic necessity. As long as land remained in unlimited supply, even the mightiest ruler could not appropriate it for his private use; neither was he able to turn his leading men into feudal magnates of the Western kind. Rebellious subjects could all too easily break away and find new homes in the distant bush. Existing methods of transport on the backs of porters likewise imposed considerable limits on the power of Bantu kingship. In Egypt Joseph, Pharaoh's minister floated grain down the Nile on river vessels; the food would be kept in repositories and serve to tide the people over in times of famine. But even the greatest Bantu ruler had no means of stockpiling grain on a comparative scale. He did not know how to build magazines in brick; he could not keep out rats, or weevils from his storage bins. Neither could he convey large quantities of manioc or sorghum from one part of his country to another.

There is much evidence nevertheless that the early Bantu engaged in different kinds of exchange. Archaeologists can document the existence of a long-distance trade in luxuries. In addition, fishermen, herdsmen, and cultivators presumably bartered their respective products through local transactions, the precise nature of which we can no longer reconstruct. Salt, an essential commodity for human existence, could be carried fairly easily, and cattle, provided a mobile source of food which could be shifted in bulk.

Some local dignitaries were enabled to acquire a permanent following, to maintain a court, as well as to feed military and labor levies for limited periods. As a result, they could more easily defend their king, enlarge the area under their control, and force neighboring peoples to pay tribute. Where nature provided suitable stone, such princes might raise permanent buildings to house the king, to defend the people, and to worship the divine forces that moved the universe. In all probability war and trade favored kingship. And kingship may have facilitated—though it did not originate—the creation of stone works. Whatever the value of these speculations, there seems good evidence that the first powerful kingly states in Central Africa emerged in Rhodesia.

The Zimbabwe culture and the Monomotapa monarchy. Southeast of Fort Victoria, a country town in the Rhodesian veld, lie the ruins of Zimbabwe, covering an area of some sixty acres. The so-called Acropolis, evidently a great stronghold of antiquity, dominates the scene. The great granite kopje is covered with huge boulders, making it a natural retreat in wartime. And Bantu builders later reinforced the strength of this position with a network of massive walls. These were fashioned of stones placed on top of one another without mortar and are comparable in certain ways to the Cyclopean architecture of ancient Etruria and Crete. Down in the valley, where aloes grow in strange shapes and kaffir booms burst out in bright red, stands the Temple, or Great Enclosure, with a high, free-standing wall. A conical tower that may have served as a fertility symbol rises above the other buildings. And there are many other structures to bewitch the imagination. The general layout shows a remarkable resemblance to that of other Bantu royal headquarters, but the architects of Zimbabwe and similar stone structures in Rhodesia were able to build in stone because of the suitability of Rhodesian granite for the purpose. The Great Enclosure presumably served as a king's palace. The ruler and his court lived in huts made of poles and dagga (a mortar made of packed, wetted clay), with floors of hardened earth. Other ruins probably were cattle kraals. Zimbabwe may have served as a natural center for royal rain cults, for there is a good deal of mist and rain and the surrounding country remains green throughout the year. Many ruins similar to Zimbabwe are scattered throughout Rhodesia, parts of Bechuanaland, and the northern Transvaal, but none have been discovered north of the Zambezi.

The Zimbabwe site has an ancient history. Archaeologists have dug up the remains of early Iron Age subsistence farmers who abandoned the Acropolis sometime during the fourth century A.D. Later on, the area was occupied by tillers who knew how to make stylized figurines of their long-horned cattle. At the beginning of the present millennium a new style of construction came into use at Zimbabwe. It involved among other things, the use of stone for walls.

In all likelihood those living in Zimbabwe and related village communities became subject to the Karanga, a Shona-speaking people who first entered Rhodesia from the north, perhaps in A.D. 850. The invaders developed an elegant style of pottery; they built numerous rain shrines, including those known today as the Dhlo-Dhlo and the Khami ruins. The Karanga widely extended their suzerainty. Zimbabwe became their royal headquarters and center of worship. During the thirteenth century they had to face new challenges in the form of intruders from Bechuanaland. The Rozwi, the dominant Karanga clan, then apparently organized their people on a more military basis. They also embarked on the construction of buildings in the valley below the Acropolis. By the fourteenth century the Karanga were trading with Muslim merchants from the coast, who gradually acquired a powerful position in the interior, where they dominated the gold trade.

Karanga culture seems to have reached its highest point during the fifteenth century. The Karanga made a name for themselves not only as builders but also as experts at carving soapstone (an art which is now reviving in Rhodesia), at weaving cloth, at fashioning gold ornaments and all manner of implements made of iron. They also acquired a great military reputation. The region between the Limpopo and the Zambezi was occupied by a number of different states; it may simply be chance that we know more about the Monomotapas, the ruling Karanga kings, than about their neighbors. However, there seems to be clear evidence that during the fifteenth century, the Karanga extended their power northward to the Zambezi. The purpose of their expansionist policy is now hard to untangle. Perhaps the Rozwi were urged on by Muslim merchants, who most likely favored a strong kingdom, capable of making the country safe for the foreigners' persons and purses. Or perhaps the Karanga needed more land for their people and their flocks. Another motive could have been the ever-present need for salt, a precious commodity for a people living a long way from the sea.

Whatever the reasons, Mutota, one of the greatest Karanga rulers, shifted the focus of his kingdom to the north, where he established his headquarters by the escarpment near the Chitako-Changonya Hill east of Gota. Visitors willing to make their way through the bush to the foot of the escarpment can still see the remains of his work. They consist of walls, built of stone slabs piled upon each other without mortar; the main stockade was scalloped, probably in order to accommodate round huts with their walls adjoining the stockade. The northern portion of the Karanga kingdom became the more important because there was convenient access to the Zambezi, and Muslim traders from the coast could reach the royal headquarters more easily. Tradition has it that later on in the fifteenth century, Matope, another great king, carried Karanga arms as far as the shores of the Indian Ocean.

Despite extensive contacts with the Muslims, Islam apparently made no impact whatever on the subjects of the Monomotapas. Traders from the coast came to buy and sell, not to convert. On the contrary, the indigenous forms of spirit worship may conceivably have become even more elaborate than they had been before. The Shona believed—and many still believe—in Mwari, the Supreme Being, the Ancient of Days. But the Deity, in their view, was not interested in the problems of individuals. The fortunes of the community were guided by tribal spirits who looked after a great variety of important matters which affected the people as a whole, especially the rains. Like the secular officeholders under the king, these spirits were graded in an intricate hierarchy. The problems of individuals were resolved by ancestral spirits. The spirits of a man's forefathers would provide help in time of trouble and would also punish evildoers. But the average man could not approach the spirit world; this must be done through spirit mediums, through men "inspired." Therefore, much of the monarch's influence apparently depended either on his own intermediary powers or on his ability to control the diviners. And the king had assistance from a select body of tribal intellectuals—part spirit mediums, part court historians—who were supposed to voice the will of ancestral kings and who maintained the traditions of the people by word of mouth, since the art of writing remained unknown.

The Karanga state developed into a powerful tribal confederacy containing many different ethnic communities. In return for tribute, the king's subjects received protection from their enemies, as well as gifts. (According to a sixteenth-century Portuguese observer, the Monomotapa always sent cattle to his subjects whenever he wanted gold.) In other words, the royal court, acted as the center of an extensive tributary exchange system which functioned without money. The king maintained an extensive court, with a complex hierarchy of dignitaries, and the royal household became the nucleus of a rudimentary state organization. Local government remained in the hands of minor chiefs and headmen, whose position continued to depend on their ability to attract followers through gifts of food. The ordinary tribesmen continued to live as they had done for centuries; they dwelt in small round huts, cultivated the soil with hoes, and kept cattle, sheep, pigs, and goats.

The Monomotapa monarchy did not succeed in welding all its disparate members into a permanent and cohesive state. On the contrary, its power became overextended, and the Monomotapas failed to maintain effective control over the outlying provinces of their empire. They may also have suffered from the fact that their various provinces remained relatively undifferentiated from an economic point of view; hence, there may not have been sufficient economic ties to hold the country together. To make matters worse, the available land surrounding the royal capital may have become exhausted by overuse. Perhaps the pressure of population placed an excessive strain on existing ways of tilling the soil. The farmers apparently used neither cow dung nor green manure to fertilize their fields. The fallow period required to recover the fertility of fields in the vicinity of great settlements must have lengthened as time went on. Farmers presumably had to go farther and farther afield to clear gardens by traditional slash-and-burn methods. And despite their impressive political and architectural achievements, the Karanga seemingly found no solution to the limitations inherent in their primitive agricultural system.

According to the findings of D. P. Abraham, an ethnohistorian, personal factors also played their part in the decline of the empire. Most of Monomotapa Matope's sons lacked their father's ability. The most competent of them, a man called Changa, born of a lowly wife, gained control over the central and southern provinces. When Matope died at the end of the fifteenth century, Changa assumed the Arab title of "Amir." The words "Changa" and "Amir" fused into "Changamire," which itself became a new title. In the end, Changamire proclaimed himself king; his new state became known as Urozwi. There was bitter fighting between the Monomotapas and the Changamires. These conflicts left both parties weakened at a time when the Karanga had to meet the greatest challenge in their history—the rising power of Portugal in their part of Africa.

4

Early Colonialism:
The Portuguese

Portugal and the Rhodesian Interior: The Sixteenth and Seventeenth Centuries

The age of the great discoveries was a time both of peril and opportunity for Western Christendom. In 1453 the Turks conquered Constantinople and, for all practical purposes, assumed the legacy of the ancient Eastern Roman Empire. In 1529 Ottoman hosts advanced to the gates of Vienna. Had they taken the city, the Crescent would have supplanted the Cross in the very heart of Europe. In the end, the Muslim assault was stayed, but the Ottoman Empire long remained the most formidable military power in Europe. Ottoman imperialism continued to dominate the Balkans and the eastern Mediterranean. The Muslims held an unshakeable grip on the land-borne trade to Asia Minor and India. They also controlled a large part of Europe's silver resources, and thereby held an apparently unassailable economic position.

Compared with Turkey, Portugal, on the other end of the Mediterranean, was but a puny power. But by the end of the fifteenth century the country was unified and relatively well administered. Portuguese merchants were enterprising and influential. Portugal was a center of scientific pursuits, and the country also came to occupy a brilliant position in the realm of letters.

For a brief span, Portugal established a huge maritime dominion, a chain of outposts that ranged from Brazil to East Africa, and from

India to China. Portuguese navigators outflanked the Muslims on the North African shore by establishing direct seaborne communications with the gold-producing kingdoms of West Africa. In 1488 Portuguese seafarers rounded the Cape of Good Hope. And in the beginning of the sixteenth century the Portuguese burst into the Indian Ocean. No Muslim power was able to offer successful resistance. The Swahili-speaking city-states of the East African littoral were too disunited and too weakened by internecine struggles to expel the invaders. The Portuguese in time set up a chain of commercial and naval bases that dominated much of the commerce of the Indian Ocean. Gold, spices, ivory, and other luxury goods enriched the Portuguese exchequer, and for a short time Portugal became one of the world's great powers.

Portugal's principal stronghold in South East Africa was Sofala, situated to the south of the modern port of Beira. The encroaching sea now covers the ruins of this fortress. When the tide recedes, a visitor can still walk across the sand, about half a mile eastward, and reach the remnants of massive walls. These stand out against a low shore, where the pale-green mangroves and lofty coconut palms make up the same kind of scenery that Portuguese adventurers must have seen four and a half centuries ago. If he digs among the rubble, the visitor can perhaps still find a rusty cannonball or some fragments of pottery. But there is not much time to search. For soon the tide comes in, and the melancholy reminders of past splendors and miseries once more sink beneath the waves.

First founded in 1506, Sofala served both as a refitting station for Portuguese vessels on their way to India and a commercial post designed to tap the gold trade to the interior. Portuguese travelers made their way to the Kingdom of Monomotapa. Impressed by the arguments of Gonçalo da Silveira, a Jesuit missionary, the reigning Monomotapa, Nogomo Mupunzagutu, even agreed to accept Christianity. But the Jesuit's success alarmed the powerful Muslim party at the king's court, for they feared Portuguese influence both for commercial and religious reasons. In 1561 Silveira was strangled at the Monomotapa's orders.

For over a century, the Portuguese tried to obtain a permanent hold over the interior, but none of their efforts attained permanent success. In 1572 a great military expedition commanded by Francisco Barreto, a former governor of India, set out from Sena in the Zambezi Valley into the interior. The reigning Monomotapa promised various commercial concessions at the expense of the Muslim merchants in Mashonaland. More important still, Shona diplomacy persuaded the Portuguese to use their arms against the Mongaze, a turbulent people on the Lower Zambezi who were constantly at war with the Karanga. Tactically, the

Portuguese, with their armor, their artillery, and their arquebuses, were superior to African infantry, armed with the weapons of the Iron Age. Strategically, however, the Portuguese were at a constant disadvantage. Portuguese armies were reduced by fever, and the presence of animal diseases prevented the use of ox wagons to carry supplies; hence, Portuguese forces could not easily operate away from the Zambezi route, where they could rely on river transport. Above all, the climate and horse sickness alike prevented extensive employment of armored cavalry, which had played such a major role in giving victory to the Spanish conquistadores over the great Indian kingdoms of America.

The Portuguese, insofar as they had a consistent policy at all, aimed to control the interior through puppet kings. The Monomotapa monarchy, which was steadily becoming weaker, had to battle against Urozwi in the south and against Manyika in the east; hence, the Karanga always aimed at playing off the Portuguese against the enemies of Monomotapa, in return for more or less temporary concessions of an economic and religious kind.

In 1607 Gatsi Rusere, the reigning king, agreed that several of his sons should be baptized, and that the Portuguese should enjoy a mining monopoly in return for military aid. Again in 1629 the Portuguese, after a series of bitter struggles, installed a new Monomotapa, Mavura Mhande, who became a Christian and promised to acknowledge Portuguese suzerainty. These temporary successes were apt to arouse bursts of optimism, and for the first time in its history, Central Africa became the subject of "best sellers" in Europe. Some of the writers depicted the Monomotapas as magnificent emperors, arrayed in gorgeous clothes, surrounded by all the fabled magnificence of the east; thus, Central Africa passed into legend as an El Dorado, where even fools might pick up golden fortunes in the bush.

Reality was more prosaic. The Portuguese could control neither the indigenous people nor their own settlers in the interior. Portuguese colonists often set themselves up as independent magnates, levied their own revenue, with their private armies waged private wars, and feared "neither God nor the King." The Portuguese policy of interfering with the legitimate succession in the kingdoms of Karanga, Manica, and Quiteve made orderly administration difficult, and many abuses flourished in the interior. The Portuguese colonizers lacked a centralized authority. Disaster was therefore not long in coming. In 1629 the Portuguese imposed a humiliating treaty on the Shona, and installed a vassal king. A short time later—the date is not absolutely clear—a country-wide rising broke out against the Portuguese; apparently this was the first anti-white insurrection in the annals of Rhodesia. According to contemporary reports, between 300 and 400 Portuguese and some 6,000 Africans in their suite were killed. Nyambo Kapararidze, a Monomotapa previously deposed by the Europeans, regained his kingdom. Luís do Espíritu Santo, a Dominican who had earlier refused to pay homage to Kapararidze, died tied to a tree, his body filled with lances. His colleague, João da Trinidade, was hurled down a cliff. It was the greatest blow that had as yet been struck against the Portuguese in South East Africa.

News of the rebellion reached Portuguese headquarters in Mozambique, in 1631. At first the Portuguese could do little, for at the same time, the Muslims of Mombasa had risen, and its garrison had been massacred. Ceylon too was in revolt; Portugal's position in the Indian Ocean was dangerously strained. Nevertheless, the Portuguese rallied with vigor. Their forces drove back an army of tribesmen that had surrounded Quelimane on the coast. Other Portuguese troops strengthened by indigenous levies, marched to Manica, installed a puppet ruler, entered the lands of the Karanga, and crushed Kapararidze's forces. The Portuguese then drew up elaborate plans for exploiting the riches of the interior by a white settlement scheme. Portuguese planners had enormously exaggerated the profits that might be made from the mines of Karanga. The men from Portugal had to contend with the English and other interlopers in the Indian Ocean. Portuguese India remained desperately short of manpower; hence, the Portuguese were unable to consolidate their position inland, and their settlement projects came to nought.

The Portuguese policy of shoring up and controlling the Monomotapas moreover did not work. The Monomotapas could not be turned into permanent satellites. At the same time their power kept declining. From the 1680s on, the Changamire dynasty began to expand its power northward from Urozwi, and the Portuguese suffered one blow after another. In 1693 Changamire's army took Dambarare, an important trading center, and slew all the Portuguese and Indians in the township. Bodies of the dead were disinterred, and the soldiers produced a medicine which supposedly made them invincible against the whites. Two resident Dominicans were flayed; their skins were carried at the head of the army to prove Changamire's might.

Again the Portuguese resisted with vigor. The residents of Sena, a fever-ridden settlement on the lower Zambezi, blocked the ends of the streets and mounted guns by the gates. Luckily for the Portuguese, Changamire died, and the Portuguese managed to restore a semblance of influence in Monomotapa's country. But they remained incapable of controlling their own colonists, who in turn were hated by the mass of the indigenous people. As a Portuguese viceroy put it, "it was the insolence of our people that caused these wars because those who possess many Kafirs and have power are guilty of such excesses that the [African] Kings and Princes, offended, break out in these disorders. Everybody in the Rivers wants to govern." [1] The Portuguese, in other words, were unable to wield any real authority away from the coast and the lower Zambezi Valley; they could make no permanent impact on the Shona, and in time Portugal's presence in Mashonaland became but a hazy memory.

The Portuguese Inland: Reflections on a Failure

The Portuguese fiasco in Central Africa strangely contrasted with the Portuguese success in Brazil. In their great American colony, as in Rhodesia, the Portuguese encountered difficulties occasioned by distance. In Brazil, the colonizers had to battle Dutch interlopers, Indian guerrillas, and African slave insurgents. They had to cope with multifarious problems created by a tropical climate and the vagaries of the seasons. Yet the Portuguese imprinted their language and their culture on the country. The Brazilian nation today numbers more than 90,000,000 people. Many influences—American Indian and African, Italian and German—have shaped them; yet the Portuguese component exceeds all others in importance. But Portugal's cultural impact on the inland regions of Central Africa remained small. Some words of Portuguese derivation entered into various indigenous tongues, including Chewa. Some Karanga turned to Christianity. These included a prince who, in 1670, became a Master of Theology and ended his days as a priest in Portuguese India; perhaps he could be considered Southern Africa's first expatriate intellectual! Portuguese colonization also affected Africa in a more indirect fashion. Portuguese colonists imported citrus fruit and other Mediterranean plants. Portuguese sailors helped to diffuse Indian corn (maize), tobacco, and other crops of American provenance on the African continent, thereby altering indigenous habits of food and consumption. Nevertheless, Portuguese colonization in the interior was a resounding failure. The Portuguese—like all their European contemporaries—could not protect their men against malaria-carrying mosquitoes nor their draft oxen against the tsetse fly. The colonizers' lack of medical and veterinary knowledge was all the more serious, since they settled in low-lying, fever-ridden country on the coast and the

---

[1] Cited by Eric Axelson, *The Portuguese in South-East Africa, 1600–1700* (Johannesburg: Witwatersrand University Press, 1960), p. 184.

Zambezi Valley. The Portuguese always suffered from lack of numbers; most Portuguese emigrants preferred Brazil to Mozambique; in any case the tiny Portuguese kingdom could not easily govern an empire that spanned the globe from the shores of the New World to the East African littoral, from the coast of India to the shores of China.

Portugal's administrative structure in the colonies was top-heavy. There were constant disagreements between the distant government at Lisbon and the men on the spot, some of them *degredados*, criminals deported from Portugal for the good of the country. For one thing, Lisbon advocated friendly relations with the Karanga, as well as a policy of conversion and of cultural assimilation. The Portuguese authorities could not easily control their own officials, much less the frontiersmen in the distant interior. Portuguese colonization inland created its own variety of bush feudalism. The Crown granted vast estates to semi-independent lords, many of mixed Afro-Portuguese or Goanese ancestry. In many ways these magnates governed their subjects like African chiefs; they lived in barbarous splendor, surrounded by their men-at-arms, their flunkies, and their concubines. They honored the king but did what appeared good in their own eyes.

The Portuguese were also unable to spread their religion in the interior. Portuguese divines above all tried to convert the mighty, hoping that the common people would ultimately follow in the footsteps of a Christian aristocracy. But the Portuguese could not Christianize the inland tribes as Christian missionaries had once converted the barbarians of Northern Europe. Christianity, it seems, became associated with Portuguese imperialism and the anti-Portuguese factions resolved to resist the Europeans' creed as well as their political pretensions. Even pro-Portuguese Monomotapas would waver in their allegiance and abandon Catholicism, as circumstances seemed to demand.

Traditional religion continued to satisfy the needs of the people. The spirit mediums spoke in the tongues of men and angels; the mediums' supernatural law satisfied the psychological needs of the Shona to a far greater extent than the sermons of Dominicans and Jesuits who knew nothing about the people's ancestors and their ways. The traditional Shona religion required no elaborate superstructure, no churches, no territorial organization of the Catholic kind. The Shona remained as impervious to Christianity as to Islam. Despite wars and commotions, there was no revolutionary change in conditions of life sufficiently great to invalidate the wisdom of the ancestors.

The Portuguese were no more successful in the economic sphere. Portuguese colonization entailed high overhead expenditures. At no time, for instance, was the supply of gold from the interior sufficient to balance Portuguese spending on the fortress and factory of Sofala. Un-like British imperialists of a later vintage, the Portuguese did not intro-duce new methods of production into the interior. They generally contented themselves with the position of middlemen, and depended on traditional African methods. As a result mining and transport costs remained heavy. African mining of the customary kind was not, how-ever, adjusted to the demands of an extensive trade. African miners did not have explosives; neither did they have pumps. Instead they labo-riously scooped out ground water with hand bowls. Africans could not therefore work the precious metal to any great depth; the resources of the "ancient workings" were often only half-used, with serious conse-quences to the economic development of the interior. Moreover, the Portuguese never solved the vital question of labor incentives. They often employed coercion, but the use of force discouraged the producers. The African tribes remained largely self-sufficient, requiring only a few foreign-made goods. "They are so lazy and given to an easy life," despair-ingly wrote a Portuguese chronicler in the seventeenth century, "that they will not seek gold unless they are constrained for want of clothes or provisions which are not wanting in the land . . . and the Kaffirs are inclined to agricultural and pastoral pursuits in which their riches consist." The Africans, in other words, had as little need for the white men's economic methods as for the white men's religion.

Portuguese mercantilism also created serious problems of its own. Portuguese empire-builders aimed at excluding or at least curtailing Muslim competition within the Portuguese sphere. According to one interpretation, the Portuguese thereby wholly disrupted the traditional network of trade and wrecked the prosperity both of the East African coast and of the interior. In actual practice, however, the Portuguese could never get rid of their Muslim rivals. Portuguese warships were never sufficiently numerous to enforce a close blockade of Muslim ports, and Portuguese seapower only operated in a sporadic fashion. Portuguese caravels might be superior to Muslim ships of the time, but even the best Portuguese vessels, dependent on favorable winds, could only cruise slowly and had to spend long periods in port for refitting and repair.

However rapacious Portuguese policy may have been, there are some indications that the Portuguese trade and the Muslim trade in fact may even have complemented one another to some extent. The Arabs brought in merchandise from the Near East; the Portuguese im-ported goods from Western Europe and the Mediterranean. Christians and Mohammedans continued to deal with one another; Arab merchants —licensed or unlicensed—could not be excluded from Portugal's immediate sphere of influence. The numerical factor moreover continued to operate against the Portuguese in the economic as well as in the political and religious fields. At its peak, the Portuguese official establishment in East Africa during the sixteenth century never exceeded 900 people. They therefore could not impose their civilization on the coast, and their influence never rivaled that of the Muslims, who created a distinctive Swahili culture on the East Africa littoral.

Portugal also encountered serious domestic problems. In 1580 the kingdom became an appendage of Spain, which used the resources of its newly acquired dependency to further the objects of Habsburg policy in Europe. It was only in 1640 that Portugal's "Babylonian Captivity" came to an end and the Portuguese once more became masters in their own house. By this time Portugal's European competitors, especially the Dutch, were making serious inroads into Portuguese strength. Above all, the Muslims, though politically divided, recovered their breath once the first Portuguese impact had spent its force. In 1698 the Portuguese finally lost Mombasa, the great trading city on the Kenyan shore. Within a few years the remnants of Portuguese power were confined to the lands south of the Rovuma river, and even here Portugal's hold remained feeble and uncertain.

State-Building North of the Zambezi

During the sixteenth and seventeenth centuries the Portuguese above all desired gold. Mozambique had not yet developed into a major supplier of slaves. Lack of capital and logistic difficulties stood in the way of building up tropical plantations of the Brazilian variety. Also the Portuguese had to contend with a difficult climate. Tete, for instance, one of the principal centers of Portuguese power on the Zambezi and a trading center on the road to the north, must have been a dreary hellhole. The rock beneath the settlement consisted of gray sandstone, which reflected the heat of the sun. Tete still enjoys the unenviable distinction of being one of the hottest places in Africa. The Portuguese fort was built close to the water; the garrison knew nothing of mosquito screens, and the Europeans suffered catastrophic mortality rate. Gold was hard to get, and even in the vicinity of the Portuguese settlements, production costs were high, and as a result the merchants' profits appear to have been exceedingly modest. The Portuguese therefore had little incentive to explore the remoter interior; hence, written sources concerning the Early Iron Age kingdoms of Zambia and Malawi remain much scarcer than those which bear on the realm of the Monomotapas. Direct contacts with the people of Malawi remained scanty. Most people in Malawi (Maravi) are matrilineal. While the Shona trace their descent to a common ancestor through the male line, the Malawi tribes, like the majority of ethnic groups in Central Africa beyond the Zambezi, trace their origin through women from a common ancestress. Children are not disciplined by their father, but by their mother's elder brother. Generational problems do not arise so much between father and son as between son and maternal uncle. Again, when a chief dies, he is not succeeded by an offspring of his own, but by the son of a sister.

The Malawi (Maravi) are today broken into a number of tribal groups, including Chewa, Chikunda, and many others. All of them, except the Nsenga, speak a common Bantu tongue known as Nyanja. Today there are Nyanja-speakers in Malawi, Zambia, and Mozambique (hence Malawi now attempts to make territorial demands on its neighbors). In recent times, the Nyanja-speaking people were organized into small village communities; there was no powerful Malawi state.

In more ancient times, their political structure seems to have been very different. Tradition states that at some time during the Middle Ages a great chief, known as Kalonga, led his people from the Luba country in what is now the Katanga into the region south and southwest of Lake Nyasa. In all probability this was not the migration of a great host but of small groups of invaders who had acquired a superior state organization and who may have attained special fighting prowess through their skill as elephant hunters. The chief Kalonga sent out various matrilineal kinsmen to colonize what is now the Chewa country in Malawi. In addition, other Nyanja-speaking dignitaries carved out spheres of influence for themselves and their followers. According to Edward Alpers, a modern historian, the various Nyanja-speaking peoples built up their power by trading ivory to the Muslims of the coast; the long-distance commerce in ivory may well have given rise to the power of the chiefs.

As Alpers interprets the situation, Portuguese intervention in the Zambezi Valley interfered with the existing network of exchange, for the Portuguese were interested in gold rather than ivory. The resultant disorders led to internal disturbances. Lundu, one of Kalonga's lieutenants, sought to create an independent state and invaded what is now northern Mozambique. In the end Kalonga, like Monomotapa south of the Zambezi, availed himself of Portuguese help, and Lundu was defeated. Malawi apparently became a kingdom which, by the beginning of the seventeenth century, reached all the way to the shore opposite Mozambique island. It formed a great tribal confederacy that was held together by war, trade, and religion.

The Malawi empire did not, however, survive the seventeenth century. The reasons for this are not quite clear; hence, we are largely reduced to speculation. Apparently, the Mbona cult (the Malawi national cult) did not sufficiently appeal to Kalonga's non-Malawian subjects. The enormous distances of central Africa probably prevented the sovereign from controlling the periphery of his state. Above all, the Malawi seem to have lost their commercial supremacy to the Yao, a Bantu-speaking people who dwelled in northwestern Mozambique. According to Alpers, the rise of Yao power went with the changed commercial position of Kilwa, a Muslim city on the coast of Tanganyika. Portuguese occupation of the Zambezi Valley interfered with Kilwa's trade and the Swahili merchants had to look for new sources of supply. The Yao made good use of the change in the commercial balance of power; by the eighteenth century they had also replaced the Malawi as the chief traders to Mozambique island. The power of the Kalongas disintegrated; the various sections of the Malawi nations developed as small, independent communities.

For reasons which are far from clear, the Congo Basin became a nursery of African monarchies. One of these empire-building peoples was the Lunda who were farmers, hunters, and fishermen. Sometime during the fourteenth and fifteenth centuries, the Lunda acquired new ideas concerning political organization from their Luba neighbors to the northeast, in the northern part of Katanga. Lunda kings came to hold power by divine right; they held extensive ritual functions, as did their headmen who were held responsible for their subjects' supernatural as well as secular well-being. Relations between the various Lunda dignitaries were apparently governed by what anthropologists call perpetual kinship. This means that whenever a great lord died, the man who stepped into his shoes inherited not merely his predecessor's status but also his name and his kinship relations. Perpetual kinship proved to be a most valuable political device; it divorced the political structure from the biological descent structure, and appears to have given the Lunda states a relatively large measure of stability. Lunda statesmen were able to establish their institutions in different kinds of country, in fertile river valleys and in regions of savanna. The Lunda do not appear to have maintained standing armies, though their so-called traveling chiefs, who journeyed through the realm on the king's business, each had an armed retinue to enforce his orders. The Congolese legacy had many other ramifications. Similar patterns of ritual, associating the chief with the welfare of the people and with the fertility of men and beasts, spread widely through Zambia. Many Zambian peoples adopted similar symbols of kingship, including scarlet feathers, iron bowstands, and slit drums.

The Lunda were outstanding as colonizers and conquerors. During the seventeenth century, they expanded to the west into what is now Angola. Here they came into contact with Umbundu middlemen who supplied them with guns and other imports in exchange for slaves. Later on, the Portuguese introduced new crops, such as maize and cassava to Lunda. In the far interior, where slave raiders did not occasion the same havoc as they did near Portuguese slave markets on the coast, the new crops enabled farmers to feed more mouths. Indirect contact with the Portuguese may therefore have led to an increase of population, thereby encouraging colonization. Certainly the possession of firearms and the expanding commerce with the coast helped to strengthen Lunda power. The Lunda built up a number of satellite states which fostered their trade and gave new opportunities for ambitious princes without a crown. For many years these minor Lunda states remained tributary to the Lunda overlord in the southern Congo, known as Mwata Yamvo, but gradually the invaders married the local people, and links with the Congo weakened.

During the eighteenth century the Lunda further strengthened the basis of their commercial power. They pushed eastward into the fertile Luapula Valley, where they set up the Kingdom of Kazembe. Kazembe became a powerful monarch, who inhabited a great "agrotown" in the Luapula Valley, a capital which served alike as a center of trade and administration of fishing and farming. Kazembe traded all the way to the Indian Ocean. Hence, by the end of the eighteenth century, the whole of Central Africa was linked by a network of commerce which stretched from coast to coast and supplied the indigenous population with all manner of merchandise, muskets, cloth, and ornaments, in exchange for slaves, copper, and ivory. Kazembe acquired despotic powers; his town was surrounded by a great stockade invulnerable to the assaults of African enemies, and by the beginning of the nineteenth century Kazembe had become one of the greatest potentates in what is now Zambia. The Lunda also seem to have brought in various technical innovations. They probably spread the cultivation of cassava. They introduced the technique of building with mud. They were skilled in the use of the talking drum, whereby villages were able to communicate over vast distances.

Another warlike people of Congo origin were the Bemba. The

Bemba, who had probably descended from the Luba, seem to have penetrated northeastern Zambia some time about 1740. According to Bemba tradition, the tribe became separated from their kindred when Chitimukulu, the Bemba captain, was killed by the Bisa people with a poisoned arrow. The Bemba then avenged their chief's death and extended their territory at the expense of various indigenous tribes, including the Bisa, the Lungu, and the Mambwe. Unlike Kazembe's people, the followers of Chitimukulu had to be content with a harsh and arid country, and it seems likely that by the middle of the eighteenth century, the region as a whole was densely populated in relation to the slender resources of its inhabitants. Competition for land may have stimulated raiding and intertribal fighting. Warfare seems to have become increasingly fierce by reason of an ever-increasing supply of firearms, which were imported into the interior. Hence the Bemba became a warrior people par excellence, organized in a centralized and despotic state.

Congolese immigrants also made their way into the Zambezi Valley, where they set up a state organized along very different principles. Sometime during the seventeenth century, the Luyi, later known as the Lozi or Barotse, moved into the Zambezi plain and gradually extended their authority right down the river. The Lozi economy rested on mixed farming, fishing, and skillful use of the agricultural opportunities offered by periodic floods that fertilized the Zambezi plain. The Lozi created an intricate tributary system that helped to distribute the diverse products from various provinces among the subjects of the king. They also built up a complex state that had some affinity to the political organization characteristic of the southern Congo. The Lozi successfully used canoe power to dominate the river. But they were also skilled diplomatists and capable legislators. Tradition has it that Mulambwa, a Lozi Solomon who reigned at the end of the eighteenth century, gained renown by reforming the law. In cases of adultery the injured party was made to sleep in public with the offender's wife or husband. Thieves, in Mulambwa's permissive view, only appropriated the other person's property because of need. Hence, a man caught stealing was brought before the king, who would either give him a cow or make him village overseer.[2] Mulambwa, unlike the great Lunda kings, refused to take part in the slave trade, a policy followed by many of his successors. In all probability, the fertile Zambezi Valley—unlike the inhospitable Bemba

[2] M. Maingo, "The Lozi Kingdom," in A Short History of Zambia, ed., Brian M. Fagan (Nairobi: Oxford University Press, 1966), p. 123.

country—required a great deal of manpower. The Lozi had domestic slaves of their own, and far from exporting their captives, used persuasion or coercion to increase the population of their valley.

The story of kingdoms and empires is easier to tell than that of stateless societies; hence, more attention is devoted in textbooks to states than to small communities. We should not forget, however, that even by the end of the eighteenth century when many monarchs held sway in parts of Central Africa, a large proportion of the indigenous peoples were not subjected to any liege lord or king. These included the Ila-Tonga peoples (probably some of the earliest inhabitants of Zambia); the Lamba-Ambo-Luano group, who supposedly came from the Congo about 1600; and many others. Even the subjects of kings had relatively little contact with their sovereign, unless they held high office. Empires might rise and fall, but the village remained the unit of social life. There were no cities, and the African remained essentially a farmer, a countryman.

5

Nineteenth-Century Invasions

Southern Backwash

Throughout the seventeenth and eighteenth centuries the fortunes of Central Africa were indirectly linked to Portuguese colonization in Angola and Mozambique, and to the activities of Muslim merchants on the East Coast. During the nineteenth century three new contenders for power appeared on the scene—Britons, Boers, and Bantu hosts who began to move northward from South Africa, thereby reversing the perennial tide of black migration that used to flow southward from the Congo Basin. The British first seized the Cape of Good Hope in 1795 as a strategic move in the war against revolutionary France. In 1806 they permanently occupied the Cape, with far-reaching consequences. Great Britain was the first great power to outlaw slavery in its dominions. The British thereby took a vital part in the worldwide struggle against a system of servile labor based on hereditary status distinctions—a system that used to dominate life in lands as far afield as the West Indies and Brazil, the southern states of the United States and Russia.

Slavery by the 1800s conflicted with the moral convictions, the religious ideals, the political assumptions, and the economic interests of British factory owners and workmen alike. Whereas slavery in the United States was abolished through a bloody civil war, British slave-owners submitted without resistance. The great planters on the British West Indian islands were cowed by British seapower. The Boer slave-owners in South Africa decided to make the best of things without

61

fighting. (The Boers are known today as Afrikaners, they are white South Africans descended from Dutch, French, and German immigrants who speak Afrikaans, a Dutch derivative.) The South African farmers did not practice plantation agriculture; hence, they required relatively few slaves. A large proportion of Afrikaners stayed on in the Cape and contented themselves with nominally free labor. Others decided to emigrate with their bondsmen beyond the Orange River, away from British jurisdiction.

The Great Trek (1836–37) formed part of a perennial migration of cattle farmers, who were always searching for new pastures. The Trek was also the frontiersmen's declaration of independence, a bloodless rebellion. The trekkers sought freedom from British rule; they objected to the abolition of slavery; they desired security against assaults from warlike "Kaffirs." And in words that were to echo again and again—in parliamentary debates at Cape Town to angry "sundowner" debates over a bottle of whiskey in some remote Rhodesian mining township—the emigrants complained against "the unjustified odium that has been cast upon us by interested and dishonest persons under the name of religion, whose testimony is believed in England to the exclusion of all evidence in our favor. . . ." [1]

By 1837, a year after American settlers had hoisted the Lone Star flag in Texas, some 5,000 Boers had crossed the Orange River. The Boer vanguard pushed farther north, into what is now the Transvaal; a few even made their way beyond the Limpopo River. The Afrikaners, though small in numbers, had a striking military superiority over the Bantu tribes who competed for good grazing land with the white pastoralists. The Boers had horses and firearms; above all, they had wagons which gave them strategic mobility in peace and war alike.

A Boer wagon, with a full span of sixteen oxen, occupied the best part of seventy feet. The driver would call the oxen by name; the animals took their place, and heavy wooden yokes were placed on their necks. A wagon in motion was a magnificent sight. Great skill was required to keep it moving smoothly. On sharp turns a wagon guided by an inexperienced driver would take short cuts and thereby throw the whole span into disorder. But the drivers knew their job; and the so-called wheelers, specially selected oxen, were almost human in the way in which they would ease a front wheel round a boulder, push through heavy sand, or hold the wagon at a steep drift. The wheelers and their wagons crushed out Bantu resistance in the end. The Boers learned the

[1] Cited by L. C. A. Knowles and C. M. Knowles, *The Economic Development of the British Overseas Empire*, vol. 3 (London: George Routledge and Sons, 1936). p. 25.

extraordinary feat of maneuvering their cumbersome vehicles into solid squares, almost impregnable to the assaults of black archers and spearmen. When caught at a disadvantage, the Afrikaners might sustain an occasional disaster, but Boer marksmanship, veldcraft, strategy, and high morale born of the conviction that they were the Chosen People of the veld, in the long run always proved superior against the military techniques of Iron Age warriors battling on foot.

The most formidable of these fighters were the Zulu and their offshoots. Early in the nineteenth century, the Zulu, a cattle-keeping people dwelling in Natal, in South Africa, elaborated a new form of political and military organization. Perhaps they had to adjust their traditional institutions to meet the exigencies derived from growing pressure on the land. Perhaps their society responded also to an increase of foreign trade at Delagoa Bay. Commercial competition led to conflicts for control over local trade routes. Foreign traffic also placed more power into the hands of the chiefs. Whatever the reason, the Zulu became a great military power. They organized their nation into regiments drafted by age; they learned how to fight in close order. They were trained to advance in crescent-shaped formations behind the cover of closely linked oxhide shields; they moved rapidly and charged home with heavy jabbing spears, while keeping a tactical reserve for the decisive thrust. The Zulu had no use for limited wars. They believed in a strategy of annihilation that allowed the enemy no time for recovery. The militarization of the Zulu had far-reaching consequences. The Zulu raided their neighbors; they slew the men, drove back the enemies' cattle, kept the women for their beds, and trained the boys for service in Zulu regiments.

The Zulu way of fighting was not overly bloody by the standards of primitive, warlike pastoral races. The pious biblical heroes of Sunday school fame seem to have preferred proceedings even more rigorous than those of the Zulu. With monotonous regularity, for instance, ". . . Joshua smote all the countries of the hills, and of the south, and of the vale, and of the springs, and all their kings; he left none remaining but utterly destroyed all that breathed. . . ." [2] The Zulu raids nevertheless occasioned widespread destruction; in turn they terrorized other peoples into fleeing from the invaders' reach and thereby caused bloodshed far from the original centers of disturbance. Zulu militarism forced other communities to improve their state organization and their fighting methods. Breakaways from the Zulu kingdom in turn initiated new migration. A number of great hordes fought their way northward, as far afield as Zambia, Malawi, and Tanzania. These were nations on the march, in search of cattle, loot, and pastures. They pillaged where they

[2] Josh. 10:4.

could; they swept other peoples in their train, developing into "snowball states," with a war-making potential of frightening efficiency. At the same time these warriors performed feats of incredible endurance. Unlike the Huns and Mongols, the Zulu armies had no horses; yet they covered distances exceeding 1,000 miles; even the march of Xenophon's Ten Thousand, recorded in the *Anabasis*, does not quite compare with such epic deeds.[3]

One of the great migrations was led by Mziligazi (Umzilikazi). Mziligazi, a man of imposing personality, a born leader, and a man of utterly ruthless disposition, began his career as one of the headmen subordinate to Shaka, the greatest of Zulu Paramount Chiefs. Mziligazi broke away from his liege lord, and led his followers across the Drakensberg Mountains, laying waste immense tracts to the north. Mziligazi's followers, known as the Ndebele (Matabele) were, however, unable to hold their own against the Boers, and sometime about 1840, the Ndebele settled in what is now Matabeleland in Rhodesia. Here they found a land where their cattle flourished; safe from the unwelcome attention of the Boers in the Transvaal, they acquired undisputed sway all the way from the Shasi River to the Zambezi. The Ndebele destroyed what was left of Karanga prosperity; though the cult of Mwari, the Shona high god, continued among the conquered and even gained the conquerors' respect.

The Ndebele state rested upon three pillars. The regimental system caused the army to remain at a high level of discipline, though in the long run the Ndebele war-making capacity declined because of military and social conservatism. In addition to employing terror against rebellious subjects and recalcitrant foreigners, the Ndebele kings also strengthened their position by skillful "cattle diplomacy," which in turn was made possible by the monarch's complete control over the Ndebele herds. Favored underlings and their followers received herds for their own use, along with other presents; royal power, in other words, facilitated a primitive system of intertribal exchange. Finally, the Ndebele kings, like other great Bantu sovereigns, kept a tight hold over the ivory trade, and thereby further strengthened Ndebele might.

Originally the Ndebele state was a strict caste society; members of the original host and their descendents stood at the top of the social pyramid. Then came the captives belonging to the Sotho and Tswana people of the highveld. The lowest stratum consisted of the Shona, who

[3] Xenophon was an Athenian general, who in 401 B.C. entered Persian service. The Greeks were forced to retreat, and Xenophon led his army all the way from the River Tigris in what is now Iraq to Trapezus on the Black Sea.

were subdued in Rhodesia. The regimental system, however, was gradually watered down. Mziligazi permitted some alien communities to live within his kingdom without being incorporated into the regimental system. Finally, there were chiefdoms on the outer periphery of the state, which were required to pay tribute.

The Ndebele kingdom was one of several "Black Spartas." Another offshoot was led by Zwangendaba, a minor chief who rose to be a nation-builder. About 1821, Zwangendaba led his people, known as the Ngoni (Angoni), into what is now southern Mozambique. Later on he marched into Rhodesia, where the Rozwi dynasty still held a semblance of power under their overlord, the Mambo. The Shona were ill-equipped to meet the barbarian invasion; the Mambo fell; his sovereignty disintegrated; and his people were decimated. Zwangendaba's host continued on the road to the north, reaching the vicinity of Lake Tanganyika about 1842. Three years later, Zwangendaba died, and his host split into several fragments.

One party commanded by Chief Mpeseni moved westward, but for the first time the Ngoni met a warrior people who matched their own valor—the Bemba. Blood-thirsty raiders, they wielded muskets supplied by Muslim traders; the Ngoni were defeated and finally settled in what is now southeastern Zambia. Other Ngoni groups, probably offshoots from Zwangendaba's host, moved to Malawi, where they founded several independent little spear-kingdoms.

Repercussions of the Zulu wars were felt even in the remote Zambezi Valley. The Kololo (Makololo), a group of cattle-keeping Bantu people with a Sotho (Basuto) core, marched northward, crossed the Vaal, fought their way through Bechuanaland, and sometime about 1840 settled in Barotseland, where they became a new aristocracy. They continued to rule the land until 1864, when the Lozi and the Tonga rose simultaneously to cast off the invaders' yoke. Weakened by fever and the unaccustomed climate of the Zambezi Valley, the highlanders from the south put up little resistance. The men were slain, the women parceled out among the victors. The Lozi continued to maintain some links with Lesotho (Basutoland), and the culture of their erstwhile lords continued to command respect.

The Slave Traders' Frontier

During the eighteenth and early nineteenth centuries, Central Africa remained relatively free from the slave trade. Kazembe and other potentates sold men for muskets, but the total number of persons affected by the commerce seems to have remained small. The Lozi and various other tribes had serfs of their own; the Lozi however did not send many captives abroad. The Ndebele did not use their prisoners as a commercial asset but incorporated them into the lower social strata of the tribe. Boer cattle farmers in the Transvaal did not require bondsmen in large numbers to look after the herds; moreover, ox wagons provided a cheaper and a more effective means of transporting merchandise than slave porters.

In the middle of the nineteenth century, however, more traders began to move into the interior in search of elephant tusks. Africa was the world's main supplier of ivory, an indispensable raw material for European makers of figurines, piano keys, and billiard balls, as well as for Indian craftsmen producing bracelets and other ornaments. The delightful ivory objets d'art that today fill museums and antique shops exacted a grim price in blood. The East Coast Arabs at first exhausted the resources along the coast. As elephants became scarce, they pushed ever farther into the interior, cutting out some of the intermediate traders. Sultan Seyid Said, the vigorous ruler of Zanzibar, encouraged this policy of expansion. By 1863 Muslims were well established on the west coast of Lake Nyasa. From there they followed the Bisa traders into the interior and penetrated into the Luangwa Valley. In addition, they opened another route across the Nyasa-Tanganyika Plateau directly to Zanzibar. The coastal traders sold guns in exchange for elephants' teeth; they also purchased slaves. Black captives were in demand as field hands on the clove plantations of Zanzibar, as domestic retainers, as concubines, even as soldiers for use on the coast and as far afield as the Near East.

In the first place the Arabs, and Swahili-speaking Afro-Arabs and Africans from Zanzibar and the adjacent mainland coast, came as mere traders who dealt with powerful monarchs such as Kazembe and Chitmukulu. But in regions where the indigenous people lacked political cohesion, the Muslims gradually began to set up autonomous little lordships of their own. The Swahili possessed firearms, even breechloaders. They knew how to fortify their headquarters with galleried stockades placed across the lines of communication, and capable of resisting even light artillery. Potentates like Mlozi, who set up a Muslim principality on the north end of Lake Nyasa, waged wars against their neighbors and sold weapons to other Africans, who in turn would use muskets to attack their local enemies. Muslim influence of course was by no means entirely negative. The commerce to the coast supplied Africans with new merchandise. In some cases Muslims arrived as permanent settlers; for instance, Swahili-speaking immigrants introduced the cultivation of rice to Malawi. They also brought new skills. Some came as smiths or tailors, who worked for local Africans.

Muslim slavery was characterized by a great number of gradations. Some slaves acquired wealth of their own; they might even be placed in authority over free laborers; a few even managed to rise to high office. Even the plantation workers, the most poorly treated of all, did not necessarily lead an unbearable existence. Sir Harry Johnston, a British administrator of great experience, thought that an African bondsman was subject to a "very tolerable form of servitude," more acceptable than life on a Christian mission station "with its regular hours of work, its plain diet, severe chastity" and ban on wild festivities.[4] But though a slave might be treated in a tolerable fashion by a regular owner, conditions in the interior were grim. From an economist's point of view, the slave trade might be described as Africa's primary form of labor migration, but people on the spot could hardly be expected to take such a detached view of the situation. "Homes were broken up, large numbers of men, women and little children were collected together and despatched on a many-hundred-mile journey overland to the coast, on which they often had to carry a heavy burden. Their slave sticks were no light weight, and they were ill-fed and provided with no clothing to shield them from the cold or wet in mountain regions. If they lagged on the way, or lay down, worn out with exhaustion, their throats were cut or they were shot. . . . The mortality among the children was terrible; the Arab slave drivers do not appear to have been educated by motives of commercial expediency in endeavouring to land as many live and healthy slaves on the coast as possible [but] . . . by something more like devilish cruelty."[5]

While Swahili coastmen were dominating the slave routes across the Tanganyika Plateau and northern Malawi, the Yao became the principal dealers to the south. According to their own tradition, the Yao had come from the regions east of Lake Nyasa. Gradually they drifted into southern Malawi, coming not as a great army but as small groups of colonists. The Yao slowly subjugated the local Nyanja-speaking population which was unable to resist the invaders' firearms. Many different pressures impelled the Yao to move westward. They suffered from tribal dissensions, were threatened by the Lomwe people, another Bantu group; and also looked for new land. In addition, like many other Bantu tribes, the

[4] Johnston to Foreign Office, July 18, 1891, Foreign Office Print 6178/91, No. 149.

[5] H. H. Johnston, *British Central Africa* (London: Methuen & Co. Ltd., 1897), pp. 158–59.

Yao employed slaves for domestic purposes. The Yao lacked a central state organization; therefore, minor chiefs competed with one another for power. This they could only obtain by getting more followers, and one of the means employed for this purpose was the slave hunt. Captives were incorporated into the headman's retinue. The women became junior wives, while the men would engage in farming, basket making, and other recognized male occupations. The chief's sons, who were not in the matrilineal line of succession, would then become the invaluable servants of the chiefs; they received important assignments as war leaders and ambassadors, since they could not play their own hand. The greater chiefs had an additional incentive for engaging in the slave commerce. Trade would bring them gunpowder and muskets; the possession of arms in turn afforded some kind of control over their turbulent vassals. David Livingstone, the great Scottish explorer, found the Yao already well established in the southern part of Malawi when he visited there in 1866. From there they pushed farther inland, trading all the way with the Portuguese in the Zambezi Valley.

Portuguese estate owners in the Zambezi Valley, most of them half-castes or Goanese, also took part in slave raiding. By the end of the nineteenth century Portuguese half-castes and allied tribes had penetrated deep into the Luangwa Valley, occasioning great destruction of life and property. Other traders came from the west. Many of these belonged to the Mbundu people who greatly extended their sphere of operations during the nineteenth century. Initially they came in search of ivory; from the 1870s onward they paid more attention to wild rubber. In addition they purchased slaves, many of whom were sold first of all to Brazil, later to the Portuguese cocoa plantations in the island of São Tomé.

The Mbundu and their allies sold guns to their customers; the new firearms, as always, upset the traditional balance of power. By the second half of the nineteenth century the Lovale people in what is now north-western Zambia began to acquire muskets, and turned against the erstwhile, powerful Lunda. Guns became new and bloody instruments of war; guns changed the techniques of hunting and accelerated the destruction of Central Africa's elephant herds; guns also turned into a new prestige symbol, a potent implement that could not be made by the customary methods of production. Muskets moreover required a steady supply of gunpowder so that the owners of firearms became even more dependent on foreign trade than before.

The various gunpowder frontiers steadily converged upon the Central African interior. By the 1880s at the very latest, merchants from

Angola had reached the country west of Lake Bangweulu in northeastern Zambia; thus, the eastern and the western trading systems merged. The effects of the expanding commerce were far-reaching. The importation of guns exalted the power of chiefs and warlords, who commanded improved weapons or who acquired local monopolies. The use of firearms may well have increased the casualty rate in war. Above all, the slave trade occasioned a great indirect destruction of life. Many were killed in raids; many more starved when the breadwinner was abducted, and the crops were looted or burned. Primitive societies, dependent largely on subsistence agriculture, probably recovered less easily from the effects of protracted warfare than modern industrial communities, which can produce more goods, which can spread the risks with greater ease, and which have far more medical knowledge at their command than primitive people.

As I see it, by the second half of the last century, the tribal societies of the interior suffered from a far-reaching internal crisis. The indigenous societies as a whole were no longer capable of dealing with the new challenges to which they were exposed. In economic terms, many African communities encountered a situation which might be likened to a balance of payments crisis. They became habituated to the use of imported goods like guns, cloth, knives, hatchets, beads—commodities which traditional craftsmen could not produce at all or which they could not produce as cheaply as foreign factories. But in order to pay for such merchandise, Africans had to rely on sources of wealth that were alike perishable and irreplaceable—elephants for their tusks and men for their labor. From the military standpoint, the expanding trade with the coasts set up an intertribal armament race, as black warriors acquired foreign-made weapons, including surplus stocks of muskets being discarded by European armies. Politically, the commerce in slaves and guns upset customary power relationships, both within the different African states, and between hostile African polities. The growth of trade, the development of new military and administrative techniques, accelerated the creation of larger states. The new kingdoms, however, had but limited resources. There were certain improvements in the method of hunting game with guns; new crops came into use; but basically the accustomed methods of production did not change a great deal. Neither the Lozi, the Bemba, the Yao, the Ngoni, or the Ndebele had sufficient power to solve the problems of the region as a whole or to impose stable government on Central Africa at large. The precolonial societies of the interior were torn by profound internal contradictions; hence, they became subject without exception to the sway of the victorious West.

White Exploration

One of the unintended and unacknowledged effects of the expanding commerce in ivory and slaves was to enlarge the information concerning Africa which was available to the Europeans. The manner in which scientific knowledge advanced becomes obvious to anyone who glances at a collection of old maps. Seventeenth- and eighteenth-century cartographers were familiar with the coast. They depicted some inland kingdoms such as the land of Monomotapa. But most of the Central African interior remained unknown; geographers populated it with strange tribes, with outlandish mountains, and with kingdoms whose names sound as if they came straight out of *Gulliver's Travels*. In the second half of the eighteenth century mapmakers adopted a more scientific approach. When they were not sure of their facts, they just plain left blank spaces. Mysterious realms such as those of "Monemug" and of similar potentates disappeared from atlases. The use of terms like "Unknown Parts" and Terra Incognita, printed boldly across the map, marked a great advance in scientific methodology. In the nineteenth century these blank spaces were gradually filled up, this time with information based on well-substantiated data. Many factors were responsible for this advance. Missionaries were looking for souls to save; merchants believed that savage warriors might one day be turned into customers. Industrialists took a greater interest in tropical products such as palm oil and cotton, while the opening of the Suez Canal in 1869 gave a much-needed stimulus to commerce with the East African coast. Central Africa once again moved into the limelight, and many explorers and missionaries turned their attention to what was still one of the last unopened "frontiers" of the Western world.

The explorers came from many nations, though the Portuguese undoubtedly enjoyed the right of primacy. The first European to visit Rhodesia and indeed Central Africa as a whole was Antonio Fernandes, a sixteenth-century traveler, probably a *degredado*, a felon condemned to death and given the chance to redeem himself by some desperate mission in the colonies. In the eighteenth and early nineteenth centuries other notable Portuguese made their way inland. One of these was Dr. Francisco José Maria de Lacerda e Almeida, once an astronomer royal, who had reached high office in the king's service. Lacerda visited Kazembe's kingdom, where he perished of fever in 1798. Thirty years later, Antonio Francisco Ferreira da Silva Portô, like Lacerda a man with a Brazilian background, settled in Angola. Here he made his name as a trader and frontiersman, and in 1848 he managed to reach the Kingdom of the Lozi.

Equally intriguing was Ladislaus Amerigo Magyar, a Hungarian originally trained as a naval officer, who made his name in Angola; he married a black princess and used the armed slaves provided by his wife to penetrate deep into the Lunda country. Silva Portô and Magyar owed their success to the expansion of the ivory trade. So did Karl Mauch, a German elementary schoolmaster with a bent for adventure. Mauch successively struck up friendships with Henry Hartley and Adam Renders, elephant hunters from the south who had penetrated beyond the Limpopo, and who helped the German on his voyages. In the 1860s Mauch visited some of the gold fields of Rhodesia and sent back glowing reports of a long-lost El Dorado in the interior. In 1871 he was guided to the Zimbabwe ruins, which further excited the imagination of European scholars who associated these Bantu structures with the biblical land of Ophir and the splendor of King Solomon. When he returned from his remarkable travels, Mauch could not get any kind of academic position in the Fatherland. The unfortunate schoolteacher lacked the coveted title of *Herr Doktor*; no scientific body would employ him, and he counted himself lucky to get a job in a cement factory whose owners were impressed by his feats. A fellow countryman of Mauch's, Karl Wiese, fared somewhat better. Wiese went to Africa—apparently in order to avoid service in the army. Instead he selected a more dangerous career, that of professional elephant hunter; he collected his own little army of black retainers and became a man of great influence in the Ngoni country. Wiese finally made some money by dealing in concessions, returned to Germany, and contributed some learned papers to the *Boletim da Sociedade de Geographia de Lisboa* and the *Zeitschrift für Ethnologie*.

It would be tedious to list all the men who filled in the map of Central Africa. Some were commissioned officers in the armed services, men trained in making maps and observing the lay of the land. Some were physicians with a general interest in science. Some were clergymen, knowledgeable in foreign languages and well schooled from the start in the anthropological information provided by the Old Testament. All of these men accomplished a remarkable amount of work on relatively little money. All of them depended on information provided by local men, Arab slave traders, Mbundu raiders, Boer elephant hunters, and many others. The European explorers' claim to fame does not so much lie, as legend would have it, in their skill as pathfinders through untrodden jungles. Most of their journeys followed local routes long known to the indigenous people. The explorers' real impact derived from their trained intelligence, from their ability to make accurate observations, and to record and publish their experiences. Many also played their part as advocates of evangelization and as theorists of empire; the greatest of these was David Livingstone (1813–1873).

Livingstone's life was one of those success stories which Victorians admired so much. He came from Scottish working-class parents, and started his career as a "piecer" in a cotton factory. He was the embodiment of the "lad of pairts," nurtured in a rigorous Calvinist tradition, endowed with high intelligence, ruthless will power and even having an obsessional strain in his makeup. By dint of hard study and saving, he managed to go to Glasgow, where he took a medical degree and then offered his services to the London Missionary Society, a Protestant group, as a doctor.

He was first sent to Bechuanaland, and subsequently severed his connection with the society to devote himself entirely to exploration. Between 1851 and 1873 Livingstone traveled right through the continent, from the Zambezi to the West Coast, and then to Malawi and to northeastern Zambia. He accumulated a vast body of geographical and ethnographic information. He was also a pioneer of tropical medicine, making a valuable contribution to the treatment of various diseases. Finally, he helped formulate a colonization policy which suited the ideals of Victorian England.

Africa, he argued—like other humanitarians of his time—must be evangelized. But it was not enough to preach the Gospel. New wine could not be poured into old bottles; the new faith would not flourish within the old social setting. "Commerce and Christianity" must go hand in hand, for the slave traders would not be beaten by gunboats alone, much less by sermons. The iniquitous traffic in human beings would only stop if "legitimate trade" was developed and if Africans found new commodities to sell—palm oil, cotton, and other tropical crops. Africans, therefore, should be taught new agricultural and industrial skills. The interior should be opened by steamships and railways which, between them, would stimulate production and free slave porters from their back-breaking labors. Where possible, Europeans should settle in Central Africa to prime the pump of progress.

Livingstone, the humanitarian, spoke for a whole generation of Victorians. In some respects there was indeed an odd likeness between Livingstone, the Christian missionary, and Karl Marx, the socialist thinker. While Livingstone was gaining fame in Africa, Marx proved in an eloquent fashion that the British bourgeoisie was playing a temporarily progressive role in the colonies. The British, according to Marx, were bestowing an extraordinary, though an unintended, boon upon countries like India by building railways, developing trade and industry, creating a modern administration, a modern army, and a modern educational system in a backward continent. In language as eloquent as any missionary's, Marx also condemned the Indian villagers' superstitions and their "brutalizing worship of nature, exhibiting its degradation in the fact that man, the sovereign of nature, fell down on his knees in adoration of Hanuman, the monkey, and Sabbala, the cow." [6]

Livingstone, likewise, had much in common with the most ardent imperialists of a later period. He was convinced that white men had a moral duty to intervene in Africa. He believed that Europe's work in Africa would benefit whites and blacks alike by providing the West with new markets, by raising Africans' living standards, and by introducing him to Western civilization. Livingstone, in a certain sense, was also a chauvinist in the tradition of his time, but he also managed to get on with Africans. On the other hand, he fiercely quarreled with his white associates and especially the foreigners. He detested the Boers. He despised the Portuguese and Swahili-speaking Muslims without whose help he could not have gained his extraordinary success. Yet Livingstone's life work gave a major impetus to exploratory work and was responsible also for the creation of the first British mission stations in Central Africa.

[6] Karl Marx, "The Government of India Bill," *New York Daily Tribune*, July 1, 1853, in Shlomo Avineri, ed., *Karl Marx on Colonialism and Modernization* . . . (New York: Doubleday and Company, 1968), p. 89.

6

Imperial Advance

Vanguard of the Gospel

The missionary movement made a considerable impact both among the bourgeoisie and the "respectable," chapel-going portion of the working class in Great Britain. Mission recruiters gained substantial successes among the intellectual elite of the British upper-working and lower-middle classes. Livingstone, as we have seen, began his career in a factory. To the millhands, he was one of them; to the entrepreneurs, he was a man who stood for social reconciliation at home, for righteousness, and better business abroad. Robert Moffat, another outstanding Scottish divine and Livingstone's father-in-law, began life as a gardener. The missionaries' creed—charity for the helpless, uplift for the deprived, humility for the proud, and hard work all around—made a profound impression among Christian congregations. In many ways missionary endeavor represented an overspill of metropolitan reform into the colonies. The missionaries believed in converting the poor at home, in improving their condition by individual self-help and by a frugal way of life rather than by collective action of the revolutionary kind. At the same time, the missionaries wished to render similar services to the "natives" abroad whom, in a sense, they mistakenly identified with the metropolitan proletariat.

The missionaries of all nations and all denominations were convinced—with few exceptions—that depraved savages should be civilized, no matter whether they guzzled gin in the slums of Glasgow or beer in the Matabele bush. Even militant black nationalists in the New World continued for a time to share most of these basic assumptions. The Universal Negro Improvement Association and African Communities League, founded by Marcus Garvey, thus proclaimed an essentially similar program designed—among other things—"to promote the spirit of race pride and love; to reclaim the fallen of the race; to administer to and assist the needy; to assist in civilizing the backward tribes of Africa; to strengthen the imperialism of independent African States . . . to promote a conscientious Christian worship among the native tribes of Africa; to establish . . . further education and culture . . . to conduct a worldwide commercial and industrial intercourse." [1]

The main missionary impulse in Central Africa derived from Great Britain. In 1859 the London Missionary Society, Livingstone's parent body, set up its first permanent station at Inyati in Matabeleland. In the 1870s, after Livingstone's death, two Scottish mission stations, belonging respectively to the Established Scottish Church and the dissident Scottish Free Church, began to work in Nyasaland. The London Missionary Society created some stations along Lake Tanganyika, which were then linked to the Lake Nyasa route by a tenuous path. In addition, François Coillard, an intrepid French Protestant married to a Scottish wife, strongly pro-British in his inclinations, made his way to Barotseland, where he became permanently established in 1884. Père F. Dupont, a Catholic priest, penetrated into the Bemba country, where he acquired an extraordinary reputation as a mighty magician and a ruler. In addition, other Catholics and also members of the Anglican Church trekked into Central Africa; so in time did Afrikaner, American, and Swedish missionaries. The Portuguese, on the other hand, who had established clerical primacy in the area, did not resume their missionary advance into the interior, a fact fraught with profound consequences for their imperial ambitions.

Whatever the early missionaries' backgrounds, they did not think of politics when they first began to build their stations of mud huts or their primitive houses made of sun-dried bricks. They were preoccupied with supply questions and with making a living from a soil that often was not as fertile as it appeared. They had to gain the confidence of their African neighbors. They often quarreled fiercely among themselves in lonely, fever-ridden settlements, where the death rate was terrifying, where only men with inflexible wills could hold out among the heathen. But they could not in fact help being drawn into both local and international

---

[1] Cited from the association's program in 1914 by Edmund David Cronon, *Black Moses: The Story of Marcus Garvey and the Universal Negro Improvement Association* (Madison: University of Wisconsin Press, 1966), p. 17.

politics. The missionaries who settled among the subjects of powerful monarchs, such as the king of the Ndebele and the paramount of the Lozi, had to fit into the framework of a tribal state. Mziligazi would not allow the missionaries to make converts. Knowledgeable alike in infantry tactics and applied sociology, Mziligazi realized perfectly well that the missionaries creed was incompatible with the structure of an Iron Age warrior state. He did, however, value the missionaries as technical advisers, as men who could repair wagons and guns, who knew English, and who could write a letter.

The Lozi state was more flexible than the Ndebele monarchy and less specialized toward war. The Lozi were more willing to train highborn youths in the white men's learning. There was also a genuine quest for new religious answers, a spiritual search which found expression in long, drawn-out discussions between, for example, Lozi princes and white men about the meaning of life, the nature of virtue, the essentials of political obligation. Whatever the Lozi may have thought of the Europeans' arguments, they could not but help respect a bearded patriarch like Coillard, a man with an immensely powerful personality and great moral courage. The Lozi, one might add, were interested not merely in the white man's lore, they were open to new ideas of all kinds, including the knowledge which Mbundu medicine men attempted to spread at a time when Mbundu economic and cultural influence was becoming increasingly important in Barotseland.

Above all, the Bible was more intelligible to an Iron Age African farmer or shepherd than to a modern European or American living in an industrial city. The grim and splendid poetry of the Old Testament spoke of a world known to Africans—one of droughts, locusts, disease, and clan wars—of a world where men feared "the terror that stalked at night and the arrow that flew at day, the pestilence that walked in darkness and the sickness that destroyed in the noon-day." And the Book of Revelations described visions that could not be outdone in dread and splendor by those of the most gifted spirit medium. The Bible—more especially the Old Testament—could be made to appeal to many classes in society, to a warlike aristocracy as well as to the poor and the outcast.

In Barotseland, as in Lesotho and Botswana, Christianity in the first place spoke to the high born—not to the lower strata. The aristocrats clearly saw a need for the white men's skills, especially for the art of reading, writing, and speaking English. The missions introduced technical skills, for instance, improvements in the art of canal building. And missionaries were called upon to give their counsel on matters of secular diplomacy as well as on clerical doctrines. In these deliberations the majority of missionaries clearly favored the imperial cause—though not necessarily the interests of their own country in particular. François Coillard in Barotseland, for instance, firmly believed that Great Britain was best fitted to protect the black people against civil strife at a time when Barotseland was shaken by bloody internal disorders; he looked to British help in order to safeguard the blacks against Boer trekkers and British goldseekers, to keep out the Ndebele, the Germans, and the Portuguese. The missionaries also had good practical reasons for desiring white rule. Not that the white evangelists were subject to capitalist blandishments. The British missionary who traveled into the interior with a Bible in one hand and a prospectus for Lancashire cotton goods in the other is a figment of the imagination of French and German chauvinists. Coillard, for instance, scrupulously refused to accept any kind of official position or salary from British empire builders. But like his colleagues, he looked forward to a time when the mission stations would be supplied by rail rather than by ox wagon or canoe, when mail would arrive regularly, when Barotseland would have all the services of a modern state. Coillard passionately demanded security for life and property; the right of slaves to offer their labor freely on the open market, the right of merchants to deal without tribal restraints on trade. He strongly objected to such aspects of "kingly socialism" (the phrase is his) as the right of royal preemption. The missionaries would not fit into the traditional network of tributary exchange. They harshly complained at measures which to them appeared as interminable exactions imposed on foreigners by tribal governments.

The missionaries' converts likewise encountered serious conflicts of loyalty. British missionaries often, though not always, considered the customs observed by African peasants and warriors to be the devil's handicraft. Moffat thus described the Ndebele way of life as of "war, rapine, beef-eating, beer-drinking and wickedness." Some critics of missionary endeavor have argued that such views derived from racial prejudice. But British Protestants (and also Catholics) were liable to use exactly the same kind of language concerning the mores of European foreigners and Englishmen. According to some mission journals, unconverted Portuguese countrymen, for example, were bound straight for hell by reason of popery, drink, and fornication. British lawmakers for long had tried to prohibit, albeit without success, the "horrid, impious and execrable vices of profane cursing so highly displeasing to God Almighty and offensive to every Christian." Sermonizing was accounted a virtue in those days; white and black alike were presented with a code of morals which, in theory, brooked of no compromise.

Black graduates of mission schools were often faced with a dilemma, a choice between European, and above all European middle-class, ideals of individualism and spiritual endeavor on the one hand and the aspirations of the "Red Heathen" and the claims of their ancestors on the other. Converts also had to make difficult decisions in the economic field. Skills acquired in mission schools—literacy, skill in crafts like printing or bricklaying—were more helpful in a European than in a traditional African setting, where there was little or no demand for such arts. Without always meaning to do so, the missionaries began to train the noncommissioned officers of empire, the literate clerks, the telegraphers, the court interpreters, without whom the colonial system could not function. Above all, the missionaries translated the Bible into indigenous languages; they provided the first written forms of the various African vernaculars. They gave Africa the Bible, a great literary treasure; they also provided dictionaries for the use of white merchants and soldiers, tools both of scholarship and of conquest.

In some regions, missionaries even set up their own petty theocracies. In Malawi and in the region south of Lake Tanganyika, the missionaries settled among stateless people. There were no powerful chiefs to whom they might appeal. There was a good deal of fighting in the vicinity of their stations. Hence mission settlements attracted crowds of refugees willing to accept the white men's Gospel in return for food and protection. The new religion, in other words, was most likely to appeal to intelligent aristocrats on the one end of the spectrum, and to marginal men, the very outcasts of society, on the other. The presence of refugees in mission villages raised complicated problems of a disciplinary and administrative kind. There were plenty of floggings—proceedings that did not peculiarly shock a generation that saw nothing wrong in beating criminals and schoolchildren—and that still remembered the atrocious corporal punishment to which British Redcoats used to be subjected.

In addition, the missionaries had to solve the ever-present supply question. The missions could not operate without a commissariat. In 1878 pious Glasgow merchants and shipbuilders therefore set up the African Lakes Company to victual the missions and introduce "legitimate trade" to the interior. The company, however, found the going hard; it stood as a shaky economic superstructure on a firm ideological foundation. The merchants prayed but made no profits. They found, like the Swahili traders before them, that only ivory would stand the high cost of transport from the interior to the coast. In order to obtain a larger supply of tusks, the Scotsmen extended their operations to the north end of Lake Nyasa. Here they soon clashed with Mlozi, an East Coast freebooter, who had become a petty sultan.

Mlozi resented interference with his local monopoly, and between

1887 and 1889 there was a good deal of skirmishing between the company's servants and the Muslims. The company could not dislodge the "North End Arabs" from their strongpoints; missionary penetration occasioned demands for imperial assistance, and thus helped to occasion wider international complications.

Prelude to Partition

Although British missionaries had early gained a foothold in Central Africa, their stations were few and far between and their hold on the people remained tenuous. Few knowledgeable men, asked to predict Central Africa's political future sometime, say, about 1881, would have foretold that the entire region between the Limpopo and Katanga was destined to pass under British suzerainty. In placing their bets, some might have put their money on Leopold II, king of the Belgians. Leopold, a rapacious leader but brilliant diplomat, was determined to hurl his little country into greatness; above all, he meant to enlarge the fortune of the House of Coburg. Leopold was, in some ways, a throwback to the eighteenth century, a daring "projector" as well as prince, intent above all on dynastic aggrandizement. Receiving little or no support from the Belgian bourgeoisie, with its parochial preoccupations, he cleverly played on the humanitarian sentiments, the geographical romanticism, and the incipient internationalism of his time. In 1876 he created the International Association for the Exploration and the Civilization of the Congo. In 1880 Leopold's associates opened the first station on the Congo. Four years later the powers recognized the sovereignty of Leopold's Congo Free State, and the king's employees soon vastly expanded the borders of this new political entity until it stretched far across Central Africa to include the mineral wealth of the Katanga.

Portugal was another claimant to the interior. True enough, it was a small country, economically backward and devoid of capital. But Portugal had recovered from the ravages of the Napoleonic wars and from long, drawn-out civil disorder. In the realm of letters and in historiography, the country ranked as high as any in the world. What was more to the point, Portuguese explorers as well as Africans in Portuguese employ had had a major share in the exploration of Central Africa.

The Portuguese had a goodly complement of tough, fearless frontiersmen, white and mulatto alike. Nothing could be further from the truth than the image of sallow, greasy dago with bemedaled chest and timid heart, created in Great Britain by a strange blend of imperial chauvinism and missionary propaganda. During the last decades of the nineteenth century Portugal produced a series of remarkable men who successfully battled against their compatriots' initial pessimism and even hostility regarding colonial entanglements; these empire builders were determined that Portugal should acquire a splendid African legacy, lest the little kingdom decline into obscurity.

The Portuguese managed to gain a good deal of foreign diplomatic support. In 1886 France recognized ancient Portuguese claims to a broad band of territory that would link Angola to Mozambique. Germany, the world's strongest military power at the time, was willing to support Portuguese pretensions. Even the British, in 1888, would have been willing to arrive at an agreement with Lisbon, recognizing the region north of the Zambezi as falling exclusively within the Portuguese sphere of influence. In exchange, the British wanted concessions south of the Zambezi and in the basin of Lake Nyasa. Had the Portuguese played their cards with more skill, Zambia today might well form part of the Portuguese Empire.

In addition, the Boers of the Transvaal seemed powerful contenders for suzerainty in the far interior. In 1881 the British suffered a sharp defeat at the Battle of Majuba Hill. Subsequently, the Redcoats retreated from the Transvaal, which they had temporarily occupied, and the British concluded a convention by which Great Britain relinquished its claim to the Transvaal. To the victorious Boers, the region between the Limpopo and the Zambezi seemed part of their natural hinterland, a vast domain where trekkers might find new grazing grounds, and where hunters could track down more game. These frontiersmen who made their way across the Limpopo—Afrikaners and some English-speaking South Africans steeped in the Afrikaner way of life—were a hardy breed. Professional hunters who would pursue elephants on horseback, these men were strong enough to fire huge muzzleloaders from the saddle—massive weapons that weighed as much as a portable cannon and kicked back with the force of a World War II bazooka.

The Transvaalers also took care to establish legal and diplomatic claims to the interior. In 1853 they signed a treaty with Mziligazi, whereby the Ndebele agreed to protect Transvaal travelers, to stop the traffic in firearms, and to hand over gunrunners to the nearest Transvaal official. A generation later, in 1887, Lobengula, Mziligazi's successor, signed yet another convention, the so-called Grobler Treaty. The Ndebele agreed to form an alliance with the Transvaal; they also consented to receive a Transvaal consul, who would wield civil and criminal jurisdiction over all Transvaalers in the kingdom.

The Ndebele of course were interested only in playing the various whites off against one another. But in the language of European diplo-

macy the Transvaalers had received what amounted almost to extraterri-
torial rights. On paper, at any rate, the concession of the Transvaal
consul gave them a strong bargaining position. Many British South
Africans entertained grave fears lest the Transvaalers might monopolize
the interior. These apprehensions grew apace when, in 1884, Great
Britain recognized the German occupation of the South West African
coast. For a long period the Germans were fully involved in the subju-
gation of their new colony. Nevertheless, some British imperialists
imagined that Germans and Boers might link up, thereby effectively
shutting out British colonists from Central Africa.

In Great Britain itself enthusiasm for colonization in Central Africa
was limited to a few lobbies. A handful of Scottish missionaries, traders,
and coffee planters in Malawi looked for British help; they hoped for
imperial support mainly against the Portuguese, whose protectionist
tariffs, obstructionist tactics toward the British inland, and popish doctrine all seemed equally objectionable. Humanitarians and evangelists
alike wanted to protect the aboriginal races of Southern and Central
Africa against the real or imagined perils of Boer depredations, Swahili
and Portuguese slave raids, and the traffic in guns and strong liquor. But
the Central African question did not involve powerful economic interests
in the motherland. The bulk of British capital exports before the First
World War did not go to tropical parts of the world but to the
Americas and regions of white settlement outside Africa. The African
trade did not count for much of Britain's commercial balance as a
whole. Most politicians were chary of African entanglements that would
lead to international complications, additional public expenditures, and
therefore higher taxes. Many of the most convinced imperialists considered the scramble for colonies more in the nature of a real estate
speculation. These vast unknown regions might prove valuable in the
future; hence, Britain should secure a lien on as much land as was going,
lest foreigners get their foot in first and exclude British merchants.

But the primary push came from South Africa, where it derived
its impetus from a new mining frontier. Perhaps the most decisive battle
in the modern history of Central Africa was waged in March, 1888, at
Kimberley. The struggle was fought not with rifles and bayonets but
with stocks and shares. The prize was the control of the Kimberley
diamond industry—one of the major financial centers of the subcontinent. The two protagonists were well matched, and the outcome of
their contest difficult to predict. On one side was Barney Barnato, a
brilliant and eccentric Jewish financier who started out as a boxer and
circus artist but later built up a fortune in Kimberley diamonds. Barnato
was as formidable on the stock exchange as in the boxing ring. He was

also endowed with a considerable degree of moral courage. "Is it true that you started your career as a clown?" he was asked in a fashionable restaurant. "Indeed I did—and I can still do the old tricks," answered Barnato, jumping on the table where he stood on his hands to the consternation of the snobbish clientele. Barnato wanted wealth and social recognition including, pathetically, membership in the exclusive Kimberley Club. He had no desire for territorial aggrandizement and favored a financial policy of caution.

Rhodes, Cecil Barnato's antagonist, was in every sense his opposite. An English parson's son, he had come to South Africa for his health; the lanky, squeaky-voiced anemic youngster could never have won one of his own Rhodes scholarships. (These were later founded to give a chance to youths with a gift for leadership and an aptitude for "manly sports," as well as academic accomplishments.) But Rhodes built up an immense fortune, which he meant to use for the purpose of imperial conquest. Rhodes had ability, ruthlessness, and drive. But he also had a quality even more difficult to define, a strange personal magnetism that made him uncommonly successful in his manifold dealings with men as different as British proconsuls, Jewish financiers, Ndebele chieftains, and Boer Commandants. In 1888 with the help of Alfred Beit, his financial lieutenant, Rhodes forced Barnato to come to terms, thereby gaining almost complete control of the Kimberley diamond industry.

From an economist's point of view the formation of De Beers Consolidated Mines, Rhodes's very own company, was merely a chapter in a much longer story. The diamond industry was started by small diggers working with little capital. But open quarrying soon gave way to subterranean mining, which required vast funds. Expensive machinery became essential. As a result, the small workers were squeezed out, and centralized control of diamond production and trade was established. Without these changes, the industry would have collapsed. But once reorganized, it went on making huge profits, the mines being able to finance their own expansion. Precious stones moreover yielded enough capital for investment in the recently discovered gold mines of the Witwatersrand, in which Rhodes acquired a substantial stake.

Rhodes's ambitions did not, however, end there. He wanted to found an empire that would secure British paramountcy in Africa and create wealth beyond the imagination of man. Rhodes read the glowing reports of Mauch and other travelers; he was convinced that there must be a "Second Rand," another great series of gold deposits such as those of the Transvaal, beyond the Limpopo where he could be undisputed master. Financial expansion however required territorial expansion. Though a British imperialist, Rhodes also thought in South African terms. Colonization in the far interior would unite Boer and Briton in a common endeavor, pushing forward the "miner's frontier," while at the same time giving more land to the Afrikaners. Inland expansion would make the Cape Colony, Rhodes's adopted home, the gateway to a great Southern African empire. British settlers would populate the hinterland and thereby help keep the region within the imperial orbit. Ultimately British territory would stretch from the Cape to Cairo, a new empire that would rival the splendor of British rule in India.

Treaties and Charter

Rhodes, having secured his financial base, methodically set out to secure a lien on the far interior. In 1888 he sent out emissaries to Lobengula and, after involved negotiations, secured a monopoly (the Rudd Concession) over all the minerals in the Ndebele kingdom. In return, Lobengula was to receive £1,200 a year, a thousand modern breech-loading rifles and a gunboat on the Zambezi (the vessel was never in fact delivered to its intended recipients, who could not have kept it afloat). From his own point of view, Lobengula was not doing badly. He would receive a regular cash income, and for the first time, the Ndebele would obtain a relatively large supply of European weapons. This was an important consideration for a people whose young warriors were rarely allowed to work in the Kimberley mines and who, unlike the Bechuana and the Lozi, could not acquire many rifles in return for labor. The demand for a gunboat was a perfectly rational one, for the Ndebele had no other means of smashing the canoe power of the Lozi, their traditional enemies to the north.

But there was also a considerable debit account on the balance sheet. The whites, who grossly misrepresented their ultimate purpose in negotiating with the king, obtained a foothold in Ndebele country. Soon they found ready excuses for further penetration. Lobengula moreover was no longer dealing with isolated hunters and concession seekers, whom he might play off against one another, but with representatives of a powerful financial company that had potent political backing. (In 1890 Rhodes actually became prime minister of the self-governing Cape Colony.) Despite his huge, imposing figure, his kingly bearing, and natural sense of generosity, Lobengula was not the equal of Mziligazi. After Mziligazi's death in 1868, he had managed to gain the throne only after a civil war. And militarily, the Ndebele army seems to have declined from its earlier standards of obedience and efficiency. Worse still, the Bechuana, the sworn enemies of the Ndebele, were acquiring firearms, while the tried tactics of the spear-crescent were becoming increasingly old-fashioned. Lobengula was thoroughly aware of the military weaknesses that beset his army. Kinsmen of the Ndebele, the Zulu, had managed to cut up a British force at Isandhlwana in 1879. But this victory, however, glorious in Zulu eyes, was followed by a smashing and irreversible Zulu defeat at Ulundi. Cetewayo, the Zulu king, fled but was captured by the British, and Lobengula had no desire to share Cetewayo's fate.

Readers schooled in Pan-African thought might well ask why Lobengula and his fellow monarchs did not attempt to form a universal alliance against the whites. Such a design, however, presupposed a community of interests which few blacks felt at the time. The Bechuana feared the Ndebele and fought them with rifles acquired from white men. According to F. S. Arnot, a British missionary who resided in Barotseland from 1882 to 1884, Lobengula sent an embassy to Lewanika, the Lozi king, inviting him to become Lobengula's blood brother and to jointly resist the whites. Arnot persuaded Lewanika to reject the Ndebele offer and to make friends rather with Khama, a powerful Bechuana chief.[2]

Khama was determined to remodel his country's institutions along missionary lines. He looked to the British for protection against the Boers, and the Ndebele with whom he had a boundary dispute of long standing. In 1885 he placed his country under the Queen's suzerainty, and Bechuana diplomacy, like the missionaries' pleading, steadily favored the British cause at the Lozi court. Even without these external influences, Ndebele and Lozi would never have made reliable allies; there was too much to divide them. At the same time, the Ndebele could not apparently resume their age-old policy of trekking beyond the reach of a more powerful enemy. Their cattle would have had to pass through tsetse country on the road to the north and also have to face the perils of the Zambezi, infested with crocodiles. Lozi war canoes moreover would have presented a serious danger to a Ndebele host trying to cross the river. Lobengula therefore tried to temporize and appease. The vacillations of Ndebele policy led to trouble within the kingdom; they also gave Rhodes more time to consolidate his financial empire.

In 1889 Rhodes submitted a scheme to the British government for the formation of a company to develop the vast regions north of British Bechuanaland and the Transvaal, to extend railways and telegraph lines northward from the Cape, and to promote mining enterprise. At a time

[2] F. S. Arnot, *Missionary Travels in Central Africa* (Bath: Office of "Echoes of Service," 1914), p. 22.

when many European statesmen were still unwilling to become directly involved in African affairs, colonization by means of chartered companies was a recognized expedient. The British authorities were reluctant to finance colonial expansion beyond the Limpopo at the taxpayers' expense. But they had no objection if private investors would share the burden, especially investors as well connected as Rhodes. The directorate of Rhodes's British South Africa Company was full of impressive names —dukes with great estates, stock exchange magnates with solid bank accounts—in a way the company symbolized an alliance between the old landed wealth and new financial fortunes. The charter of the company gave it extensive financial and administrative powers over a huge and ill-defined area. Having gained these rights, Rhodes, in 1890, set up a privately paid force to secure the golden North.

Rhodes's methods would have befitted a Renaissance condottiere. In 1889 he made a confidential agreement with Frank Johnson, a former prospector who had worked his way up to be a company manager, and with Maurice Heany, a former American cavalry officer and frontier fighter. By this document the two bound themselves to raise a force of 500 whites and carry by sudden assault all the principal strongholds of the Ndebele nation. Johnson himself, as he put it, had an open mind as to whether the king was to be captured or killed. Heany and Johnson were to be paid £150,000 between them if they succeeded. If they failed, that is to say if they were speared by the Ndebele, the agreement solemnly stated that "the parties of the second part . . . shall have no claims whatever on the parties of the first part."

Johnson proceeded to prepare his force in secrecy, but apparently Heany, while under the influence of drink, could not control his tongue. Heany's indulgence in liquor probably served him well, for the scheme was a wild gamble; the raid might easily have failed, and defeat might have occasioned the slaughter of every mercenary as well as of every white civilian in Matabeleland. Johnson then contracted to take a column of pioneers to Mashonaland on a circuitous route skirting Matabeleland; they would avoid any clash with Lobengula's warriors. Johnson, an able man, half soldier, half entrepreneur, collected a picked body of men, comprising 180 pioneers and some 500 British South Africa Company police. The expedition curiously combined the military technology of the backveld with that of the Industrial Revolution. There were eighty-four ox wagons trained to maneuver with military precision. There were automatic weapons and seven-pounders. The pioneers also had a steam tractor and an electric searchlight, which could sweep the bush in the event of a night attack. Lobengula's only chance would have been to take the column by surprise in broken country or to attempt a night assault. With an army supposedly numbering 18,000 men, the Ndebele might have tried to win by sheer force of shock and numbers. But Lobengula was too conscious of the difficulties involved in beating the whites; he did however try to repudiate the Rudd Concession.

In 1890 Johnson's pioneers reached their destination; they built a small stronghold—Fort Salisbury—now the Rhodesian capital, and dispersed to look for the promised Ophir. In the meantime Rhodes was looking even farther north. In 1889 he had offered to make a financial contribution to the cost of administering Malawi (then referred to as British Central Africa) if the imperial authorities would set up a protectorate in the lakeside country. The Scottish missionaries and the traders were under considerable pressure from the Muslims in the north. Intent on making good on old claims to the interior, the Portuguese sent a military expedition to take over what British missionaries considered to be their chosen preserve. The imperial government stepped in at last, and in 1889 a British protectorate was declared over the Shire Highlands. Between 1889 and 1891 the British annexed the whole of Nyasaland—at any rate on paper. In deference to the opinion of local missionaries and traders, the country was placed under imperial rather than chartered company administration, with its avowed South African bias.

Rhodes finally took steps to establish paper claims over what is now Zambia. Some of the most important kings in the country—men like Chitimukulu, the Bemba monarch, and Mpeseni, the lord of the Ngoni—never sought British Protection. Rhodes's men did, however, secure a treaty from Kazembe. More important still, Rhodes concluded a convention with Lewanika, who thereby placed himself under British suzerainty and gave extensive concessions to the chartered company. The Lozi were divided on the advisability of such a course. But Lewanika, their king, was determined to use British help to secure his throne against internal disturbances and his kingdom against aggression from Ndebele and the Portuguese. Pro-British arguments put forward by Khama's envoys in the Lozi capital carried the day, and in 1890 the chief dignitaries in the kingdom affixed their names to the so-called Lochner Concession.

At the same time foreign opposition to Rhodes's schemes was brushed aside. In 1890 Germany signed a treaty which recognized Rhodesia and Malawi as in the British sphere of influence, while Tanganyika was adjudged to be in the German. Upon receiving a British ultimatum, which for long rankled at Lisbon, Portugal was compelled to abandon her claims. The Boers in the Transvaal were firmly warned, and in 1890 company forces peacefully headed off an attempted Boer trek across the Limpopo. The next year chartered police inflicted a severe local defeat on a Portuguese detachment at a lonely border post. In 1891 also the charter was formally extended over the lands north of the Zambezi (excluding Malawi). By the beginnings of the 1890s, the political borders of Central Africa had frozen into something like their present shape. Rhodes had been unable to acquire a port for his company lands on the Indian Ocean, where the littoral remained under Portuguese control. He had likewise failed to acquire the copper-rich Katanga, which fell under Belgian sway. But the bulk of the interior was firmly in British hands. Portuguese and Transvaalers were excluded from the far interior. And British empire builders had laid the foundations of three new territories which later developed respectively into the republics of Zambia, Malawi, and Rhodesia.

7

Pacification

The Ndebele War, 1893

A junior Ndebele officer asked to comment on his country's military situation sometime about 1892 would probably have expressed a feeling of thorough satisfaction. The Ndebele could mobilize something like 18,000 warriors, trained in an iron code of discipline and valor. The whites in Mashonaland could not even raise one-tenth of that number. The Europeans were traders, a handful of farmers, and a good many fortune seekers anxious to find the reputed El Dorado of the interior. But the prospectors could not find the expected Second Rand. The modern miners faced difficulties similar to those experienced by the "Ancients." Also the British South Africa Company was in financial difficulties. Rhodes had recourse to all kinds of expedients in attempts to raise money. The chartered company's *raison d'être* was to make money, but its investors received no dividends. (In fact chartered stock only began to yield returns after 1923, when the company had abandoned its administrative responsibilities.) The company, far from anxious to shoulder new military responsibilities, cut its forces to the bone. In 1892 the police force had been reduced to forty whites and thirty-five Africans. The railroad had not yet advanced into the interior; the whites still relied on horses, mules, and ox wagons; their supply lines from the Cape remained impossibly long. Chartered policymakers anticipated that Ndebele power would have to be liquidated in the more distant future. But Dr. Leander Starr Jameson, the company's local administrator, initially believed that this end might perhaps be achieved by peaceful means. The ideal solution, from the company's point of view, would have been to turn Lobengula into a royal labor recruiter. Hoping apparently that a warrior king could be turned into a minor entrepreneur, the chartered company even sent some gold mining equipment.

While chartered company planners looked to a period of peace for reasons of economy, Lobengula wanted to avoid hostilities for reasons of military expediency. He had no desire to stop the whites from digging holes in the ground for gold. He had no wish to forego the promised chartered subsidy. He had no intention of risking his army in a desperate war—provided always that the European presence interfered neither with his sovereign rights, the Ndebele way of life, nor his claims to raid or extort tribute in western Mashonaland. A compromise between British and Ndebele was, however, hardly possible. Had the Ndebele dwelled a long way from the area of British settlement, peaceful coexistence might perhaps have been achieved. But a capitalist economy depending on wage labor and a tribal warrior state depending on war could not live as neighbors for long. Jameson was conciliatory at first. Had he wished for a blitzkrieg against the Ndebele, he would not have practically disbanded his military police force in 1892. He could have struck earlier on in 1893, when a considerable portion of Lobengula's forces had gone on the warpath to the north. But Jameson was firmly resolved that the Ndebele should not penetrate into the British area of settlement. To Lobengula, on the other hand, the very concept of a defined border was unacceptable. The king had never agreed to the demarcation of a frontier; western Mashonaland was his to raid and rob, provided always that his soldiers let the whites alone. In this tragic encounter Lobengula and Jameson alike both assumed that absolute justice was on their side. In the long run, neither could draw back.

Relations between the Ndebele and the British were not, however, determined by the king and the administrator alone. Both the British and the Ndebele were divided into factions. Among the Ndebele the peace party had support from men of caution, usually older chiefs who had already made their reputation in past wars and built up their influence in the nation. The war party drew strength above all from younger chiefs who still had their way to make in the Ndebele military hierarchy, and who did not regard white gold miners as a very formidable lot. Lobengula thus faced a dilemma: either he fought and risked defeat or he appeased and compromised, and might thereby lose his crown.

The British were equally divided. The company at first wanted a policy of peace, with economy. So did the colonists in regions free from Ndebele incursions, such as Umtali in the east. But the settlers who had to cope with the Ndebele wanted war. From 1892 on, the Ndebele had carried out a number of raids into the Fort Victoria area. No European was hurt; but every section of the settler community, the whites argued, suffered financial loss. Mine managers and prospectors were left stranded without African labor. Transport riders would no longer forward mining equipment. Shopkeepers found themselves without customers. The settlers could not make a living if their workmen were killed or, indeed, if there was any kind of local disorganization.

There were also wider political considerations. British radicals loathed the "Chartered Millions" and later were quick to accuse the British South Africa Company of having forced a war on the hapless Ndebele. But the charter itself obliged the company to secure "law and order" within its sphere of operations. Had the company cooperated with the Ndebele, a warlike people denounced by missionaries of many kinds, the chartered directors might equally have come under humanitarian attack, not as warmongers but as men responsible for an unholy alliance between capitalism and a bloodstained system of African feudalism. Whatever the if's and but's, in July, 1893, Jameson, having apprised himself of the situation at Fort Victoria, decided on war.

A settler force, armed, led, and equipped by the chartered company advanced quickly into Matabeleland, and the Ndebele army collapsed with surprising swiftness. Ndebele strategy was built on a rapid offensive; there was little planning for defensive warfare. Tactically, the methods of the Ndebele had become petrified. The Ndebele had acquired a good many guns, but they did not know how to repair or maintain them in good working order; neither did they make good use of firearms in action. In some ways the Ndebele commanders had come to resemble diehard British Guards officers of the period; both had become equally preoccupied with the colorful and ceremonial aspects of war; both had become addicted to the unthinking cult of cold steel.

Ndebele shock tactics, however, proved no match for the mobility and firepower of mounted white sharpshooters. The settlers moreover successfully employed Maxim guns, a weapon which professional soldiers still tended to underestimate. The Ndebele had no intelligence network. On the other hand, the whites received valuable assistance from Ndebele guides whose relatives had been executed by Lobengula and who were anxious to avenge the deaths of their kinsmen. The Lozi rejoiced at every Ndebele defeat. The Shona, though sometimes treated harshly by the whites, had no desire to help Lobengula's warriors. The settlers' base in Mashonaland therefore remained secure, and the whites were able to advance swiftly. After a few bloody battles, Ndebele resistance collapsed. Lobengula, having chivalrously safeguarded the lives of the European residents in Matabeleland, tried to escape to the north, but he perished during the flight. With no more than 672 whites and some black auxiliaries, the chartered columns had managed to crush an opponent who enjoyed a numerical superiority of twenty or thirty to one. The British now occupied Matabeleland. Victory however had not come to imperial forces but to the chartered company, with its South African orientation.

The Africans in Matabeleland had learned that the spear-crescent would no longer win victories in war; they acquired a healthy respect for European tactics. For the Europeans, the war produced a legend. The only reverse suffered by the colonists was the destruction of the so-called Shangani patrol under Major Allan Wilson, which attempted to capture Lobengula by a risky *coup de main*. Wilson, a courageous but undisciplined officer, perished with all his men. Their final fight, comparable in certain respects with Custer's Last Stand, made a deep impression on the whites. This was the 1890s, an age of general peace. Men's sensibilities had not yet become blunted by the holocausts of the Somme or Verdun, of Stalingrad or Hiroshima. In the Shangani engagement fewer lives were lost than in many an unrecorded "incident" during the London blitz. But the psychological impact of the fight was infinitely greater. To the colonists, the contest became a symbol of white courage against black barbarism, part of white Rhodesia's first indigenous tradition, that would become richly embroidered by later legend.

The Great Rebellion: 1896–1897

When the German armies collapsed after the Second World War, the soldiers of the *Wehrmacht* were utterly stunned. High-ranking officers who, a few weeks earlier, had been proud of their rank, sold their Iron Crosses, their assault badges, and other highly prized decorations for a few cigarettes. Many Ndebele warriors reacted in exactly the same fashion. Famous fighters sold for a song all their plumed headgear and other marks of valor, as if to express despair for the future as much as to meet the wants of the present. The Europeans indeed tried to make a clean sweep of the old system; a whole world seemed to disintegrate. The regimental system was broken up, at least in theory. The various Ndebele castes were placed on a level of equality, for the whites were determined to turn warriors into wage earners.

Ndebele aristocrats now had to work side by side with the despised *Holi* (the lowliest status group). Many *Holi* indeed took the opportunity of moving away from their former masters' reach. The Europeans believed themselves to be benefactors of the oppressed. But what they gave with one hand, they took away with the other. The Ndebele lost a large portion of their cattle to the victors. The whites appropriated huge areas of Ndebele land. Admittedly, company plans of confining the Ndebele to two large reserves in poorly watered country came to nought. All together, there were only a few thousand whites in the country. There were no population displacements of the size that rearranged the ethnic boundaries of Eastern Europe after the Second World War or that robbed seventeenth-century Ulstermen of their land in favor of English and Scottish immigrants. Few Ndebele were faced with the prospect of "Hell or Connaught." Most Ndebele however suffered from the European presence to a greater or lesser extent.

The whites confiscated a great proportion of Ndebele cattle; soon afterwards a terrible rinderpest epidemic swept down from the north and destroyed most of the livestock in the country. The Ndebele and the Shona alike tended to blame European magic for this terrible disaster, especially as the British killed infected beasts in order to stop the progress of the disease. To some extent the Europeans managed to shield themselves from the worst effects of the outbreak by importing new stock from Barotseland. The Ndebele had no cash to do likewise and angrily blamed the whites for shooting native stock out of pure spite. Europeans carved out huge farms for themselves on the most fertile soil. The new owners would tell the people on the land that if they wanted to stay, they would have to help as herdsmen and farmhands. These labor services in fact turned out to be unsatisfactory. They made sense only as long as the Europeans farmed with methods little superior to those of the indigenous people; they could no longer be used when white farmers began to import steam plows and other expensive machinery that could not be entrusted to unwilling conscripts. But forced labor, whether recruited by direct pressure or by indirect pressure of money taxes, proved bitterly unpopular. The new *corvées* did not even provide the Ndebele with the security of feudal tenure, for farms tended to change hands quickly; hence, many African villagers were faced with a constant succession of new masters.

The grievances of the people were compounded not so much by misgovernment as by nongovernment. The administration remained understaffed, for the chartered company was anxious to save money and to spend as little cash on its administrative responsibilities as possible. There were numerous abuses and outrages, both on the part of white ruffians and African policemen in the company's service, who often used their position to loot or pay off old family scores. The Ndebele, a proud and warlike people, suddenly found themselves reduced to the status of a conquered race, without intermediaries, without a stake in a new order which seemed as unintelligible as it was obnoxious.

Many Shona were equally discontented. The whites had put an end to the Ndebele menace, but vast stretches of Mashonaland had never been subject to Lobengula in any shape or form. Hence the people owed no debt of gratitude to the British, who regarded the local people as a conquered race. Even those Shona communities that had welcomed the destruction of Ndebele power grumbled at the new masters. The Ndebele war parties had been an occasional menace; the British had come to stay! They imposed taxes; they interfered with customary land rights; they interrupted long-established trade connections between the Shona and the Portuguese. They often tried to impose labor services.

In addition, the British came to dominate local politics. Initially, the Shona chiefs had tried to play off the whites against local opponents. In many instances relations between individual farmers and administrators were cordial enough. But the Europeans were determined to reduce chiefs to the status of minor constables, and they made enemies apace. There was also friction between local Africans and the Cape-born aristocracy of labor—Africans from the south who worked for the whites as wagon drivers and foremen, who sometimes even bought small farms of their own and became a power in local politics. Above all, the whites in Mashonaland as in Matabeleland lacked a stable system of administration. All too often the mailed fist served as a substitute for settled administrative routine. Many Africans, though by no means all of them, therefore tried to solve their problem by spears and guns.

As time went on, logistics and white politics combined to give African insurgents the best chance for a rising ever given to revolutionaries in the modern history of Rhodesia. Initially, the pioneers were almost isolated. The railway line from the south only reached Bulawayo in 1897.

The pioneers found themselves stranded on the highveld, hundreds of miles from the nearest railhead. The cost of living rocketed sky-high, and for a time an ordinary bottle of brandy cost £50 in Salisbury. The situation was rectified by speculators who rushed in supplies by ox wagons. Advertisements then gravely informed the public that "the

cost of living had now fallen to 5 shillings a bottle." But the pioneers
had few other consolations. Disease was rife on the malaria-ridden
veld. Few pioneers managed to make money, for the Second Rand
was never found.

The pioneers' troubles did not end at this point. The majority of
the indigenous people remained unreconciled to the white invaders and
also to their black auxiliaries, mostly Africans from the Cape, who
came as transport riders, evangelists, and sometimes as small farmers.
Rhodes's spirit of overconfidence and his proclivity for taking chances
further weakened the settlers' position. Revolution always stands an
exceptionally good chance of success when the ruler's army suffers defeat
in a foreign war. On a small scale this happened to the forces of the
British South Africa Company. The "charter" became implicated in an
attempted *coup d'état* against the Transvaal, where Rhodes had extensive mining interests and where British townsmen in Johannesburg
were at loggerheads with the local government composed of Afrikaans-
speaking farmers. Rhodes hoped to start a British rebellion on the
Rand against the Boers. Chartered forces from Rhodesia would assist
the rebels. But the *Putsch* was bungled. For once Rhodes did not rely
on experts like Frank Johnson, who would have been quite willing to
sign a contract for starting an insurrection on a cost-plus basis. Johnson
wisely suggested that volunteers should gradually infiltrate into Johannesburg in the guise of mineworkers. They would be clandestinely armed
on the spot and then could strike without warning. But Rhodes preferred to rely on Jameson, a man of mercurial temperament and a
gambler to the core. The chartered police was diverted from Rhodesia
to Bechuanaland, leaving Rhodesia inadequately secured. At the end
of 1895 a startled public learned that Jameson had made a dash into
the Transvaal at the head of 600 horsemen. Jameson's filibusters probably comprised more well-connected young men than any comparable
force in history. But breeding proved no substitute for sense, and the
projected rising in Johannesburg turned out to be a fiasco of the operetta
variety. Jameson's little band was quickly forced to surrender. There was
an inquiry. There was plenty of whitewashing. The knowledge the imperial authorities possessed of the planning—though not of the actual
raid—was hushed up. Jameson's career, however, was not affected. He
subsequently became prime minister of the Cape, was made a baronet,
and immortalized in Kipling's poem "If."

The political effects of the raid however were far-reaching. Relations
between Boers and Britons were poisoned; the raid was a milestone on
the way to the South African War. The Ndebele moreover found the
chance for which they had been waiting. The redoubtable *Doktela*

(Doctor) Jameson was in jail, together with his best soldiers. The Ndebele, who still retained something of their military organization, were strengthened by black deserters from the chartered company's police, who had acquired European training and arms. To the incredulous surprise of the whites, many Shona communities—though by no means all—also joined in the rising. The insurrection thus assumed a transtribal character which had been absent from previous wars. As Terence Ranger, the historian of the rebellion, sees it, the revolutionary leadership derived from two connected religious systems. There was the cult of Mwari, the high god; this was connected with an extensive system of spirit mediums. Worship of Mwari had been taken over by the Ndebele. In fact the Ndebele defeat at British hands seems to have brought about a theological revolution to give new hope to the vanquished. The cult of Mwari and the system of spirit mediums wielded tremendous power in Mashonaland. Sacred shrines became centers of revolt. Specially appointed messengers traveled through the country, taking back prayers and presents to the chiefs. Upstart leaders like Mkwati, a former slave, and Kagubi, an ordinary husbandman, spoke not only of the past but also in terms of a splendid future, of a time when a new Mambo would unite the Rozwi people.

At first the company's position looked desperate. The bulk of the company's police were prisoners in Boer hands. For a while white power was confined to a few townships. The rebels enjoyed tremendous numerical superiority. They had guns, and they knew how to use them. In fact the insurgents displayed much greater tactical skill than the old-fashioned Ndebele generals. The total technological discrepancy between the white mounted riflemen, on the one hand, and the irregular black foot soldiers, on the other, was in fact smaller than that which exists in modern times between colonial armies employing helicopters, transport planes, tracked vehicles, wireless, and all the paraphernalia of modern war, and the forces of rebel partisans, equipped with automatics, bazookas, and other light weapons. The insurgents for a time held the strategic initiative. About one-tenth of the white settlers lost their lives; the European population suffered an exceptionally high rate of casualties, incomparably greater than the rate of losses sustained by Europeans in the Mau Mau rising or the Algerian rising after the Second World War. The Europeans moreover were taken utterly by surprise. Their intelligence could not penetrate the enemy network of spirit mediums. And unbeknown to the revolutionaries, the British South Africa Company faced grave political and financial problems in Great Britain. All the omens seemed to favor the insurgents.

But in the end organization, technology, and superior morale began to tell. The colonists displayed great resilience and courage. Above all, they never at any time despaired of victory; defeat to them seemed inconceivable. In their estimation, the whole civilized world stood behind them. This, after all, was the time when Alfred Austin, the British poet laureate, wrote without embarrassment of

> Africa's Cape, where loyal watchdogs bark
> And Britain's Sceptre ne'er shall be withdrawn—

when the young Bertrand Russell was an imperialist, when intellectuals like H. G. Wells and Sidney Webb looked to the Empire for improving the world, when professors vied with music hall singers to extol the splendor of British governance abroad. The chartered company, aided by imperial units, made a determined military effort. A force of imperial mounted riflemen rushed to Rhodesia to assist the colonists. Despite their enormous numerical inferiority, the whites soon regained the initiative. Mobile squads broke up the guerrilla units and kept them on the move. The enemy's crops and cattle were seized by the Europeans. The insurgents never dared to attack the well-fortified *laagers* (encampments), and resistance became hopeless.

The Ndebele who still possessed the remnants of a state organization negotiated as a body. After an untold amount of suffering, they concluded peace with Rhodes, who risked going unarmed into the wild Matapo Hills to meet the Ndebele chiefs, and thereby enjoyed his finest hour. The Shona held out much longer; their guerrilla tactics proved superior to the old-style Ndebele methods, but the rebels could not reverse the tide. Tribes in the extreme north and the extreme south had not joined the insurrection, any more than had all the Ndebele. The whites gradually concentrated their forces against the disaffected districts, and the rising petered out. By 1897, in the year when Queen Victoria celebrated her diamond jubilee, and the British Empire had risen to its very zenith, all resistance came to an end. Rhodesia at last was firmly in the British grip.

Winning the Lakeland

The indigenous people called him Mlozi, sorcerer, though he probably had an Islamic name. He did not in the least look like a freebooter —more like a sage. He wore a fine beard; thoughtful eyes gazed gravely at the photographer from beneath a white skullcap. Seated on a carpet, in a flowing white robe, he seemed more like a theologian, apt to dispute on some obscure point of Islamic practice, than a professional slave trader. Mlozi, however, was a redoubtable fighter, and in a way, he represented what might be called the southernmost extension of the Islamic mercantile frontier. Of Zanzibari origin, he had begun trafficking with the tribes of the interior. In Malawi there were no powerful indigenous kingdoms, and Mlozi made his own laws. He gradually surrounded his trading posts with stockades, and took possession of the country north of Lake Nyasa. There were other chiefs like him, adventurers from the East Coast who came inland as settlers or, more usually, as ivory and slave traders. There were also independent Yao lords who affected Muslim ways and carried on an extensive trade with the East Coast. In what is now Malawi and in parts of eastern Zambia, Islamic currents mingled with the northernmost waves of the South African Bantu dispersion. Swahili merchants hailing from Zanzibar or Kilwa dealt with Ngoni chiefs, whose ancestors had trekked northward all the way from Natal.

Accordingly, when the British declared a protectorate over the whole of Malawi in 1891, they seemed to face an insoluble task. The local whites—a handful of missionaries, traders, coffee planters, and hunters —were no match for Swahili or Yao warlords armed with modern rifles. The imperial power, represented by Harry Johnston, Her Majesty's Commissioner and Consul General, had few resources at its disposal, but Johnston was a remarkable man. An ex-art student, undersized, squeaky-voiced, he was as unlike the beefy, Rugby-playing empire builder of fiction as might be imagined. He was good at everything. He wrote a shelfful of books that would have made the reputation of an academic; his works range from an autobiographical novel, which H. G. Wells considered worthy of a laudatory preface, to studies of colonial history and Bantu linguistics. He was a capable photographer, draftsman, naturalist, ethnographer, and an energetic administrator.

Above all, Johnston, like Cromwell, was a splendid self-taught soldier. With the help of officers from the British Indian army, he at first subdued the Yao of southern Malawi. By 1896 the most dangerous chiefs had fled to Portuguese territory, and Johnston was in a position to turn his attention to the "North End Arabs." A seaborne force supplied with light artillery proceeded against Mlozi. After heavy fighting, the British stormed Mlozi's stockade, a powerful fortification whose design displayed much military ingenuity. Mlozi's slaves were freed. The chief was caught, tried, and hanged.

Once the British had broken Muslim power in Malawi (and once the Germans had taken similar action in neighboring Tanganyika), African associates in the Islamic inland trade found themselves in a difficult position. The chiefs of the interior were largely cut off from their supplies. Mlozi's defeat moreover made a great moral impression. The Bemba were unable to agree on a concerted policy. Mwamba, one of the most powerful dignitaries in the Bemba hierarchy, succumbed to the influence of Père Dupont, a remarkable French missionary. Dupont acquired the reputation of being a master magician. When Mwamba died, the missionary, for a time, assumed chiefly authority over Mwamba's people, an extraordinary achievement apparently made possible only by the manner in which the Bemba had lost their former political cohesion. It is not surprising, therefore, that after a few skirmishes, the Bemba submitted to the whites. In 1898 a small expedition from Malawi destroyed the Ngoni state in the Fort Jameson region of Zambia, and the last of the Zulu-descended "Black Spartas" thus disappeared from history. In 1899 yet another small force from Malawi forced Kazembe to surrender. The British gradually extended their hold over Zambia, stamped out the remainder of the slave trade and constructed *bomas* (government stations) in the most distant bush. When the First World War was about to break out, the British effectively controlled the most remote portions of Central Africa.

Once again, the colonizers had accomplished an enormous military task with a minimum of force. In 1898 the entire armed units of Nyasaland—including hospital assistants, camp followers, interpreters, and porters—amounted to no more than 1,200 men, nearly all of them Indian or African mercenaries under British command. Yet in Nyasaland, at any rate, the British were dealing with a determined and well-armed enemy. There were the Yao, skillfully fighting from behind cover. There were Swahili-speaking coastmen, strongly entrenched in their stockades and supplied, more often than not, with up-to-date breechloaders.

But the British had two tremendous assets—Sikhs and seapower. Sikhs (who could stand the climate better than white troops), formed the backbone of Johnston's force in Nyasaland. They supplied that element of discipline which local levies lacked, and thus provided an essential stiffening for Johnston's force. Seapower, in the shape of a few imperial gunboats, allowed the British to control Lake Nyasa. Seapower made up for lack of numbers and for difficulties in the way of communications by enabling Johnston to suddenly throw relatively large bodies of men against enemies like Mlozi. Gunboats also supplied Johnston with floating artillery against enemies ashore. Another British asset—an important one—was that the Africans and the Swahili immigrants lacked any kind of unity. The Yao would not cooperate among themselves; even the Swahili chiefs were at odds with one another. The bulk of the original Nyanja-speaking population, whom the Yao had largely subjugated, firmly took the British side. Once defeated, even the Yao were ready enough to enlist in Johnston's little army. In time Yao fighting men indeed became the "Swiss of Central Africa," fighting for pay under the Union Jack in the most remote corners of Africa. Without African aid, Johnston could never have occupied so immense a territory with so small a force.

The shape assumed by Johnston's military operations helped to establish an important difference between early Nyasaland, on the one hand, and Southern Rhodesia, on the other. Rhodesia was essentially conquered by European colonists. In Nyasaland, victory lay with the imperial power. The settler element, in the shape of the African Lakes Company, had been incapable of dislodging the North End Arabs from their strongholds. The same was true in northeastern Zambia. The Ngoni were vanquished by imperial forces. The local white colonists were few in numbers and never took any serious part in the fighting.

Johnston himself, though as passionate an advocate of empire as Rhodes, represented a concept of colonization very different from the South African school. Rhodes believed in development through white mining enterprise and European farms, while Johnston stood for the "Indian-East African" school of empire. The Europeans should not come as permanent settlers but as temporary residents, as planters, officials, missionaries, technicians, and as employees of commercial companies. Johnston hoped to develop European plantations that would produce tropical crops for the world market. He also encouraged Indian immigration. He respected the Sikhs for their valor; he believed that Indian traders, with their willingness to accept low profits and high risks, would stimulate enterprise in African villages. India would also supply the country with telegraphists, clerks, postmasters, and other subordinate officials. Lastly, Johnston held that farming ought to be encouraged among African peasants; black villagers were to improve their land on the basis of individual rather than tribal land tenure.

Johnston's views went with a curious concept of the "colonizability of Africa," a view ultimately based on current medical misconceptions. In 1899 Johnston published a book where he set forth the prejudices of his age in a cartographic fashion. The lands up to the Zambezi were described as "healthy . . . where European races may be expected to become in time the prevailing type." Zambia and Malawi were supposedly "unhealthy but exploitable; impossible for European colonization but for the most part of great commercial value and inhabited by fairly docile, governable races; the Africa of the trader and planter and of despotic European control." [1] In fact, Johnston's map was already scientifically obsolete by the time it appeared in print. Between 1897 and 1898 Ronald Ross, an Indian army surgeon, discovered the life cycle of the malaria parasite. His was the colonial discovery of the century. Soon Europeans learned how to protect themselves against malaria and other diseases; from then onwards white men could live in comparative safety anywhere in Africa. But Victorian theories concerning African diseases continued to influence practical policy long after they had ceased to be scientifically tenable. Zambia and Malawi were somehow considered to be part of tropical Africa, while Southern Rhodesia continued to be viewed as a "white man's land."

Johnston and other imperial administrators cast in his mold, continued to believe, however, that permanent white settlers should have no say in Malawi. Instead Johnston envisaged a stratified society, run by expatriate officials who would act as trustees for the natives. The ruling class would consist of a migrant elite of Britons who would spend their working lives in the colonies and finally draw their pensions in England, or die with their boots on in Africa as befitted gentlemen. Asians would serve as minor officials and as the middlemen of empire. They would also make up the working class. Johnston's view on colonial society found striking expression in a flag of his own design for British Central Africa. There were three horizontal stripes: white on top; yellow in the middle; black at the bottom. Johnston's race-bound tricolor never found official acceptance. But for two generations to come, it more or less expressed the social realities in the lakeside protectorate. Nyasaland became part of the British planters', traders', and missionaries' frontier, resembling in some sense the Indian Empire which had helped to subdue the country. Rhodesia formed the extension of the South African miners' and farmers' frontier. In Zambia the two imperial currents mingled but ultimately receded into historical oblivion.

[1] Sir Harry Johnston, A History of the Colonization of Africa by Alien Races (Cambridge: Cambridge University Press, 1899), p. 275 facing.

8

The Birth of a New Economy

Pacification and Its Social Impact

Just about one hundred and twenty years ago, Karl Marx arrived at a striking analysis of British colonialism in India. British interference on the subcontinent, according to Marx, produced the greatest social revolution that had ever come upon Asia.[1] The Raj broke traditional forms of society, introduced railways, telegraphs, modern means of instruction, and a host of other innovations. By these and other means, the British laid the foundations of capitalism in India, and thus set in motion a series of revolutionary changes with incalculable consequences. The British conquests in Central Africa had comparable effects. It occasioned the most radical social transformation ever experienced in Central Africa.

The British realized that white (or, for that matter, brown) merchants could not prosper, while potential customers were being murdered by warrior bands without manufactured goods to sell. European railway builders, miners, or plantation owners could not get to work so long as African labor was abducted to provide Zanzibaris with plantation hands or Ngoni chiefs with military recruits. A wage-earning and a slave-raiding economy could not exist side by side; neither could a wage-earning and a warrior economy. The British were determined to end

---

[1] Karl Marx in *The New York Daily Tribune*, June 24, 1853, quoted by Karl A. Wittfogel, "The Marxist View of Russian Society," *World Politics*, XII, No. 4 (July, 1960), 497.

all traditional restraints of trade such as local ivory monopolies; royal rights or preemption, which gave kings advantages at the expense of commoners; or sumptuary laws that prevented men of low degree from acquiring prestigious luxury goods. The British were equally resolved to do away with all local forms of servitude, domestic slavery, obligatory military service, or any kind of labor dues that interfered with the working of a wage economy.

The British accomplished their object with rapidity and great economy of force. Within two decades, they gained undisputed mastery over a region of approximately 485,000 square miles, an area approaching the size of Europe. Yet so tight was the colonizers' hold that, for two generations, they did not have to reckon with serious revolutionary challenges. Over a glass of whiskey, settlers might darkly predict "native troubles." Staff officers might draw up elaborate designs for withdrawing the white population into *laagers* in the event of an African rising. But the military plans formulated during the first two decades of the present century were all pigeonholed and today form no more than archival curiosities. European fears proved unfounded. During three great armed conflicts, the Anglo-Boer War (1899–1902), and the First and Second World Wars, Southern Rhodesia and its sister colonies were in fact able to mobilize most young Europeans capable of bearing arms. In each of these wars well over 10 percent of Rhodesia's white population departed to fight abroad. Yet no indigenous rebels attempted to use these favorable circumstances to start a rising and to repeat the feats performed by black rebels between 1896 and 1897. The British had to face a great deal of discontent, but they did not have to reckon with a revolutionary situation.

The new conquerors were able to maintain their rule with a minimum of military outlay. To an extraordinary extent they relied upon administrative ability, personal integrity, diplomatic skill, and the prestige of their arms and technology. Indeed when Lewanika, king of the Lozi, returned from a visit to England to attend the coronation of King Edward VII, his stories seemed so marvelous that his subjects imagined the British must have bewitched the monarch. British power might spring partly from gun barrels, but in Central Africa there were precious few Britons to carry guns. By 1913, for instance, the Southern Rhodesian police (deceptively known today as the British South Africa Police) amounted to no more than 550 whites and 600 blacks; between them, they constituted an elite corps charged with the dual duty of ensuring both external defense and internal security. The Northern Rhodesian police, then a semimilitary body, numbered 750 Africans, led by a grand total of 27 British sergeants and officers. British rule, in other words, was profoundly civilian, both in structure and ethos. At a period when even a small neutral and pacific European country like Norway kept nearly one out of every 200 inhabitants in uniform, the Rhodesian ratio of military personnel to civilians probably amounted to less than one-tenth of 1 percent.[2]

The British presence, though insignificant in terms of military statistics, had far-reaching political effects. The British had forestalled all their rivals. The Portuguese were unable to make good their ambition of creating a great territorial bloc stretching all the way from the Atlantic to the Indian Ocean, a design that had appeared far from foolish in the 1880s. The Transvaal was cut off from its natural hinterland. The British had outtrekked the Boer *voortrekkers*. Afrikaners however continued to make their way into Rhodesia; some of their great ox wagons even managed to cross the Zambezi; small parties of Boers settled as far north as Lusaka, where the trekker's frontier at last petered out. But the Afrikaners could no longer hope to establish political control over the region between the Limpopo and the Zambezi, most of which would almost certainly have fallen under their sway had it not been for Rhodes's intervention. British colonization likewise put an end to Islamic expansion. Swahili traders and freebooters could no longer move into present-day Malawi and northeastern Zambia. The Islamic religion, which many missionaries had regarded as the most desperate threat to the evangelization of Africa, ceased to gain converts in Zambia. The southernmost frontier of Islam was first brought to a halt and then rolled back.

The British occupation also prevented the growth of what might be called "bush feudalism" among stateless peoples. Tough adventurers armed with rifles and followed by their own retainers could easily have set up independent lordships on the distant veld. These depended on trade in ivory, on traffic with neighboring chiefs, and on the exaction of tribute. Their suzerains spoke Afrikaans, Portuguese, Swahili, or even English like "Changa Changa," a British frontiersman who carved out a short-lived principality in a remote area of Zambia where he levied his own "taxes." But the "Arabs" and the "Mambari" (that is to say Portuguese-speaking Africans engaged in the exchange of slaves and elephant tusks) were driven out. "Changa Changa" experienced in his own person the transition from feudalism to capitalism; he ended his working days as a personnel manager on a mine; and to this time his title denotes a gang boss.

[2] In 1913 the estimated population of Southern Rhodesia was just under 800,000 and the estimated population of Northern Rhodesia just over 1,000,000. Both figures were probably underestimates.

Pacification also put a stop to all tribal power independent of European control. For the first time warfare between the various indigenous groups came to an end. The whites set a limit to tribal migrations; *Völkerwanderungen* on the part of great armed hosts became a matter of history; the geographical locations of the various indigenous peoples became more stabilized. The British tightened their hold by controlling the distribution of firearms to Africans. This did not of course mean that all guns disappeared from African ownership, but they lost much of their former military significance. Powder became expensive; good weapons were hard to acquire. The guns that stayed in African hands were usually inefficient and no match for modern magazine rifles. In many parts of Central Africa guns still retained some value, but not so much for military purposes. They constituted a kind of investment, especially for people without cattle. They could be used as a dowry, as pledges for loans, as a mark of prestige, or as a means of frightening away baboons and other pests. But they no longer played any part in intertribal or private conflicts, which came to be settled in the courts of the administration.

The demographic effects of pacification are hard to assess. No one knows how many people were killed in intertribal affrays or slaving *razzias* that shook the country before the advent of the *Pax Britannica*. No one can make an exact estimate of the recuperative capacity possessed by primitive societies faced with the loss of men, cattle, or seed grain as a result of internecine strife. All we can say for certain is that pacification was a success in biological terms. From about the turn of the present century the population of Central Africa as a whole seems to have experienced a steady increase. In all probability, its numbers roughly doubled every generation. In any event, prowess in war ceased to count for survival; the weaker tribes at last found physical safety.

Pacification also had unintended consequences. In various parts of Central Africa, the white man's peace seems to have enabled villagers to make more adequate use of their land. Tillers could move farther afield without having to worry about problems of defense. Discontented groups broke away from unpopular chiefs or from overly large parent villages without fear of reprisal. Indeed British administrators in time began to deplore this process of physical dispersion, which they could not prevent.

The colonial impact put an end to traditional agrotowns, such as Kazembe's capital on the Luapula. At the end of the nineteenth century Kazembe's city had contained nearly 20,000 people; it was surrounded by a great stockade and combined in varying degrees the functions of a fortress, a trading center, a capital, and a convenient settlement for farmers and fishermen. The British conquest removed the social and political *raison d'être* for such aggregates; Kazembe's town disappeared, and its inhabitants moved farther away. The whites were the colonial city builders par excellence. All the existing cities in Central Africa owe their existence to European initiative, but they were designed to function within a totally different system of production and sited according to considerations that would not have concerned an agricultural community of the traditional kind—considerations such as proximity to the rail line or to great mineral deposits.

Having conquered the country, the British liquidated the slave trade; they also abolished domestic servitude of the indigenous kind. In doing so, the colonizers acted from motives both of humanity and self-interest. The British considered themselves as harbingers of liberty, and there is good evidence that they were thus regarded by various servile groups such as the Lozi bondsmen. Slavery was also incompatible with a wage economy; the British found that Lozi serfs would not work for remuneration if their earnings could be confiscated by the ruling aristocracy. Even if the labor migrants were allowed to keep their cash, they could not at the same time perform traditional *corvées* and work in white employment. In 1906 Lewanika, under considerable pressure from the British, thus allowed the serfs in his country to purchase their freedom for a cash payment of £2.

Colonization also did away with the various forms of bondage that existed among stateless peoples like the Ila who dwell in Central Zambia. In precolonial days, men, women and children might lose their liberty in various ways. They might be kidnapped, convicted for crimes, sold in payment for debt, or purchased from Mambari merchants; they might even voluntarily put themselves into the hands of some great man. The treatment of these dependents varied a great deal. Some were practically treated as members of the family. Others might suffer a more unhappy fate. Some girls practically served as prostitutes. The most miserable of them all—aging women, shivering with the cold, and dressed in ragged skins—were looked upon as beasts of burden.[3] Critics of colonialism have since tried to reinterpret such features of preimperial society by referring to them as relationships of a patriarchic kind. There seems to be no evidence that the ex-serfs themselves shared this assessment. Despite the assumed advantages of a precapitalist labor nexus, the British never had to worry about lobbies of black wage workers anxious to exchange their new condition for earlier forms of bondage.

[3] See Edwin W. Smith and Andrew Dale, *The Ila-Speaking Peoples of Northern Rhodesia* (London: Macmillan & Co. Ltd., 1920), pp. 408–12.

British rule finally did away with the more lurid forms of punishment customary in many tribal societies, punishments that compared in savagery with those employed on the European continent before the Age of Enlightenment, and again in modern totalitarian states. The British no longer permitted the mutilation of convicted criminals (a chastisement widely employed among the Bemba). Lozi prisoners could no longer be burned at the stake, thrown to the crocodiles, or be eaten alive by fearsome black ants.[4] The British did their best to stamp out ordeals by poison and fire, reminiscent of those used in medieval Europe; they tried to prevent the execution of alleged witches. The new rulers thereby earned the gratitude of suspected witches and the hatred of the witchfinders and their adherents, who accused the government of permitting witchcraft to flourish and even increase. The British likewise prevented the killing of newborn twins, supposed harbingers of misfortune. The colonizers thereby greatly reduced the "killing capacity" of government; judicial executions became rare under the Union Jack, and the new rulers thus laid down the very standards of humanity against which they were later destined to be judged.

Economic Development Before 1914: The Immigrant Sector

The nineteenth century might be called the age of steam-power optimism. Poets versified and parsons preached concerning the moral and physical improvements to be expected from the application of steam to transport. Livingstone, Marx, and Kipling agreed on one thing— steam would revolutionize the world, and steam power would prove a boon to humanity. The greatest railway builders of all were the British who had pioneered most of the new steam-powered technology in the first place. British engineers, commonly backed by British bankers, played a decisive part in building railroads as far afield as the United States, India, and Australia. Britons constructed the greater portion of the railway on the African continent, perhaps the most important economic achievement of the "New Imperialism" before the First World War.

Railway development began on a small scale at the Cape of Good Hope. The big impulse came with the discovery of gold and diamonds, and the new lines were designed above all to serve the needs of miners. Engineers were enabled to transport heavy machinery from the ports to

[4] See, for instance, Frederick S. Arnot, *Garenganze or Seven Years' Pioneer Mission Work in Central Africa* (London: James E. Hawkins, 1889), pp. 66, 77–78.

the distant interior; ores could travel to the sea in bulk; merchants could carry goods more cheaply and in larger quantities than before. Railways also had more indirect effects. Equipment had to be mended and maintained; hence the companies set up repair shops and other facilities, which in turn provided a stimulus for further innovation. The steam engine, and the gasoline motor successively did away with the need both for ox wagons and human porterage. For the first time in history the sweating carrier was relieved of his back-breaking labor and could be put to more productive employment. And the railways provided a tremendous incentive for agricultural enterprise, for farmers were enabled to produce bulky cash crops for distant markets.

British policymakers were well aware of these sociological implications. The construction of a line to the Zambezi was indeed one of the conditions for the grant of a charter to Rhodes. The British South Africa Company acquitted itself well; already in 1897 the line from the south reached Bulawayo, where its arrival became an occasion for patriotic celebrations. British engineers also extended the Rhodesian system to Beira on the Indian Ocean. But theirs was a grim achievement. During the five years required to build the line from the shore to Umtali in Rhodesia, nearly 500 Indians and 400 Europeans perished from tropical disease. The men ran sweepstakes on the temperatures of the sick; the gambler with the highest curve would win the pool, if he lived.[5] Aged pioneers who told their tales to posterity indeed underplayed their suffering when they said that the line cost a man a mile.

Rhodes had even more extensive plans; in 1898, he induced his stockholders to authorize extending the line beyond the Zambezi, a remarkable undertaking in view of the fact that the existing network already covered huge areas having a sparse population so that at first there was little traffic, and less profit. Rhodes intended the new track to go to Lake Tanganyika; it would ultimately be laid to the Indian Ocean. The scheme came to naught however, as the British government would not furnish the required support. The line was then replanned to go via the great coalfields of Wankie in Rhodesia, where the chartered company held a financial interest; it then passed through the mineral-rich regions of Zambia and in 1909 was finally linked to the Belgian Congo system.

The completion of the railway system was a triumph for the chartered company. Rhodes and his associates managed to construct the Rhodesian lines as private rather than state enterprise, as was done else-

---

[5] James Morris, *Pax Britannica: The Climax of an Empire* (New York: Harcourt, Brace & World, Inc., 1968), p. 374.

where in Southern Africa. By dint of sound financial management, Rhodesia obtained its tracks at a relatively low cost. The chartered company managed to raise capital at favorable rates, and its railway builders spent less money per mile than their confreres in South Africa or in tropical colonies like Uganda and the Gold Coast.

Development in Malawi was much more laggard. Between 1906 and 1916 railway builders linked Blantyre in the highlands to Chindio on the Zambezi. By doing so, they enabled planters to export coffee, tea, and other crops. But the Protectorate lacked exploitable mineral resources; its internal revenue remained tiny. The line could not be extended, and for many years passengers had to rely on slow, uncomfortable little steamers that chugged upriver from Chindio. The story might have been different had Malawi been opened to the influence of the chartered company. But the combined pressure of missionaries, local white planters, and traders, and also of determined advocates of imperial colonization of the "tropical" kind, helped to keep Rhodes's influence out of Malawi. Unfortunately there was little money to spare for capital investment under the imperial aegis. Continuous railway communication with Beira did not come into being until 1935; hence, Malawi remained a poverty-stricken backwater, many of whose people had to eke out their living by working for employers in the south.

In building the railways, Rhodes looked for a Second Rand, but Rhodesia was founded upon a gigantic miscalculation; there was no second Johannesburg; Rhodesia—unlike Zambia or the Transvaal—contained only widely disseminated bodies of low-grade gold ores. These small deposits could, however, often be worked by petty white entrepreneurs with small amounts of capital. These small workers, a tough and enterprising backveld bourgeoisie, laid the foundations of Rhodesia's modern gold industry. They also exercised a considerable influence on Rhodesia's white political attitudes. But the future lay with larger companies with sufficient financial reserves to tide their firms over bad times and long periods of development work, and sufficient technical knowledge to work metal at great depths. The extraction of base minerals like copper, zinc, chrome, and coal was a task totally beyond the financial strength of the small workers; but again larger capitalists (most of them with South African connections) stepped in, so that Rhodesia gradually began to diversify its mineral production.

In the northern territories development was much slower. A good deal of prospecting, however, was done at the behest of two outstanding magnates associated with Rhodes—Edmund Davis and Robert Williams (both later raised to knighthood). Davis was a Jew from Australia, Williams a Scotsman from Aberdeen. Both started at the bottom of the ladder; both possessed equally that business acumen which tradition ascribes in exaggerated measure to their respective communities. Each man grasped the potential of the lands beyond the Zambezi, and from the late 1890s onward, a number of expeditions under their direction, prospected in the far interior and marked out copper claims. For a variety of technical and financial reasons, however, development was slow, and for long Northern Rhodesia remained a sleepy, poverty-stricken backveld colony, which mainly served as a reservoir of African labor for the wealthier south.

The Rhodesian and Katangan mines provided markets for European farmers, most of whom settled on the cool highveld along the rail line. Agriculture at first depended almost entirely on maize and cattle; methods were primitive; life was hard. But as mining compounds grew in size, the mining companies needed more food. The chartered company vigorously promoted local enterprise, and the newcomers gradually improved their technology. Ranchers imported breeding stock; veterinarians introduced successful ways of treating cattle disease; planters improved the strains of maize and experimented with all manner of new cash crops, especially tobacco, which turned out to be an unexpectedly precious resource. The pioneers began to construct dams, cattle dips, and tobacco barns; they fenced in land. In time they often changed the very appearance of the countryside.

Initially the results of their intervention were frequently far from happy. The native woodland suffered considerable destruction through the depredations of white miners in search of fuel, and also through intensified slash-and-burn agriculture on the part of Africans. Unwise use of plows and sledges likewise occasioned soil erosion. But the immigrants gradually began to master some of these ecological problems. Using coal for fuel gave protection to the woods, and the more enlightened farmers learned how to safeguard the soil. The colonists altered the very pattern of indigenous vegetation, often with striking results; they planted various types of Australian eucalyptus, tall trees capable of quick growth, which made excellent windbreaks and also provided long, straight poles. Wattle, a splendid acacia, also from Australia, with bark useful for tanning, flourished in the Eastern District, where the dark green foliage of the black and the golden variety came to give a characteristic touch to the hillsides. Various kinds of pine trees were acclimatized in the country. The jacaranda with its lilac flowers became a familiar ornamental tree; so did the bougainvillea, another South American plant, which grew in profusion and added bright splashes of color to dusty, straggling townships and homesteads built of brick, and drearily covered with corrugated iron.

Just before the outbreak of World War I, farming received considerable encouragement, when private entrepreneurs and cooperative enterprises began to lay the first foundations of a secondary industry. Much of this depended on processing primary products. Bacon and cheese required elaborate treatment for export; ranching gave rise to creameries. The railways set up workshops of their own; during the Boer War, Rhodesians even created rudimentary armories and fitted out several armored trains. Timber was being cut in small mills. By 1914 Southern Rhodesia, now a settled country, had assumed a decisive lead over its northern neighbors; the territory had begun to emerge from the initial stage of being a producer of primary products, and in a small way, had entered the manufacturing business.

The Beginnings of the African Cash Economy

When the chartered company first assumed power in Rhodesia, the directors placed all their hopes for economic improvement in European enterprise. The attitude taken by the board was in no wise peculiar. In 1924 the Colonial Office took over the governance of what is now Zambia; at first the new administrators followed in their predecessors' tracks, and assumed that only white farmers could supply a surplus of food sufficiently large and dependable to provide the mines with their needs.

Quite unexpectedly, however, African cultivators also began to enter the new network of exchange, and paradoxically, this process began south of the Zambezi, where a considerable proportion of the arable land belonged to whites. (By 1930 some 31,000,000 acres of a total 96,000,000 had been sold to whites.) The regions available for black tillage thus contracted. But there were no wholesale land expropriations on the scale experienced earlier by North American Indians, by Araucanians in Chile, by Maori in New Zealand, or by Scottish clansmen during the Highland "clearings." Africans retained a foothold in the countryside. They could not help but benefit from the indirect effects of colonization, from improvements in communications, from veterinary measures against cattle disease, from the end of raiding, from increased demands for food on the part of mineworkers and townsmen.

The new economic revolution began in what is now Rhodesia. From the first decade of the present century, enterprising Africans—some of them chiefs, some of them settlers from the Cape—began to use plows and wagons, to purchase breeding stock from whites, and to sink boreholes on their land. The white and the black economies started to interact, and the Europeans divided along class lines over how they should respond. Town-dwelling European workers thought that Africans should be allowed to grow food but that they should not advance into skilled trades. European farmers were willing enough to employ black bricklayers and painters; they complained, however, about the way in which expanding local markets for African-grown food "spoiled" their native labor supplies. But even white farmers might buy African grain, especially rural entrepreneurs engaged in specialized occupations such as tobacco growing and dairy farming.

Perhaps the principal agent of change was the rural trader, often a Jew, a Greek, or an East Indian, who traveled to the villages with his wagon and in time set up a store, ultimately perhaps a whole chain of stores, each of them under African management. "The natives near a mine are idle," wrote an angry European in the period that preceded World War I. "The reason is not far to seek; a considerable proportion of the wages earned at the mines finds its way to the native villages." The main culprit for lifting the blacks beyond what the writer considered to be their appointed station in life was the itinerant hawker who purchased indigenous goods and created new demands. "With his wagon full of cloth, ornaments and European food, [he] barters his wares for the grain and meal of the natives; he encourages their vanity and their taste for luxuries . . . the children who are growing into young men take their parents' luxuries as necessities and require to gratify their tastes still further." [6]

Moralizing of this kind could not, however, prevent the working of the new exchange economy. European manufactured goods, such as pots and pans, knives, and hatchets, soon became necessities. Africans started to dress in the European fashion. Later on, the use of bicycles, wheelbarrows, sewing machines, wagons and other capital goods spread into many villages. The growing demand for such commodities in turn gave a stimulus to agricultural production.

The history of African farming remains to be written. All we can say for certain is that the process of innovation initially centered mainly in Southern Rhodesia, economically the most developed part of the region. Despite large-scale white land appropriations, the acreage of cultivated African land began to increase rapidly from the first decade of the present century and kept growing; African-owned cattle multiplied in an aston-

[6] Percy F. Hone, *Southern Rhodesia* (London: G. Bell & Sons, Ltd., 1909), p. 63.

ishing fashion, until the vast increase in stock itself began to pose ecological problems.[7]

Malawians and Zambians found much greater difficulties in securing jobs than Rhodesian Africans, and Malawi especially became a major exporter of manpower, comparable in some respects to the Scottish Highlands of old. The migrants included mercenaries who served with distinction under the Union Jack in many parts of Africa. Malawi also experienced an extensive "brain drain," for the Protectorate could not give employment to all its mission-trained teachers, evangelists, and clerks, many of them schooled by Scottish divines, who often imprinted something of their own dour Calvinist viewpoint upon their converts.

The great majority of work seekers were unskilled men, but even they did not by any means form a homogeneous labor force; there were indeed subtle differences of ethnic background and personal temperament among those who chose to work in different occupations. The boldest spirits commonly went into mining. They had to face the terrors of dark tunnels lit only by the dim flicker of carbide lights; they had to cope with industrial accidents and with the ever-present peril of disease. During the pioneering days of Zambia and Rhodesia, white and black migrants alike sustained a death rate comparable to that suffered by an army in action. White and black miners acquired the tough outlook common to soldiers wont to believe that a man should live for the present and not worry about the future and that every bullet has its billet. Europeans perished primarily from malaria and its aftereffects; Africans succumbed above all to diseases of the lungs.

During the first two decades of the present century, however, Central Africa experienced a medical revolution. New safety regulations and mine inspection; improvements in management, diet, and medical care; the application of Western urban technology to unromantic subjects like sewage disposal and water purification occasioned a striking decrease in the death rate of African miners. Mining, once regarded as among the worst jobs going, gradually became one of the most desirable occupations. At the same time, malaria was gradually eradicated from the various settlements. The European death rate in Rhodesia, once tremendously high, dropped to a level lower than in Great Britain, and the territory became physically safe for permanent white settlement.

The improvements occasioned in the conditions of mineworkers indirectly affected employers throughout Rhodesia. White planters and

[7] By 1897 the African cattle population had been reduced to 43,000 as the result of rinderpest and war. By 1913 it was estimated at 380,000; by 1943 it amounted to over 1,800,000.

farmers might complain bitterly about competition for labor from large enterprises, but rural entrepreneurs could not escape from the restraints of an exchange economy. Some employers might be harsh taskmasters; others were plainly brutal. The great majority, however, assumed an attitude of paternalistic authority that helped modify the nature of labor relations. Unpopular masters, and even more so, unpopular mistresses would find themselves boycotted, as Africans from different ethnic backgrounds developed their own lingua franca, known disparagingly as "kitchen kaffir," a form of basic Zulu understood on every mine and every farm. African workmen built up an unofficial and amazingly effective system of information concerning bad employers, a network that was perhaps as effective in ameliorating labor conditions as the overt efforts made by officials and legislators.

The ultimate effects of labor migration are hard to assess. White employers at first disliked the system; in the early 1900s mine owners agitated for a "non-spasmodic labor supply," for proletarians without a stake in tribal lands. If the capitalists had had their way, Rhodesia would have imported Chinese and other Asian workmen on a large scale, but this met with such bitter opposition from white workers and humanitarians that employers had to rely on black men alone to do the unskilled jobs. In some ways the system of labor migration helped to shield Africans against the worst abuses of the Industrial Revolution. Unemployed workers could return to the reserves; women and children never labored in mine shafts, as they had done in eighteenth-century England or, for that matter, in the empire of Monomotapa. Migrant labor however remained inefficient and economically expensive—despite the low wages paid. Africans, for a time, had no intention of giving up their traditional land rights; hence, the system unwittingly delayed the emergence of a class-conscious urban proletariat. Its impact on the countryside was equally double-edged in nature. Among people like the Bemba, whose particular method of slash-and-burn agriculture entailed heavy physical toil at tree-lopping time, the shortage of men occasioned severe difficulties. Among communities practicing forms of agriculture like mound farming that did not require so many strong young men, labor migration seems to have enriched the economy. All communities involved in the system, however, acquired new wants and goods. New ideas started to circulate in the remotest parts of the backveld. As one aged official put it, the migrants left the villages as children, they returned as rebellious men.

Yet the growth of discontent was often a measure of social progress. After the abuses of the early days, labor legislation enforced by the British South Africa Company came to compare favorably in design and execution with the laws current in the African colonies of France and Portugal and those in British African territories governed directly from London. The workers' lot was indeed far from enviable: the Africans' standard of living generally remained low; urban Africans lived in segregated quarters, subject to all kinds of administrative controls including pass laws. Yet declining mortality rates alone bore silent witness to gradual improvements in the condition of the black workmen.

At the same time, some workmen began to remain in employment over longer periods, without returning to their villages. A certain proportion of migrants even became more or less full-time workers, depending solely on wages and no longer obliged to work on their ancestral plots. Such men were apt to acquire specialized skills. In the early days of white settlement there had already existed a small aristocracy of labor, consisting mostly of black immigrants. They had usually worked in service occupations, as cooks or wagon drivers, as teachers and preachers. Economic development slowly increased both the number and kind of jobs available. The growth of farms and cities, for instance, created a demand for bricklayers, carpenters, painters, and such like. And after World War I Africans, for the first time, began to move into other erstwhile "white" preserves such as truck driving. The increasing complexity of colonial administration provided opportunities for African court interpreters, detectives, telegraphers, and government clerks. The diffusion of trade necessitated employing African commercial assistants. Improving facilities for social welfare entailed the employment of hospital assistants, sanitary supervisors, welfare officers, and others with specialized training. The more highly schooled Africans in turn began to compete in the labor market with certain groups of whites. And ultimately the "new Africans" clashed with the Europeans in a struggle for political supremacy.

9

Postwar Settlement

The Growth of Black Consciousness

The impact of the new economy profoundly upset accustomed modes of behavior. On the one hand there was a fresh outburst of energy, as Africans turned to new occupations, and eagerly absorbed all manner of new learning, secular and missionary. The whites, for instance, taught to a select elite the art of storing ideas. In the past, tradition had depended on memory and on word of mouth. The old knew most and the young knew least. But missionary and other teachers gradually showed people how words could be committed to paper and permanently preserved. Labor migrants could now communicate with their villages by letter; in time they were also enabled to enter the white man's world by learning English, by reading his books, his newspapers, and even the published debates of colonial legislatures. Of equal significance was the creation of a vernacular literature. In Central Africa, as in many European countries, this began with missionary translations of the Scriptures and the compilation of hymn books in indigenous tongues. These laid the foundations of new literary languages.

Perhaps the most revolutionary concepts introduced by white men concerned space and time. The Bantu, of course, could reckon time quite accurately for their purposes by studying the position of the sun or by using the growth cycle of a stable crop, the work cycle of a village, or by similar devices. But in a village there were neither printed calendars nor mechanical clocks. The peasants thought of time in terms like those of the ancient Hebrews who wrote that ". . . to every thing there is a season and a time to every purpose under the heaven: a time to be born and a time to die; a time to plant and a time to pluck up that which is planted."[1] To the European, however, time was something to be minutely subdivided like a loaf, a commodity for sale. Time was money, and this was the first lesson in philosophy taught to the labor migrant when he went to work off his "ticket," his labor certificate indicating a monthly period in employment. New terms for hours, minutes, months of the year, and times of the day began to enter into Bantu languages, often characteristically in English dress. Linked to these novel concepts was a new sense of space, one that slowly percolated into the villages. To the tribesman, land was a continuum which was in unlimited supply and went on forever, like time. In traditional African society, huts were round; gardens naturally assumed oval shapes; so did the outlines of great building complexes like Zimbabwe. The Europeans, however, had a different idea. Their houses were square, and so were their city blocks. They conceived of land as a commodity which was limited in supply and which should be apportioned on the basis of individual tenure. Space was subdivided by imaginary grids. Each of the resulting little bits became marketable pieces of merchandise like the hours specified in a labor contract.

The intellectual and spiritual impact of these intangibles are hard to assess—harder even than the physical impact of railways, boreholes, and similar technological innovations. Some Africans apparently found the new learning exhilarating, to judge from the extraordinary eagerness for it shown by a minority. Others must have been seized by a sense that the very universe was cleaving apart, that the Ancient of Days himself was failing. As an old Ila Chief put it shortly after the First World War:

> To-day Leza [God] has turned over and abandoned his old ways. To-day he is not the same, he is altogether different, for he is not as he was in the distant years before the white chiefs came. At that time he was truly the Watergiver and all things were still sufficient on earth . . . to-day we say: Leza has grown old. . . . There is no flood to-day—no great giver of floods.[2]

Africans wrestled with these problems in many different forms. They had ancient prophetic traditions of their own; indeed biblical prophecy

[1] Eccles. 2:1–2.
[2] Edwin W. Smith and Andrew Dale, *The Ila-Speaking Peoples of Northern Rhodesia* (London: Macmillan & Co. Ltd., 1920), pp. 198–99.

was much more intelligible to Bantu people than to Europeans, for an African—like an ancient Hebrew—considered it perfectly natural that a spirit medium should arise and declare that the spirit of the Lord was upon him. African prophecy was enriched by the Scriptures which, at first, had a decidedly more profound impact than any secular work. The Old Testament especially was much nearer in spirit to the people of Malawi or Zambia than to contemporary Europeans. The climatic and geographic setting of the Bible resembled that of the African veld more than that of England. Bantu-speakers had no trouble understanding about the dread plagues of Egypt, or echoing ancient fears—for any terror by night: or for the arrow that flieth by day, for the pestilence that walketh in darkness or the destruction that wasteth at noon-tide. Many of the prophetic portions of the Old Testament moreover served as a revolutionary's handbook, for Isaiah and Ezekiel had condemned the proud, the rich, and the mighty in terms more picturesque than any used by modern European revolutionaries. Africans thus listened to prophets; some also joined orthodox European churches; others founded separatist churches of their own. The distinction between the adherents of these various bodies was not rigid, for many missionary converts in fact held tenets that surprised or shocked their white mentors, while numerous separatist leaders expressed views that were perfectly orthodox by the standards of European churchmen.

Black dissenters also derived inspiration from other sources, from antigovernment propaganda current among white settlers and from the teachings of radical white sectarians, who believed that the world would soon come to an end and that the evil trinity of church, government, and business would soon perish in some millennial cataclysm. Africans were influenced also by black Americans who came as teachers and missionaries, as well as by a handful of Africans who managed to go to the New World.

Some of these strands were woven into the career of John Chilembwe, an early Malawi rebel. Chilembwe was born sometime during the 1860s, the son of a Yao father and a Chewa mother. He went to school at a Church of Scotland mission and later became an associate of Joseph Booth, a fervent fundamentalist preacher. Booth and Chilembwe subsequently went to the United States, where Chilembwe attended a black Baptist seminary in Virginia and where he learned about revolutionary American leaders like John Brown. In 1900 Chilembwe returned to Malawi and set up his own mission station with the support of the black American Baptists. The mission at first gained the approval of British officials. Chilembwe established independent black schools and a kind of embryo chamber of commerce for Africans; his followers planted cash crops and gained a modest degree of prosperity. But popular grievances concerning the harsh treatment of African workers on white estates, governmental favoritism shown to European planters and traders, brutalities inflicted on the people by black soldiers, the employment of African troops in foreign conflicts all contributed to bring about a change in Chilembwe's political position.

Above all there was the ideological shock occasioned by the First World War. Many Europeans used to believe that the employment of African soldiers in European wars would radicalize the askaris, who would learn that the white man might succumb in battle and white women in bed. But the argument rests on a gross oversimplification. Africans never believed that whites were like God. Black policemen and soldiers moreover on the whole formed a conservative element in society, and the British never had to cope with black mutinies in Central Africa, either during the First or the Second World War, or during the aftermath of war. On the contrary, British officers, particularly white settlers, habituated to the use of authority and familiar with black people usually got on well with their men. Hence Rhodesian colonists gained an exceptionally large number of commissions in black fighting formations, and successfully commanded troops from many parts of British Africa. The war did however shatter the appearance of white solidarity. Black men seemed to be dragged into Armageddon, as black mercenaries were sent into the firing line, and as carriers were conscripted in the thousands to transport supplies to the soldiers.

In 1915 Chilembwe decided on an insurrection and mobilized a few hundred followers. From the military point of view, the *coup* was hopeless. It did not interfere with operations against the Germans in East Africa. It did not mobilize the elites, who continued to put their trust in reformist solutions. It did not appeal to the masses, who had no desire to be mixed up in an ill-considered *Putsch*. Chilembwe stood for a policy of sacrificial demonstration; he called on the people to "strike a blow and die" in an enterprise that would make the ruler's moral position impossible. Few Africans were willing to lose their lives in such a cause. The rising quickly collapsed; Chilembwe perished. His enterprise, however, had a significance which went beyond purely military considerations. Chilembwe, a man of mixed tribal origins, was willing to transcend ethnic policies, and to use violence for his purposes. He also appealed to an incipient feeling of black solidarity, and though he failed, Chilembwe's ideas—unlike those of Marx or Lenin—made some immediate impression in the backveld.

The October Revolution of 1917 struck no answering chords in

Central Africa. Russia was far away; its affairs were unknown. The Communist Party of South Africa (founded in 1921, the first Communist party in Sub-Saharan Africa) was soon reduced to total dependence on the ever-shifting line laid down by the Comintern with an eye to Soviet rather than African problems; the party appealed only to a tiny elite; its leaders were Europeans, who failed to make any converts among the army of labor migrants on the mines and farms of South Africa, and who exercised no influence whatever beyond the Limpopo. Industrial organization centered on the Industrial and Commercial Workers' Union (ICU), a black South African body, part trade union, part protest organization, led by Clements Kadalie, a Nyasalander. The ICU set up branches in Southern Rhodesia, but among a laboring class containing a large percentage of migrants with strong links to the reserves, trade union principles did not easily strike root. The leadership was unstable, and the movement collapsed.

Central Africans also continued to derive some inspiration from American sources; America at the time made a much greater impact than the Soviet Union. Throughout the 1920s rumors kept circulating in various villages and compounds that aircraft and other technical innovations imported by the British were really of American provenance, and that a great army of black Americans would come to throw out the British. Wishful thinking of this kind often went with Messianic expectations. According to one prophet, God had sent the whites to Africa in order to bring free gifts to the blacks and teach them about God. The Europeans however had kept the divine presents and their superior knowledge to themselves; hence they could be justly expelled; ultimately there would be a new heaven and a new earth, and the blacks would at long last get their due. These and other related kinds of socioreligious escapism helped to shape a peculiar form of rural radicalism, which paralleled, and sometimes interpenetrated reformist concepts popular among the black elite.

The bulk of educated Africans—junior civil servants, telegraphists, teachers, clerks, court interpreters, and detectives—mainly depended on jobs in the European administration, the churches, and the larger firms. They generally had no desire openly to challenge their employers, especially at a period when paid positions were not easy to get. The elite did, however, wish to bring about a great variety of improvements; they also wished to be treated in a fashion different from that applied to the common people. (Clerks, for instance, objected to serving jail sentences under the same conditions as those meted out to ordinary laborers.) The "new Africans" gradually became conscious of their special position.

From the early 1920s, they banded themselves into "native welfare societies," whose members conducted their transactions in English, and which gradually acquired wider political influence.

White Politics

A time-traveler suddenly transported to Salisbury during the First World War would have found himself in a strange land. The Rhodesian capital, now a great city, was no more than a dusty township in the backwoods; most of its streets were dirt roads; there was little traffic; even the well-born rode around on bicycles, and His Honor, the Administrator, liked to make his dignity known by riding on a two-wheeler painted red with a golden crown at the rear. Life was leisurely; there was a spirit of white camaraderie. Yet in other ways conditions were grim. Nearly 7,000 Europeans, approximately a quarter of the country's European population, had put on khaki, and the war cast a shadow over the land.

The most pressing local political issue for the whites concerned the constitutional position of the two Rhodesias. The British South Africa Company wished to unify the two territories, and the chartered initiative served to divide the Europeans along the lines of class and status. The chartered company looked to administrative reform in order to save money and to simplify its problems of government. Well-to-do mining men backed the government. The opposition was led by Sir Charles Coghlan, a prominent Bulawayo lawyer of Irish descent, who acted as the spokesman of the less affluent settlers. Amalgamation, Coghlan argued, would strengthen the chartered company's position, delay self-government for Southern Rhodesia, and saddle Southern Rhodesia with a "Black North"; as a result the settlers would ultimately be swamped by a huge African majority. In 1917 the chartered company steamrollered its proposal through the Southern Rhodesian Legislative Council. But the Colonial Office would not sanction the scheme. Rhodesia and Zambia stayed apart at the settlers' behest, and the separate existence of the two territories was never successfully challenged thereafter.

London's decision brought about bitter disappointment on the chartered board. The trouble was, argued the British South Africa Company's policymakers, that white settlers could always make a great deal of noise through left-wing members of the British Parliament. British progressive opinion at the time tended to side with the colonists, who

were often looked upon in much the same way as Africans were forty
years later—oppressed people ground down by a ruthless financial
monopoly. The main Rhodesian bugbear of British missionaries, humanitarians, and Labourites in those days was the British South Africa
Company; the tacit alliance between the settlers and the British "conscience vote" (reminiscent in some ways of the understanding between
Boers, on the one hand, and British liberals and antiimperialists, on the
other, during the Anglo-Boer War) continued to influence the fortunes
of Rhodesia during an era when the constitutional future of the whole
region became a matter of debate.

After 1918 the settlers wanted no more of chartered rule. Neither
did the British South Africa Company itself, for the task of administration was unexpectedly expensive; governmental responsibilities interfered
with the commercial pursuits of the concern, which had never paid a
single dividend to its stockholders since its inception. The British Government had no desire to assume new responsibilities south of the
Zambezi at a time when the Empire was experiencing trouble in Ireland
as well as India. Not even the most militant critics of imperialism
thought of turning Rhodesia into a black republic like Liberia or Haiti.
The only practicable choice for Southern Rhodesia was apparently to
join South Africa or to assume some form of local autonomy under
settler auspices.

Rhodes himself had always desired the former alternative, and
when General Smuts became prime minister of South Africa in 1921,
the British South Africa Company waxed enthusiastic over union. Smuts,
the former Boer general, had long since become an ardent advocate of
empire. He was willing to offer excellent terms to the company and to
Rhodesia at large; he enjoyed the support of the Johannesburg mine-
owners to whom the chartered company was tied with financial bonds. By
taking in a new English-speaking territory, the general would strengthen
his hand against Afrikaner nationalism and against white radicalism in
town and country alike. Union was also favored for a time by Winston
Churchill, who was British colonial secretary for part of the period.
Churchill felt at first that the imperial cause would gain by Rhodesia's
inclusion in the union. A powerful union was better than a struggling
little colony which one day might go bankrupt and therefore become a
charge on the imperial exchequer.

The cause of union however met with strong opposition, especially
from the ranks of the less prosperous whites. To indulge in some bold
generalizing, the people who opposed union in 1922 had much in common with those who had opposed amalgamation of the two Rhodesias

in 1917, and who were to oppose the creation of the Federation of Rhodesia and Nyasaland in 1953. Many European miners, railway workers, and artisans feared Smuts because of the manner in which he had put down the Rand Rising of 1922—an armed rebellion of skilled white workers in Johannesburg, the only large urban insurrection ever to take place in Sub-Saharan Africa. The white workers in Rhodesia and South Africa alike opposed the "Randlords'" policy of reducing costs by substituting black labor for skilled white labor. There were numerous economic rivalries between South Africa and Southern Rhodesia. There was also, however, a deeply felt appeal to British patriotism and a considerable distrust of the Afrikaner minority (which amounted to nearly one-fifth of the white population). The great majority of Rhodesians were of British descent; they did not wish to be absorbed by a country likely to fall under the sway of Afrikaners. Rhodesian autonomy moreover was supported by missionaries, humanitarians, Indians, and Coloreds—all of whom preferred the existing Rhodesian regime to South Africa's. The matter was finally decided by a referendum. Despite opposition on the part of the Establishment, including the major mining interests and the press, the majority of the electorate decided in favor of Responsible Government.

In 1923 Southern Rhodesia changed its status to that of a self-governing colony, run by a premier and cabinet drawn from the leading party in the newly established Legislative Assembly; the latter was elected under a formally "color-blind," but largely white franchise. The new state controlled its own army and its own civil service; for all practical purposes the new state enjoyed full internal autonomy. The British Government insisted above all on the interests of British investors. Owing to some complex legal reasoning, the Southern Rhodesian taxpayers had to dole out money to acquire the public works, the unalienated lands, and the mineral rights of their territory; later on they also purchased the railways from the company. The Southern Rhodesian settlers formed the only community in imperial history which ever had to pay for the privilege of self-government.

The Europeans nevertheless got a good bargain. The new government took over a remarkably effective civil service. Coghlan, the new premier, and his successors all resisted the temptation of using the bureaucracy for the purpose of political patronage. Public services, though locally based, retained the standards of technical efficiency, financial probity, and administrative continuity built up under Sir William Milton and Sir Drummond Chaplin, the company's previous "administrators." Southern Rhodesia continued to govern its African rural population in the accustomed fashion. There was direct rule through white officials; the chiefs were looked upon as local constables without recognized judicial powers, responsible in all matters to the colony's own Native Department. The system was reflected in the country's military structure. Southern Rhodesia retained the police as its first line of defense. In addition, the new administration created a short-service European citizens' army, similar in ethos and organization to Australia's; this was, so to speak, the white electorate in arms, which could be mobilized at short notice and small expense.

From 1924 Zambia passed under the control of the Colonial Office, for the local settlers were too few to assume administrative powers, and they actually desired imperial governance. Administration fell to the Colonial Service; militarily the two northern territories remained dependent on small forces of professional black soldiers officered by a handful of whites drawn from the same strata as the native commissioners, that is to say, from British middle- and upper-middle-class people with something of a gentry outlook and, for the greater part, with an Oxford education. The terms of political handover favored the chartered company, which retained mineral and land rights. Political reorganization was followed by swift economic expansion. Experts discovered ways in which the low-grade ores of the Copper Belt could be worked profitably.

By 1925 far-sighted investors had come to realize that enormous wealth must be hidden beneath the Zambian bush. Despite the government's initial skepticism, mining magnates realized that Rhodes's Second Rand had turned up at last. The Zambian copper resources could not be worked by small investors; they required a vast capital outlay, for mining companies had to dig great depths; they also had to create a vast range of facilities—health services, local communications, indeed whole new cities—which alone permitted the new copper wealth to be mined. Investors moreover had to wait a long time for a return on their money; substantial profits only started coming in from 1937 onward, twelve years after Zambia's "Copper Revolution" had first begun. The Zambian mineral industry came to be dominated by two great financial groups. The first of these centered on the Anglo-American Corporation, which had close links with the chartered company and the South African gold industry. The second rested on the Rhodesian Selection Trust, in which American influence was strong; these transatlantic ties proved of great technological value owing to the experience which the United States, the biggest copper producer, had accumulated in the mining and distribution of these ores. Zambia became "company country" par excellence, and the local white bourgeoisie remained infinitely weaker there than south of the Zambezi.

In Malawi, the white estate owners continued to be an influential group, particularly as tea became a profitable crop that replaced coffee. But the tea growers never developed into a plantocracy. Effective power remained with the British administration, which gradually became more conscious of the opportunities offered to economic development by native peasant farming. In 1936 a new ordinance indeed prohibited the alienation of additional land as freehold, and Malawi never became a settler's country in the true meaning of those words.

The colonists in Malawi and Zambia did, however, attain representation in the local colonial legislatures, especially in Zambia. Africans north of the Zambezi, unlike their compatriots to the south, could not cast a direct vote in elections for these chambers, for legally the blacks in Zambia and Malawi were only "British Protected Persons," not British subjects. The distinction was far from academic. Appointments to administrative positions in the British civil service and to regular (as distinct from temporary wartime) commissions in the British army were reserved to native-born British subjects, even naturalized white foreigners were excluded.

Africans did, however, secure a measure of responsibility in local government in the villages. From the 1930s onward, the British abandoned the company's tradition of "Direct Rule" and gave some formally defined powers to indigenous chiefs of traditional or supposedly traditional provenance. "Indirect Rule" did not mark a radical break with the past; even the chartered company had employed the power of kings like Lewanika for its purposes, and in practice, the new regime still required a great deal of European supervision. Indirect rule made for peaceful and inexpensive rural governance at a time when many other parts of the world were beset by tyranny and torn by bloodshed. But Indirect Rule raised as many problems as it solved. It did not apply to the cities, where Africans were supposed to be no more than temporary sojourners, and where administrative powers rested with municipal officers—hard-working whites, often men born in Africa who lacked the prestige and the financial prerequisites attached to the British Colonial Service. In the countryside the British found that many chiefs were unaccustomed to the new responsibilities placed upon them by the administration. Rain-makers could not easily be turned into road-makers. The chiefs thus were forced to send their sons to school or to recruit educated Africans to their service; hence, the emerging class of literate blacks imperceptibly gained in influence. At the same time the elite remained wed to a policy of political caution that did not as yet challenge the basic assumptions of British colonialism. For the time being the elite continued to back Indirect Rule in which they continued to have a stake.[3]

Slump and Recovery

The worldwide slump occasioned a temporary crisis in Central Africa. There was widespread unemployment. Jobless labor migrants returned to their villages. Out-of-work Europeans, lacking the scanty security afforded either by a stake in the land or by regular unemployment insurance, became all the more resolute in protecting their livelihood against African competition. The slump struck Zambia with such severity that, in 1933, the administration considered ending white settlement altogether. Instead of pushing European colonization, as hitherto, the British considered economy measures that would have turned the country into "a superior kind of Bechuanaland." The mining companies, however, argued that their industry could not be run within the framework of a purely African territory; in the end the administration continued to provide the services regarded as essential for keeping a white population in the country. The settlers in Zambia, however, abandoned previous hopes of ultimately turning the country into a white dominion. Instead, they looked to Salisbury for their salvation, an attitude further encouraged when in 1930 the British Labour Government issued the so-called Passfield Memorandum, which reiterated an earlier promise that African interests should be "paramount" in East Africa.

In Southern Rhodesia, the Europeans had to deal with an emerging African opposition that took many different forms. Educated Africans demanded some form of direct representation in the Legislative Assembly and criticized many aspects of Rhodesia's African policy. Traditionalists wished to restore the Ndebele state in some form. Prophets foretold a day of reckoning when God would "blow out the whites with a big wind." In addition, Africans for the first time employed the strike as a weapon; in 1927 the miners at Shamva downed their tools (a foretaste of much severer labor troubles in the Copper Belt in 1935 and 1940).

Howard Unwin Moffat, a descendent of the famous missionary fam-

---

[3] The first organization to call itself a congress, on the pattern of the South African National Congress, was formed in 1937 with the support of the wealthier Tonga farmers, traders, and chiefs. The new body called itself the Northern Rhodesian African Congress and put forward an ultramoderate program, which did, however, call for cooperation with Africans in other territories.

ily and Coghlan's successor in the premier's office, tried to cope with prevailing unrest through the Land Apportionment Act in 1930. Moffat argued that by 1930 European settlers had bought some 31,000,000 acres of unalienated land. Africans were legally entitled to acquire more farms, but lacking both capital and knowledge of commercial and administrative procedure, they failed to hold their own, having purchased no more than 45,000 acres. If a free land market continued to operate, the Africans would become a landless proletariat with revolutionary proclivities. The new legislation abolished the free land market. It increased the area immediately available for Africans, and made special provision for Africans willing to buy land on individual tenure.[4] Later on the act aroused bitter controversy, but at the time it was looked upon as a pro-African measure. Missionary opinion as well as leading liberal theoreticians like Professor E. H. Brookes supported Moffat.

Once again it is worth pointing out that, at the time, the principle of territorial separation was acceptable to the majority of British academics, missionaries, and administrators. The fundamental assumptions then current influenced imperial civil servants and experts as much as it did the settlers. In 1930, for instance, the British appointed Professor S. D. Adshead, a prominent town planner from London University, to design a new capital for Zambia; the new consultant based his plans on the assumption that whites and blacks must dwell apart. Earlier, the Missionary Conference of Southern Rhodesia had supported separate development; so did the Rev. A. S. Cripps, a militant Christian socialist who lived in Rhodesia; he denounced the settlers' sins and at the same time defended separatism, in a work characteristically entitled *An Africa for Africans: A Plea on Behalf of Territorial Segregation Areas.*

Moffat, a modest unassuming man, thus had little trouble gaining the approval of the British Labour Government for his Land Apportionment Act. He did not, however, manage to cope with the hardships occasioned by the slump; he was accused of not doing enough for the whites, and in 1933 Godfrey Martin Huggins (later Lord Malvern), a successful British surgeon, formed a new Cabinet. The Huggins government started off as a crisis administration, comparable in many ways with the national government, which then exercised power in Great Britain. Huggins took stringent measures to protect the smaller white maize farmers against their two main competitors: the big European

---

[4] In 1930, some 21,594,957 acres were set aside as native reserves, and 6,851,876 for native purchase areas; 31,033,050 areas were by this time alienated to whites; 17,423,815 remained available for Europeans.

growers with substantial capital reserves, and the African villagers who worked with lower overheads than the whites. Huggins likewise safeguarded the skilled European workmen against being undercut by African artisans, and also by nonunionized whites willing to work at lower wages than those acceptable to European trade unionists. Huggins's policy thus benefited the less affluent whites. It also tended to work against the interests of consumers as a group. Yet, Huggins's policy gained widespread approval; some white Rhodesians indeed compared it to Roosevelt's "New Deal." Whatever the merits or the demerits of Huggins's economic policy, the Rhodesian economy revived relatively quickly. The British policy of devaluing the pound gave an unintended subsidy to Rhodesian and South African gold producers alike, and the economy of southern Africa as a whole proved to be unexpectedly resilient under pressure.

The Zambian copper mines likewise recovered their prosperity within a relatively short time. The industry benefited especially from the growing demand for copper occasioned by expansion of the motor car and electrical industries, and the Copper Belt became the economic heart of Zambia. The British then decided that Livingstone, the territory's existing headquarter, should no longer serve as the country's capital. Instead they would build a center more favorably situated than the hot and oppressive little township on the Zambezi. Thus in 1935 Lusaka was opened as the country's new capital; a backveld Canberra, it was as yet half empty but destined to grow into a large city.

The copper revolution also affected Zambia in other ways. More and more Europeans came to the country as railwaymen, artisans, and mineworkers, determined to defend their living standards against any subsequent "dilution of labor" by lower-paid Africans. The whites pioneered trade unions in the country, but Africans soon learned from the Europeans and attempted to employ the strike weapon on the black man's behalf. Zambia, during this period, attracted a larger number of educated men from Malawi—black evangelists, court interpreters, teachers, and mine clerks who contributed to the emergence of a new political consciousness. At the time the British were becoming increasingly unwilling to surrender any part of Zambia to Southern Rhodesian control. As late as 1926, when neither the imperial nor the Southern Rhodesian authorities had as yet fully awakened to the opportunities offered by Zambia's fantastic mineral potential, Southern Rhodesia might still have acquired the Zambian Railway Belt up to the Congolese border. In that case Barotseland would perhaps have become a separate protectorate, and northeastern Rhodesia would probably have been joined to Malawi.

But the white Rhodesians missed their chance. Later on, when they took up the amalgamation issue again, the imperial authorities would no longer agree to a full merger between Southern Rhodesia and any part of the "Black North." Such a policy would have gone contrary to imperial professions of trusteeship. Also, the imperial authorities would have lost direct control over Zambia's copper, a raw material of vital strategic importance.[5] Imperial policy thoroughly appealed to emergent African opinion in the northern territories; educated Africans almost universally rejected any form of closer union, and as long as they remained politically weak, they looked to London for defense against any encroachment on the part of Salisbury.

New Modes of Thought

The changing climate of intellect. The Passfield Memorandum, as well as growing British opposition to any form of amalgamation between the two Rhodesias, was symptomatic of a change in the prevailing climate of intellectual opinion. In 1920 the Reverend John H. Harris, secretary of the Anti-Slavery and Aborigines Protection Society, an influential British association dedicated to the cause of colonial reform, still praised the Rhodesian settlers as fine people who had a sense of justice and the ability to run Rhodesia without depriving qualified black voters of their suffrage. As time went on, such judgments became increasingly rare within the ranks of British missionaries, scholars, and the more widely read journalists. The white settlers' moral stock began to slump in Great Britain, and the settlers in turn began to denounce clergymen, academics, and progressive politicians for practicing "philanthropy by proxy" at the colonists' expense.

At the same time there was a revolution in scholarship which affected British Central Africa as well as many other parts of the colonial world. The bulk of the early work concerning the cultures of Africa derived from the pens of missionaries and government officials with an academic bent. These pioneers included men like David Clement Ruffelle Scott, a missionary distinguished both as a builder and as a linguistic scholar. He was responsible for building the monumental mission church at Blantyre, an astonishing example of untutored architecture,

---

[5] L. H. Gann, *A History of Northern Rhodesia: Early Days to 1953* (London: Chatto & Windus Ltd., 1964), pp. 245–51, 267–78. L. H. Gann, *A History of Southern Rhodesia: Early Days to 1934* (London: Chatto & Windus Ltd., 1965), pp. 256–57.

and for compiling the equally impressive *Encyclopaedic Dictionary of the Mang'anja Language,* both completed in 1897.[6]

During the 1930s, specialization of academic labor steadily increased in the field of Central African studies; professional scholars came to dominate the intellectual scene. Anthropologists, museum curators, and archivists laid the foundations of modern African history. In 1931, for instance, Gertrude Caton-Thompson published her great work concerning the Bantu origins of Zimbabwe, which finally put an end to romantic speculations on the supposed mysteries of King Solomon's Mines. In 1938 a key date in the intellectual history of Central Africa, the Rhodes-Livingstone Institute opened its doors in Zambia. The institute, a sociological research body, received strong support from Sir Hubert Young, then governor of Northern Rhodesia, who felt that the administration required more information concerning the new social problems thrust upon Central Africa by economic change. Institute officers had been reared, for the most part, in the secular, egalitarian, and optimistic traditions derived from the Age of Enlightenment. They were determined both to understand the world and to improve it. As Godfrey Wilson, the first director of the institute, put it with almost missionary fervor:

> Radical social contradictions cannot be maintained . . . in the structure of Northern Rhodesia (as of the world at large) radical social contradictions are evident today . . . in consequence that structure must be changed, in one way or the other, so as to resolve them. This necessity is not a moral necessity; it is objective and material.[7]

Theoretically, this point of view need not have operated against the settlers. Indeed the firm aim of the institute was "to analyse scientifically the social life of modern man, White and Black in Central Africa, to furnish information to the government and to disseminate the findings of the Institute to a wider public.[8]

In actual practice the new scholarship was double-edged in its impact. There was a major breakthrough in the study of African society. There was also a new spirit of critical inquiry, which frequently merged

---

[6] James Morris, *Pax Britannica; The Climax of an Empire* (New York: Harcourt, Brace & World, Inc., 1968), pp. 502–503.

[7] Godfrey Wilson, *An Essay on the Economics of Detribalization in Northern Rhodesia.* Part 2. Rhodes-Livingstone Paper No. 6, 1942, p. 82.

[8] Max Gluckman, "The Rhodes-Livingstone Institute and Museum," *The Rhodes-Livingstone Journal,* No. 1, 1942, p. 5.

imperceptibly into social criticism; this mood was often unaware of the extent to which social research was itself both indebted to and influenced by the conditions created through the *Pax Britannica*, a system of governance that managed to create revolutionary changes without the time-honored totalitarian methods of trial and terror. Anthropological research sometimes was accompanied by a sense of self-identification, conscious or unconscious, with the African peoples who formed the subject of the professional studies. An anthropologist would proudly speak of "my people." His Afrocentric and phil-african approach provided a strong emotional incentive for sound scholarly work. At the same time it helped to modify the climate of academic opinion in a sense inimical to settler interests.

A pervasive new mode of thought also affected missionary attitudes. The simple convictions of early backveld evangelists, willing to risk death from disease for themselves and their families in order to battle against Satan, gradually disappeared. As the realities of precolonial Africa receded from the memory of living men, missionaries became less willing to condemn, and more willing to praise the olden ways. Before the First World War clergymen could write without embarrassment about the assumed depravities of an African village, where "mere bairns are corrupted and tainted at the cradle" by "heathen hovel life" and where the most eloquent sermons against the evil instruction offered by parents to their children were answered by the equally eloquent African proverb asking, "What baby lion ever trembled at his father's roaring?" [9] The writer who had spent twenty-two uninterrupted years in Africa, thought of himself as the member of Kipling's

> . . . legion that never was listed
> that carries no colors nor crest,
> but split in a thousand detachments
> is breaking the road for the rest.

But his ideological successors lacked some of the old certainties. They were, however, deeply influenced by the "overspill" of social consciousness from the metropolitan countries into the colonies. Christian leaders slowly began to appreciate the importance of bringing the Gospel to the mining compounds as well as to the kraals. The town-oriented approach owed a good deal to sociological inspirations.

Outstanding among the new breed of missionaries were men like

[9] D. Crawford, *Thinking Back: 22 Years without a Break in the Long Grass of Central Africa* (New York: George H. Doran Company, 1912), p. 442.

John Merle Davis, an American churchman who first made a name for himself by a survey of multiracial problems on the Pacific Coast, by his work as secretary of the Institute of Pacific Relations. Davis's work made a considerable impression on the International Missionary Council, which placed him in charge of its newly created Department of Social and Industrial Research, and which supported a major study concerning the problems of industrialization in the Copper Belt.[10]

At the same time the academics' influence on colonial government began to increase. Beginning in the late 1930s senior civil servants were sent to summer courses at Oxford. Summer schools of this kind would have met with snorts from the earlier generation of officials who got their leadership training in the Bechuanaland Border police, the Indian army, or the ivory business. The new trend, however, fitted in with the requirements of a period when government became increasingly complex, when government officials themselves began to undertake extensive research projects, and when district officials had to cooperate with specialists drawn from many different fields.

The change in the intellectual climate was quickened by the growing antipathy felt by many British intellectuals against entrepreneurs in general, an antipathy by no means unknown among senior colonial officials. During the 1840s and the 1850s, Marx had eulogized the progressive role by British capitalism in the colonies; Engels had rejoiced over the defeat suffered by Algerian tribesmen at the hands of the French. Seventy years later, Marxists had repudiated colonialism in all its forms, except the Russian. Imperialism had come under heavy fire from most of those who called themselves progressive. The reaction against imperialism in turn worsened the image of the settlers who had once been praised as pioneers of middle class values in the bush. Journals in southern Africa began to complain of being misrepresented or of not being heard at all. As one writer put it, British radio commentators chosen to discuss colonial problems always assumed an attitude of being "irritatingly impartial and broadminded," but in fact they were always "hostile to the European settlers in British Africa" who had a living to make.[11] Despite these complaints, the settlers could not reverse the tide of opinion, and the gulf between the colonists and academic opinion became increasingly wide. Whereas the missionaries had placed their trust in African clergymen and evangelists, the intelligentsia began to support educated Africans having more secular aspirations. Literate

[10] John Merle Davis et al., *Modern Industry and the African* (London: Macmillan & Co. Ltd., 1933).

[11] *The African Observer*, I, No. 5 (September, 1934), 2.

Africans (the kind of men who began to group themselves into African welfare societies) came to be looked upon as the new agents of progress, destined to free Africa from the burdens of the past, to transcend the bonds of tribalism, and to preach a new Gospel of development and self-government, capable of regenerating a continent.

Matrix of color. As time went on, the educational gap between whites and the black elite began to narrow. Some Europeans became convinced that rigid segregation between the races was wrong and that the principles of social equality accepted in England should also be applied in Africa. As the elite improved its position, European (and also Indian) color bar practices became emotionally harder to bear precisely for those who had benefited most from European rule. In the early days of European colonization, the rank and file of Africans probably accepted the social color bar enforced by white men in much the same way as, in 1945, the defeated Germans put up with the airs of superiority and the segregated facilities available to the victorious allied army, and indeed to every victorious army in history stationed on enemy soil. The victors in Africa at first did not question their own superiority; the vanquished at long last preferred caution; they were moreover separated from the whites by profound barriers of culture and custom which most Africans did not wish to cross.

Gradually, however, more Africans went to school; the level of black education improved; more Africans became convinced that they should fill European jobs at European pay. African workmen advanced into a variety of so-called white trades. After 1918, for instance, truck driving and operating taxis were jobs for the white man. A generation later most professional drivers were Africans, and the process was speeded up by British army training schemes initiated during the Second World War. Africans learned better farming methods from agricultural officers or by the example of white farmers or from their own black neighbors. The progressive black farmer began to resent his inability to buy "white" land; the better-off African storekeeper realized with anger that he could not invest money in real estate situated in the European part of a city. At the same time, educated Africans became more sensitive to personal slights. Illiterate laborers did not expect courtesies from white or Colored foremen. But African clergymen who had read, not only the Gospel, but also such secular works as the plays of Shaw or historical studies from the pen of the well-known British socialist, Harold Laski would no longer bear slights from white shopgirls. Black sergeants who came back from the war with a well-merited Distinguished Conduct Medal (DCM) pinned to their tunic would not tolerate bad manners that might have appeared to their fathers as offensive but inescapable concomitants of white conquest. The elite responded with bitterness; in his auto-biography Kenneth Kaunda recorded how he could move strong men to tears by reminding them of insults inflicted upon them by Europeans.[12]

In theory the Colored (Eurafrican) community might have served as a bridge between black and white. In practice this did not happen. Miscegenation merely created a new color caste. In any case miscegenation did not become a way of life. In the early days of white colonization most pioneers were young bachelors; many of them took African mistresses; a few even contracted proper marriages, either by African or by European law. Among the first generation of native commissioners the practice was so widely spread that the acting administrator of North Eastern Rhodesia even defended concubinage in a secret dispatch. Illegitimate unions between British officials and African women did no harm, the memo argued, provided such alliances were "decently veiled," and did not degenerate into "mere libertinage." Concubinage had been of material comfort to the well-being of many officials in the lonely bush; it had served to protect whites from contempt and from the imputation of more offensive sexual pleasures on the part of ribald Africans. By living with African women, Europeans might be apprised of impending native troubles. Above all, concubinage "facilitated the acquisition of native languages and modes of thought." [13]

The British high commissioner for South Africa was shocked by these views, which offended Victorian sensibilities. The chartered company tried to get rid of officials who flaunted their paramours. Many Africans perhaps complained, as did some Germans after 1945, at the real or alleged iniquities of government by interpreters and mistresses. Concubinage could not, however, be eliminated as long as there were few white women in Africa. The number of Eurafricans increased, not only through unions between white men and black women, but also through the immigration of Coloreds from South Africa, who came as wagon drivers, traders, hunters, foremen, and artisans. The Colored community, however, remained numerically small. It was also ridden by internal divisions, for it contained people who had been brought up to all intents and purposes as Africans by African mothers as well as people who lived like Europeans and spoke English as their native tongue.

[12] Kenneth D. Kaunda, *Zambia Shall be Free* (London: William Heinemann Ltd., 1962), p. 42.
[13] Acting Administrator of North Eastern Rhodesia to High Commissioner, October 4, 1910. Confidential 2/1/3, North Eastern Rhodesia Public Records, Lusaka.

Miscegenation between whites and blacks and, to a lesser extent, between Indians and blacks, diminished, as transport facilities and health standards improved. British women could join their husbands in Central Africa by using regular steamboat and railway services. The proportion of white women to white men steadily increased. (In Southern Rhodesia the ratio of white females to 1,000 males grew from 407 in 1904 to 864 in 1936.) As soon as European women arrived in some station however remote, they almost at once insisted on "respectability," on ironed shirts, and proper table cloths but, above all, on the banishment of African mistresses. Europeans who lived with African girls and even Europeans legally married to African wives were no longer invited to white households (though the partners in mixed unions might still receive visits from white men). The children of black-white alliances mostly labored under the stigma of illegitimacy, no matter whether the European father looked after his offspring or ran away from his responsibilities. Eurafricans were hardly ever accepted into a color-conscious white community; Indo-Africans rarely entered the Indian community.

The psychology of racial segregation transcended mere economic considerations, for even well-to-do Coloreds rarely broke through the color bar. (All the same, there were some exceptions. There are some examples of white farmers who married Colored wives and apparently lived happily ever after.) The chief barriers were raised by white women. Their most obvious motive was sexual jealousy, the kind of sentiment that frequently led British ATS (Auxiliary Territorial Service) girls attached to the postwar army of occupation in Germany to denounce fraternization in the most intemperate language. But the color bar had psychological roots deeper than those derived from a search for sexual monopoly. In Central Africa European women were initially scarce; almost any girl—pretty or ugly, kind or quarrelsome—could find herself a husband. Probably, however, segregation derived from deeper cultural cleavages. Women bear a greater responsibility than men for bringing up children and for passing on the cultural heritage of their respective community to the very young. Women generally seem to resist changes in their religious and cultural legacy with greater tenacity than men. However this may be, profound changes would certainly have taken place within the European value system had numerous marriages been contracted between Europeans and Africans. Intermarriage, however, never came into fashion, and even though the social color bar was largely broken by the advent of independence in Zambia and Malawi, white and Indian endogamy froze into an almost inflexible pattern.

10

The Second World War and
Its Aftermath

The New Politics

The battles of the Second World War were fought far from the borders of Central Africa. Yet hostilities exerted a profound influence on the region as a whole. Southern Rhodesia mobilized approximately 15 percent of its white population. In addition, Godfrey Huggins, to the consternation of many of his white countrymen, increased the colony's military potential by permitting Africans to enlist in fighting units. Africans also served with distinction in the Northern Rhodesia Regiment and the King's African Rifles, seeing action in such far-flung areas as Ethiopia and Burma. In Malawi especially "military labor migration" reached great proportions, and there was a more distinct sense of national consciousness. Protests increased against missionary paternalism, against poor working conditions on white plantations, against the inadequate wages of black workmen in Southern Rhodesia, and related ills. In 1944 educated Africans formed the Nyasaland African Congress, a countrywide body designed to represent Africans who had as yet no black spokesman on the local legislative councils either in Zambia or Malawi. Organizers set up branches in many parts of the country, special care being taken not to alienate the chiefs.

Economically, however, Malawi still remained a backward country; development centered above all in Southern Rhodesia. The country was cut off from many of its overseas supplies, and there was an almost insatiable demand for manufactured goods both in Rhodesia and the northern territories. The country's infant industries made enormous strides; Southern Rhodesia built up its own iron and steel industry as well as many other enterprises. Economic development influenced every aspect of Rhodesian society. The poor white gradually disappeared from Rhodesia just as he disappeared from South Africa. Manufacturers also required increasing numbers of semiskilled and skilled black workmen; factory owners thus began to call for stabilized African rather than migrant black labor, on the grounds that a permanently established and better-paid work force would prove more efficient and thus economically more advantageous than a reserve army of semirural proletarians. Huggins, once a convinced supporter of segregation (known in Rhodesia as the "Two Pyramid Policy"), came to agree with these arguments. He became convinced that—both for administrative and for economic reasons—segregation would not work; African urbanization would have to be accepted, and African social stratification should be encouraged. Huggins thus began to embark on a policy of cautious social reform designed to improve farming standards in the reserves, to alleviate the worst miseries of town life, and above all to avoid violence in any shape or form, both by resisting the "gunpowder and grapeshot" school of settlers and by making economic concessions at the right time and the right place.

The war had equally profound effects on Zambia. The copper industry continued to expand. The Second World War was fought with the internal combustion engine and other specialized machines. Tanks, trucks, planes, radios, and radar equipment all needed enormous supplies of copper. Great Britain's main supplier in the Commonwealth, Zambia emerged from the war with its metal-producing capacity greatly increased. Politically, the local shortage of goods and raw materials at first benefited the settlers, who played such an important part in the process of production. The imperial authorities in Central Africa looked to Southern Rhodesia for all kinds of economic favors, ranging from rail facilities to priorities in the delivery of manufactured goods. In fact the British became more dependent on Rhodesian goodwill, as Great Britain had to rely to an ever-increasing extent on raw materials from the sterling area. In 1941 the three Central African territories set up a permanent secretariat at Salisbury to facilitate functional cooperation between them; this body became a precursor of the ill-fated federation established twelve years later between the three countries.

In Northern Rhodesia the imperial authorities had to make all kinds of concessions to white miners. The British at the time did not worry about black insurrections; they were much more concerned instead that white rebels in the Copper Belt might stage another "Rand Rising," thereby disrupting the copper industry, which was vital to the British war effort. Thus, in 1942 the British in Zambia gratefully availed themselves of a white Rhodesian armored division supplied by Huggins to nip European subversion in the bud. The most dangerous European leaders in the Copper Belt were arrested; the British thereby crushed an incipient alliance between militant Afrikaner nationalists and equally militant British left-wing socialists.

European militance gave unintended inspiration to African workers. The white Copper Belt strike was followed by a major African strike. Later on, Africans goaded by low wages and the sharply rising cost of living, likewise employed the strike weapon in Southern Rhodesia; in 1945 the railwaymen laid down their tools; in 1948 there were even more extensive work stoppages, though bloodshed was avoided. Labor unrest soon led to the formation of black trade unions. In Malawi the truck drivers were the first to organize. In Zambia the formation of trade unions was furthered by the British Labour Government, which sent out an adviser to assist Africans in their endeavor. In 1949 African miners thus established the African Mineworkers' Trade Union, a reformist body dedicated to improving wages within the existing economic framework.

The growth of trade unionism among the workers was paralleled by the development of new political organization. The British, anxious to set up sounding boards for African opinion, created a number of African representative bodies with advisory functions; these African Regional Councils, composed of African urban delegates and representatives from the Native Authorities, provided educated Africans with a schooling in Western parliamentary techniques and voting procedures which in turn influenced the structure of territorial politics. The British Labour Government, installed in 1945, made further political concessions to Africans. In 1948 two African members took their seats on the Northern Rhodesia Legislative Council; a year later two Africans joined the Nyasaland Legislative Council. For the first time Africans obtained direct representation on local legislative chambers, and the process, once begun, was hard to halt. During the same period African welfare societies founded a countrywide federation which later became the Northern Rhodesia African National Congress. The new congresses derived considerable encouragement from India, which in 1947 obtained independence from Great Britain without having had to fight, thereby setting a prestigious example to an emergent African elite that lacked any kind of military background.

The growth of African political consciousness did not preclude a certain amount of cooperation between white and black politicians with regard to specific issues. In Zambia, for instance, the colonists supported the creation of African regional councils, the provision of agricultural help for black villagers, and other concessions that did not go counter to European interests. Black members of the Legislative Council for their part supported the European members in their demand for curbs on the British South Africa Company's liberal rights. But on the broader issues of policy, agreement was impossible. The white and black elites alike regarded themselves as the residual legatees of empire. The Europeans in Zambia looked to Salisbury to protect their interests. The blacks in Zambia and Malawi felt that their respective countries should be treated no differently from the British colonies in West Africa. The emergent class of African schoolteachers, junior civil servants, and clerical employees gradually became convinced that both their personal interests and national advancement would best be served by capturing the machinery of national administration. The new doctrines also made progress among semiskilled workers, such as miners and truck drivers, who hoped that political and economic advancement would go hand in hand. African nationalism seeped into the villages through the activities of elected African representatives, of returned labor migrants, of preachers and of village schoolteachers. African politicians struck many answering chords. They appealed to the villagers' distrust of government-sponsored improvement schemes whose purpose was often crudely misrepresented; to the countryfolk's concern with rising prices; to widespread exasperation concerning pass legislation and other grievances, as well as to superstitious fears. From the early 1950s politically conscious Africans became convinced that after a period of "caretaker" government under the British Colonial Office, the black elites would be able to take over control in Zambia and Malawi, and that Southern Rhodesia must in time follow suit.

The Federation of Rhodesia and Nyasaland

On October 15, 1945, shortly after the end of the Second World War, a major Pan-Africanist Congress met at Chorlton Town Hall in Manchester, England. The delegates included a whole brain trust of future prime ministers including Jomo Kenyatta, Kwame Nkrumah, and Hastings Kamuzu Banda, a thirty-three-year-old Malawian. Banda, like Livingstone, Jameson, and Huggins before him, was a medical man. He represented a new generation of Africans who had come up in the world the hard way. Whereas Livingstone had started his career as a textile worker, Banda had begun as an engine room "oiler" in a Witswatersrand mine. Later Banda managed to get an education; he obtained a medical degree from a black college in Tennessee in the United States and advanced professional qualifications at Edinburgh and Glasgow. The congress in which Banda participated stood out as a landmark in African history. It adopted a philosophy of reformist socialism, vigorously denounced imperial rule, and called for independence to cure the ills of Africa. By the standards of a subsequent generation, its program was moderate, but at the time its demands appeared almost utopian. Except for the defeated Italians, the Western empires in Africa had emerged from the war unscratched. Great Britain's military might stood unchallenged in its colonies; the British Commonwealth Prime Ministers' Conference as yet contained only two members from Africa, Sir Godfrey Huggins from Rhodesia and General Smuts from South Africa. Their prestige ranked high both at home and abroad. Their respective countries had loyally stood by Great Britain in the dark days from 1939 to 1941, when the Soviet Union and the United States remained neutral in the war against Germany. South African and Rhodesian war production had assumed an important role in the Commonwealth's African war effort. South African and Rhodesian troops had played a distinguished part in liberating Ethiopia from Italian rule, and in the North African and Italian campaigns. Great Britain, plagued by the perennial dollar gap, looked to Pretoria and, to a lesser extent, Salisbury for various economic favors; the gold resources of Southern Africa remained vital to the economic well-being of the sterling area as a whole. Smuts especially had gained new laurels as one of Churchill's wartime advisers. Smuts had also played a major role in drafting the United Nations charter. His friend and ally, Huggins was widely regarded as a kind of Rhodesian Smuts, a known opponent of "white extremism" and very much *persona grata* with the British Establishment.

Under the prevailing circumstances Southern Rhodesia would hardly have experienced effective opposition had Huggins gone all out to secure dominion status, provided also he had made some minor concessions regarding African policy. The British "conscience vote" was as yet little concerned with Central Africa. During the late 1940s, the average British university student was indeed no more interested in the internal affairs of Rhodesia than in those of Tasmania or Prince Edward Island. The British governing circles had more pressing concerns connected above all with their country's postwar economic problems and, to a lesser extent, with the Soviet threat in Europe and decolonization in Asia and the Near East. Huggins, however, wanted a great deal more than a Rhodesian "midget dominion." The colony was booming; its industrial production kept increasing at a phenomenal rate. The Rhodesian manufacturers however had only a restricted home market and looked for a bigger Central African state, where they would enjoy protection against foreign competition, including that from South Africa. A large Central African state, with a wider economic base, would more easily secure scarce loan capital from overseas. A central government would be more easily enabled to make decisions of a transterritorial character concerning the allocation of priorities in transport, the provision of technical services, and so forth. A federated state with larger resources and a more balanced economy might be better placed to overcome the effects of a recession. The federal scheme also made a considerable appeal to the copper companies in Zambia. A united Central African state would be well placed to initiate large-scale hydroelectric developments essential for progress in the industry. A mildly liberal labor policy would favor African advancement and thereby reduce costs.

But Huggins and his associates did not think in economic terms alone. They were British patriots determined to build a powerful British dominion, an imperial bastion that would resist both the immediate threat from white Afrikanerdom in the south and the long-range menace from black nationalism to the north. There was a curious feeling of imperial idealism and a sense of having to seize a last chance, the one and only opportunity left for maintaining "civilized standards" in the heart of Africa.

Huggins's hand was strengthened when in 1948 the Afrikaner nationalists secured a decisive and probably irreversible victory at the polls in South Africa, and when Smuts fell from power. The Afrikaner triumph produced a strong British national reaction in Rhodesia. Huggins, who previously had occupied a precarious position in the postwar Rhodesian parliament, was returned with a towering majority. The imperial government would not consent to Huggins's original demand for an all-out amalgamation between Rhodesia and Zambia, the type of amalgamation which the settlers had themselves rejected thirty years before. The British Labour Government and their Tory successors were however willing to consider a looser federation, which they hoped would liberalize Southern Rhodesia's racial practices; form a counterweight to South African power; and promote economic and social development in Central Africa. At British insistence Malawi was also forced into the new association, even though Huggins would have been willing to leave the lakeside protectorate to its own devices.

The federal scheme aroused bitter opposition from British advocates of "Native Trusteeship," as well as from European right-wingers who feared that white interests would be swamped in a federal flood. Federation also encountered strong hostility from Africans in the north-

rn territories. Federation, their argument went, would make Southern
Rhodesian influence supreme in Central Africa; Rhodesian color bar
ractices would be extended beyond the Zambezi; white settlers would
ob the blacks of their land; constitutional safeguards were so much
yewash. "Once upon a time there was a tortoise," said an African
toryteller. "The stupid beast wanted to go out flying with two pigeons.
The pigeons got hold of a little stick; the tortoise held on to it with its
nouth, and up they went into the air. But when the villagers saw the
trange trio, they burst out laughing. The tortoise opened its mouth
o rebuke them, but it could not fly and miserably crashed to the ground
nd died." The moral was obvious. The African was the tortoise, the
vhites were the pigeons. Let no black man throw in his lot with Euro-
eans unless he could fly equally well. African political and economic
ears were enhanced by preoccupations with magic. And grim stories
vent around the Copper Belt of white men who butchered blacks to
an their meat or who poisoned sugar to render Africans impotent.

The Africans however lacked an effective combat organization.
Their opposition was brushed aside, and in 1953 the new ship of state
t last set sail with the clumsy title of "Federation of Rhodesia and
Nyasaland," and the Kiplingesque motto *magni esse mereamur*, "Let
s deserve to be great." From the economic and the administrative point
f view, the federation was an outstanding success. The federal govern-
ent created competent and relatively inexpensive services; those con-
erned with noncontroversial matters like medicine and meteorological
esearch operated with exemplary efficiency. There was a staggering
ise in national production, which set an example to the underdeveloped
vorld at large. Farmers increased their crops; mining companies turned
ut more metals; secondary industries grew apace, not only in Southern
Rhodesia but also in Zambia. Rhodesian capitalists saved extensively;
etween 1954 and 1960, gross capital formation averaged about 31 per-
ent of the gross national product, a record that exceeded alike that of
Vest Germany, the Soviet Union, and the United States. A spirit of
Victorian optimism was in the air, a mood that would have delighted
amuel Smiles. "Non-Africans" during the period saved approximately
3 percent of their disposable incomes; (the corresponding figure for
Great Britain, with its welfare and consumption economy, amounted
o little more than 5 percent). Impressive new engineering works went
p, including the giant Kariba Dam. Money became available for
igher education and the arts. For instance, in 1957 the University
College of Rhodesia and Nyasaland started its first teaching courses; in
he same year the Rhodes National Gallery opened its doors in Salisbury
vith the express purpose of encouraging local artists, both black and

white. The cities expanded, new immigrants poured into the country and real wages increased for Europeans, Asians, and Africans alike.

Even politically, the federation seemed to be making some head way. In 1956 Huggins retired as federal prime minister; he was raise to the peerage as Viscount Malvern of Rhodesia and of Bexley, loade with honorary doctorates from great British universities, and com memorated as a great statesman by David Low, most pungent of radica British cartoonists. Roy Welensky, ex-slum boy, ex-engine driver, ex Rhodesian boxing champion, and ex-trade unionist, succeeded to Hug gins's office. Like Huggins, his mentor, Welensky provided the ele torate with the unusual example of a politician who veered to a mor moderate stance from his former uncompromising commitment t apartheid and white supremacy.

In 1957 Welensky went to London, where he secured what—o: the face of it—was a solid British promise to stand fast to the federa cause. The Tory Government in power at the time announced its firr opposition to the secession of any constituent territory from the fec eration. It also gave an understanding that Great Britain would no initiate, amend, or repeal any federal legislation or deal with any matte within the competence of the federal parliament. Welensky and hi political allies firmly controlled the federal and the Southern Rhodesia: legislatures, whose system of representation was designed to maintai a European majority for a long time to come. The federal army, con posed both of European conscripts and African askari remained firml loyal; there was no armed underground of the Algerian or the Indc chinese variety. Contrary to the predictions of Banda and his fellov nationalists, Africans in Malawi and Zambia were not deprived of thei ancestral acres; also, white color bar practices in industry lost some o their sting as the demand for skilled labor kept increasing, and eve white trade unionists began to make concessions. The Rhodesian Estab lishment got by without terror; there was cautious reform of the piece meal variety and despite widespread discontent and deep-seated fear; the new state seemed firmly established. In spite of the apprehension of the British conscience vote, the federation appeared set to become permanent British bastion in Africa.

The Federation Totters

For all its imposing appearance, the federation rested on shak foundations. The new state was plagued not only by open and laten conflicts between Europeans and Africans but also by profound cor radictions within the European governing strata. These found expres-ion, for instance, in a bizarre constitution. By 1956 the Rhodesias and Nyasaland had to pay for a federal governor, three territorial governors, federal and a Southern Rhodesian cabinet, a federal and a territorial parliament at Salisbury, two executive and two legislative councils in the northern territories, as well as mayors and municipal councils in the major cities—all to serve a population smaller than London's. None of the successive governor generals had been well known before they came to Rhodesia; none could be built into a symbol of federal unity. Many senior officials in the governors' lodges and the secretariats of the north remained skeptical of the federal experiments. Governor Sir Arthur Benson of Northern Rhodesia, for instance, turned into a bitter critic of the federation. Carbon copies of his most secret dispatches had surreptitiously found their way into Huggins's in-box before they even reached London, a practice that reduced the customary level of cordiality between senior British policymakers. The architects of the federation had anticipated that their handiwork would facilitate admin-istrative saving. But the territorial services kept expanding as fast as their administrative responsibilities diminished.

The division of functions between the federal and the territorial governments rested on the old trusteeship assumption that native affairs could be neatly sliced off from ordinary administrative work. African administration, African agriculture, African education up to university standards, and related subjects all remained subject to territorial con-trol. The federal government thus had little chance of establishing any real contacts with Africans, except in health matters. Few people how-ever understood this division, and federal authorities incurred the blame for sins of commission and omission for which they bore no constitu-tional responsibility.

There were countless administrative anomalies. For instance, an engine driver starting from Wankie in Southern Rhodesia came under one workmen's compensation code if he ran off the rails south of the Zambezi and under another if he crashed north of the river. The terri-torial authorities dealt with African agriculture; the federal government was responsible for most aspects of European farming, though locusts still ate white- and black-owned crops with equal voracity. Territories ran their own police; the federal government ran the army. If a terri-torial governor required military support, he would have to call on federal troops; as a consequence, federal authorities would take the blame in the popular mind for using force. Above all, London retained the right to alter the balance of power in the territorial legislatures of Zambia and Malawi. This did not matter a great deal as long as London

and Salisbury saw eye to eye; but once their views diverged, and Africa
secessionists came to dominate the northern legislatures, the machiner
of government would break down.

The federation also had to meet new economic and political cha
lenges. At the end of the 1950s world copper prices began to fall; th
hectic boom slowed down, and federal and local authorities had t
contend with all sorts of unforeseen problems. The two dominant coppe
trusts moreover disagreed among themselves on various important i
sues, including the speed of African advancement and the siting of th
federation's main hydroelectric projects. Their records are not yet ope
to the historian's inspection, but apparently by the late 1950s the Ame
ican-controlled Rhodesian Selection Trust, which had originally sup
ported federation, became convinced that federation would not las
and that the investors' interests would be better served by a moderat
African government in Zambia.

Moreover, during the period as a whole, the climate of oversea
opinion underwent a rapid change. The United Nations became a
influential forum of anticolonial and antisettler opinion. The whit
settler was often cast in the role once reserved for the "Unspeakabl
Turk" in the liberal nonconformist demonology of late-Victorian En;
land. Africans frequently came to be looked upon in much the sam
way as liberals and socialists had looked upon the Boers about 1900,
brave people heroically defending their heritage against British "methoc
of barbarism." Africans moreover benefited by the new transvaluatio
that began to stand Victorian concepts on their heads. Victorians con
monly (and quite mistakenly) used to identify black Africans with th
"lower orders of society" in England; hence Africans had incurred th
censure commonly given to "the vicious and idle poor." Under the ne
intellectual dispensation, Africans began to gain from this suppose
(and inaccurate) parallel, as the suburban protest culture belabore
all things bourgeois and praised all matters proletarian. The new a]
proach was as missionary-oriented and as ethnocentric as the old; th
British still wanted to refashion Africa in their own image, into peac
ful, prosperous democracies of the Northern European pattern. Bt
now they dropped their former local agents—the settlers and the chie
—in whom they had once placed so much trust. Instead they centere
all their hopes on the educated African—the new white-collar class—wt
was supposed to be able to transcend existing ethnic differences ar
who was assumed to be both technically fitted and ideologically equippe
to set up new nations run on the Westminster model.

Perhaps even more important was the wider shift in world powe
The Suez campaign of 1956, the last exercise of British gunboat-an

cruiser-imperialism, turned out to be a fiasco. In 1957 Ghana became independent. In 1958 France began on a course of all-out decolonization in Black Africa. The end of empire seemed in sight.

In the meantime, Africans improved their political organization; they also acquired a greater sense of unity. The campaign for federation had the unanticipated effect of heightening the Africans' political consciousness. Africans might be in a minority in the federal parliament; the central legislature did, however, serve the unintended purpose of providing a forum to black parliamentarians from all three territories. The Europeans' slogan of "partnership" between the races (with the Africans as junior partners for a long time to come) became itself a measuring stick against which white intentions came to be evaluated, judged, and condemned.

To discuss the development of African political organization during this period would require a volume of its own; we can only point to a few salient facts. The leading cadres continued to be made up of the new administrative bourgeoisie—of African teachers, welfare officers, clerks, and other educated people. The activists formed a small minority, but gradually they gained wider support, often by making the most fantastic promises of benefits to be derived from independence, when Africans would inherit the earth. The radical wings of the independence movements gained particular strength among unemployed youngsters in the cities; but in addition villagers began to enlist in nationalist parties, convinced that freedom would provide more land and that it would also put an end to unpopular government regulations designed to enhance agricultural productivity. In 1957 the Southern Rhodesian African National Congress came into being, an outgrowth of the City Youth League. The new organization (which ultimately became the Zimbabwe African People's Union) was led by Joshua Nkomo, a trained welfare officer, a trade unionist, and originally one of Huggins's political protégés. A year later Banda returned to Nyasaland, after a lengthy absence, to reorganize the congress movement.

In Zambia the existing African Congress split. Kenneth Kaunda, the party's erstwhile secretary general, built up a more militant organization, destined to develop into Zambia's present ruling party. Kaunda, a dedicated man, in many respects represented an entirely new class of politically conscious Africans. He had grown to political maturity at a time when traditional village life was being profoundly changed. Townmade goods were becoming more widely used even in the remoter areas. The spread of the money economy was increasing the villagers' contacts with the outside world. It also created new professional openings in village trade, in the lower rungs of the administration, in teaching and similar service occupations. Even the most backward cultivators began to realize that literacy was a desirable skill for their children. The art of reading helped to diffuse new ideas and new tastes among the country people. Industrialization occasioned new opportunities and also new discontents. Black expectations were able to gain a measure of legitimate expression by reason of the civic protection extended to all subjects of the Crown. For all their social and political disabilities, African dissenters enjoyed a degree of physical security unimaginable to the subjects of Hitler and Stalin. The institutions created through the *Pax Britannica* itself played an important part during a critical time of African political development.

The vanguard of African dissenters now mainly consisted of African white-collar workers. Like African millenarian prophets, these secular reformers were descended from African villagers; they were still familiar with the ways of the villagers, but they were better acquainted with the Europeans' intellectual and governmental techniques than were unlettered country folk.

Kaunda, one of the most impressive of the "new men" had grown up on a mission station; the son of a Malawi clergyman who had been employed by a Scottish mission to preach the Gospel to the Bemba. Later on, young Kaunda went to the Copper Belt, where, for the first time in his life, he felt the full shock of the color bar. He joined an African welfare society, and subsequently became a member of Congress. Political work soon made so many demands on him that he gave up teaching and returned to his mother's farm, where he combined politics with petty trade. He started to deal in second-hand clothes, and in doing so, he had to cycle over great distances, a tough job, but one that provided excellent training for the difficult job of organizing Congress Party branches over the length and breadth of the northern province. During this period Kaunda came into conflict with his former teachers at his old mission station at Lubwa, and fervently quoted George Bernard Shaw to white clergymen. In the end he built up a powerful organization that secured widespread backing among the Bemba cultivators of the northeast and also in the Copper Belt, where Bemba miners made up a considerable proportion of the labor force. The federation issue now provided a common bond for African nationalists of many different kinds. The struggle over federation also helped to place the problems of Central Africa in the arena of international politics. In 1958 a strong delegation of Central African leaders attended a major Pan-Africanist Congress at Accra in independent Ghana, where they signed a declaration pledging themselves to destroy the federation.

End of Empire

Early in 1959 Dr. Hastings Banda initiated a policy of controlled violence; government supporters were attacked, roadblocks were set up, government property was destroyed, and administrative officials were harried. Violence also burst out in Southern Rhodesia, where African nationalists skillfully nursed grievances of many kinds, including grievances over the so-called Native Land Husbandry Act, a measure designed to raise farming standards in the reserves. From the military point of view alone, these disorders presented no serious difficulties. Tough, sardonic men like "Bobo" Young, an ex-private in the Scots Guard, who in the days of the charter had once policed the huge Chinsali district with a handful of black auxiliaries, would not have been impressed by such outbreaks. In fact the federal forces put down the incipient rebellion in Malawi without difficulty. A state of emergency was declared in Southern Rhodesia, and on the face of it the African offensive was a complete failure. The federal army remained intact; black soldiers in the federal army, unlike the Africans in the Congolese *Force Publique*, never seem to have thought of mutiny. The state machinery could not be captured. The settlers' morale was unaffected. The use of gasoline bombs, the practice of enforcing the payment of political levies by threats, the internecine disagreements between the nationalists, and also the activities of thugs masquerading under the nationalist label created many enemies for the nationalists. There was never any shortage of informers willing to betray to the security forces the real or alleged plans of the militant opposition.

But then nationalists in fact gained a decisive political victory. The bulk of British metropolitan opinion was no longer willing to put up with the methods and ideals of such men as "Bobo" Young. Banda and Kaunda were arrested but soon released, thereby gaining the coveted honor of being "prison graduates." New parties replaced those that had been banned. These included the Malawi Congress Party, the United National Independence Party in Zambia, the National Democratic Party (later the Zimbabwe African People's Union) in Southern Rhodesia.[1] The new groups were more tightly organized than their predeces-

---

[1] The development of the various African parties was a complex process which can only be briefly summarized. In Southern Rhodesia, a youth league, which drew its main strength from militant Africans in Salisbury, united with a group of African nationalists from Bulawayo to form the African National Congress. In 1959 the party was banned, but it was reconstituted in the following year as the National Demo-

sors. They enjoyed wide support at home and gained the confidence of numerous well-wishers abroad. Banda especially exercised an almost Messianic fascination. "The national leader is there," wrote an enthusiastic British liberal in the manner once reserved for missionary publications, "a hero who has arisen from the people, mysterious, confident, certain, . . . not . . . a personal demagogue but . . . the embodiment of the will and spirit of the people." [2]

But above all, the African nationalist cause now came to appeal also to Tory politicians of a more practical kind, to men without the slightest interest in the romantic personality cult extended to Banda. In 1959, Ian Macleod, a distinguished wartime soldier, became secretary of state for the colonies in the British Tory Government in power at the time. Macleod, in Welensky's opinion, was "probably the most powerful holder of this office since Joseph Chamberlain—not excluding Churchill . . . ," [3] and Macleod and his colleagues became convinced that decolonization was unavoidable. There was more violence; there were further negotiations, and after a series of complex constitutional changes, the African naitonalist parties gained decisive majorities in the northern legislatures.

Southern Rhodesia tried to respond to the new challenges by a cautious policy of reform that primarily represented the aspirations of

---

cratic Party. In 1961 the party was again outlawed, on the grounds that it had organized violence. It was then replaced by the Zimbabwe African People's Union (ZAPU), which was declared illegal in Southern Rhodesia in 1962. ZAPU in turn suffered from severe internal dissensions. In 1963 these led to the secession of a group of dissidents led by Ndabaningi Sithole, who formed the Zimbabwe African National Union. In Malawi, the Malawi Congress Party was formed in 1959 to replace the banned Nyasaland African National Congress.

In Zambia, Kaunda and his followers seceded from the Northern Rhodesia African National Congress. The dissidents formed the Zambia African National Congress, which was banned in 1959. It was replaced in the same year by the United National Independence Party, which merged several nationalist bodies under Kaunda's leadership.

[2] Guy Clutton-Brock, *Dawn in Nyasaland* (London: Hodder and Stoughton Limited, 1959), pp. 55–56.

A decade later, such enthusiastic assessments had ceased to be fashionable. Militant African intellectuals now expressed sentiments of a very different kind, views which oddly brought to mind earlier settler critiques of the African nationalist leadership. Thus "Banda joined the freedom movement with zest and zeal. Wilful provocation of the British administration, soap-box rabble-rousing and a term in prison—the usual requisites for heroism in nationalist struggles—earned him a popular following." Quoted from Peter Enahoro, "The Juju Orator," *The African Scholar*, 1, No. 3 (March–May, 1969), p. 11.

[3] Sir Roy Welensky, *Welensky's 4,000 Days* (London: William Collins Sons, 1964), p. 162.

the industrial bourgeoisie. In 1958 Sir Edgar Whitehead, a brilliant but arrogant man became prime minister. Whitehead considered that only rapid industrialization under white auspices would provide sufficient jobs for a black population that kept doubling its numbers every twenty-five years. The system of migrant black labor would no longer serve the country's needs. Land apportionment should gradually be liquidated. A free land market would contribute to growing agricultural productivity. Traditional systems of landholding in the reserves must ultimately give way to individual tenure for a technically competent and politically conservative class of African smallholders. The black "surplus" labor from the villages would move to the towns, get permanent jobs in the factories, and become a settled and reasonably remunerated proletariat, capable of buying Rhodesian manufactures. Whitehead realized that his policy would entail some political as well as social and economic concessions to the Africans. In 1961 Southern Rhodesia adopted a new constitution, which for the first time gave some direct representation to Africans and which would ultimately have provided for an African majority in the legislature, based on the votes of black smallholders, skilled workers, and the emergent African petty bourgeoisie. (In South Africa, Whitehead would have found himself at home in the Progressive Party.) Whitehead and his partisans considered the African workers as consumers as well as producers; they meant to make economic concessions; they also proposed to grant the franchise in such a way as to give the vote to the African petty bourgeoisie and the emergent black "aristocracy of labor" so that the European right might be permanently kept out of power.

In retrospect, Whitehead's failure seems inevitable. Yet in 1958, when he became prime minister, a right-wing victory seemed beyond the bounds of possibility. Whitehead enjoyed much more personal prestige than R. S. G. Todd, his predecessor in the Southern Rhodesian prime minister's office, who, from the average European's point of view, labored under the disability of having been an ex-missionary. Whitehead had a distinguished career at Oxford; he had served his country in many senior capacities; he was an eccentric (rumor had it quite wrongly that he was wont to invite the prize bull from his farm into his parlor), and Rhodesians liked tough-minded eccentrics. The European right wing was disunited and demoralized; within a few years leadership passed to four different politicians in succession, none of whom had much personal influence. Whitehead had the backing of big business, the mining companies, the English-speaking churches, the entire daily press (to this day, the Rhodesian Front, the new government party of the right, has no daily newspaper at its disposal). But Whitehead was caught in a political vise. His policy was predicated on the continued existence of the federation, and by the late 1950s, the bulk of the British Tory Party was losing faith in the federal experiment.

In Rhodesia itself, Whitehead had to battle against a substantial European opposition comprising many farmers, men who feared for their land or for their jobs, and who had commonly opposed the federal solution in the first place. Whitehead received no support from the intelligentsia, because Rhodesia was supposed to be drifting steadily toward the right. From Whitehead's view this was unfortunate, for African advancement was more rapid under him than in any previous period of Rhodesian history. But once the Europeans realized that cautious reform would neither conciliate the African nationalists nor ensure the future of the federal state, they turned against Whitehead. In 1962 the European right wing, recognized as the Rhodesian Front, gained a decisive victory at the polls. By now all territorial legislatures were dominated by antifederal majorities. Two years later the federal state broke up amidst bitter mutual recrimination. Zambia and Malawi became independent states within the Commonwealth. Rhodesia (the word "Southern" was dropped from its designation) drifted into South Africa's political orbit. On November 11, 1965, the country declared its unilateral independence (UDI) from Great Britain under Ian Smith, a farmer who had seen distinguished wartime service as squadron leader in the Royal Air Force and as a guerrilla fighter behind the German lines in Italy. White Rhodesians, supposedly the staunchest of British royalists, bade good-bye to the Queen, hauled down the Union Jack, raised their own green, white and green banner; in 1970 they finally turned their country into a republic, a small state subject to United Nations sanctions, recognized by no powers in the world but sublimely confident of its ability to resist all comers. From the Cape to Cairo the British colors had been hauled down—by an ironic twist of history, remaining only as a tiny inset within the flag of South Africa, a country which Great Britain now snubbed in politics and courted in commerce.

11

White Counterrevolution

The Sociopolitical Problem

Long before the UDI (unilateral declaration of independence), the issue had created a profound cleavage within the European community. There were heated debates, not only in public but also privately among businessmen and civil servants. Moral issues apart, the opponents of UDI argued that a government based primarily on European farmers and artisans would lack the intellectual suppleness to deal with Rhodesia's problems. Rhodesia would succumb to the disruption of trade brought about by international sanctions, especially the loss of its British and its Zambian markets; the Rhodesian currency would decline in value. The Rhodesian industries, having already become dangerously dependent on the protected markets of the Federation of Rhodesia and Nyasaland, would face breakdown. An economic slump would lead to a steady deterioration of the public services; white morale would decay; the settlers would gradually leave the country in search of greener pastures. South Africa would never dare to shore up the tottering Rhodesian structure, for South Africa supposedly faced a revolution from within and possible intervention from abroad. Ultimately there would be military interference, either from Great Britain, the nominal sovereign, the United Nations, the Organization of African Unity, or from indigenous guerrillas, familiar with all the hideouts in their native bush. Rhodesia might become the sort of international fighting issue that during the 1930s had caused volunteers from all over the world to join the international brigades during the Spanish Civil War.

In practice, however, these predictions mostly failed to come true. British and United Nations planners alike had failed, for instance, to study the conditions of the country against which they proposed to wage economic warfare. They did not take into account the surprising economic resilience displayed by Rhodesia in the past, especially during the Second World War, with its attendant shortages. Between 1939 and 1945, Rhodesia had vastly expanded the range of its manufactures, increased its war production, and mobilized some 15 percent of its white population as well as a substantial number of Africans. To cap it, under the guidance of Max Danziger, a brilliant but vitriolic Jewish lawyer (Southern Rhodesian minister of finance 1942–1946), the country had succeeded in largely paying for its war effort out of current income.

The Rhodesians now staged an economic repeat performance. The economic sanctions imposed by the United Nations were insufficiently severe to crush the country but were harsh enough to act as an economic stimulus. The Rhodesian tobacco farmers, for example, had to restrict their production, thereby benefiting in all probability their American competitors. But the farming industry proved sufficiently adaptable to make the required adjustments. Rhodesian manufacturers were forced to diversify their industrial production. Rhodesian merchants lessened their dependence on the British market by trading more extensively with other countries. Sanctions were applied moreover in a highly selective fashion. The Americans denied themselves the use of American-owned chromite resources in Rhodesia and instead imported more ores from the Soviet Union. This policy increased American dependence on the Soviet Union for a strategically vital raw material, increased costs for the American producer, possibly placed existing owners in America under pressure to sell their stock to other interests, but did not achieve its declared object of preventing the export of Rhodesian ores. But the Americans, the British, and indeed all the nations of the so-called First, Second, and Third World continued to trade with South Africa; the South Africans in turn refused to participate in the boycott; hence, the wall of sanctions became more like a sieve. Even Zambia, out of necessity, continued to deal with Rhodesia sub rosa; had it not, the Zambian mineral industry would have been wrecked, and the mines would have been denied access to electricity generated at Kariba. Malawian labor migrants continued to come to Rhodesia. Economic warfare would not work. Hence the Rhodesian level of prices remained stable in relation to that of most other developing countries. (Between 1954 and 1968, for instance, it rose an average of less than 2.5 percent.) Like its neighbors, Rhodesia suffered from urban unemployment, unemployment hit the blacks especially, yet the real wages of African workers with jobs continued to go up. (They rose from about £88 in 1954 to about £133 in 1968.) In fact, the white regimes of Southern Africa received a number of unintended economic subsidies. When Great Britain devalued the pound sterling, the gold production of South Africa and Rhodesia went up in value. When Arab-Israeli hostilities led to the closing of the Suez Canal, the shippers of the world became more dependent on the Cape route and on South African facilities.

The Rhodesian Front also enjoyed other advantages which derived from the country's history. The quality of the Rhodesian civil service remained high. Good organization played an essential part in the preliminary planning that helped to defeat sanctions. Rhodesian public services continued to stay free from graft. Rhodesia moreover enjoyed the advantage of having a small and cohesive bureaucracy. Decisions could be quickly made; communications did not get clogged in a complex paper jungle, as they did so often in the immensely more extensive British administration.

Foreign critics who predicted a speedy breakdown in the Rhodesian power structure had also failed to take account of the way in which the Rhodesian Right had itself been transformed both by ideological and sociological changes. Ian Smith's new republican constitution provided for limited African representation and ultimate parliamentary parity between black and white in the remote future, as the level of the Africans' tax contribution kept rising. Such a scheme would have appeared to be the work of an unbalanced Negrophile to a man like Coghlan. Even the bulk of the right-wing voters were no longer willing to speak simply of "keeping the Kaffirs down." Volkswagen salesmen after all wished to sell cars to blacks as well as whites. Even conservative-minded merchants discovered the value of the African market. White as well as black artisans got work when the government initiated a housing scheme for blacks. Rhodesia no longer depended on a backveld economy. The country needed more educated Africans, and the Rhodesian Front perforce had to expand the number of African schools.[1] At the same time, the social composition of the white electorate had undergone an immense change since Coghlan's days. The urban worker was more highly trained in the technical or administrative field than his predecessor a generation earlier. The average white farmer was quite likely to

---

[1] Between 1962 and 1969, that is to say, during the first seven years of Rhodesian Front rule, the number of African primary pupils rose from 560,356 to 664,706. The number of secondary school pupils rose from 5,860 to 18,466.

have a degree in engineering, agronomy, or some similar subject. (Ian Smith himself had a degree in business administration, and in some respects, thus characterized the new class.) The Rhodesian Front was not in the least a "Cowboy Cabinet." In 1968 about two-thirds of the party's representatives in the legislature had university degrees or equivalent qualifications.

The white Rhodesian electorate moreover retained a great degree of political cohesion. The country was too backward economically to sustain a substantial intelligentsia; the clergymen and university lecturers consisted largely of labor migrants; hence the upper-class white conscience vote remained small. An oligarchical franchise and a restricted electorate made for an archaic political style in which electors felt that their suffrage mattered a great deal. Parliamentary seats, after all, might be won or lost by a few dozen votes. Cabinet ministers still had to justify their policies at "sundowners" and tea parties. The voters did not suffer from a sense of alienation. Neither could there be a cult of personality as long as practically any elector might secure an interview with a minister. Election campaigns remained inexpensive. (Even during the heyday of federation, the ruling United Federal Party never spent more than a few thousand pounds a year.) Hence powerful financial donors could not acquire an anonymous influence; the parties depended primarily on smaller contributions from their members. The Argus Press (which remained linked to Johannesburg mining interests) continued to dominate the world of Rhodesian journalism. But Rhodesian voters steadily opposed the newspapers whose editorials they read over the breakfast table.

Many British opinion makers had depicted the settlers as an effete ruling class, doomed to speedy extinction by their own ineptitude and love of luxury. But the settlers, unlike many other oligarchies, were willing to draft their own sons for universal military service; the children of the rich could not escape the draft by purchasing substitutes or by working toward advanced degrees. In the same way, the settlers were willing to tax themselves in return for their privileges; the whites in fact supplied the bulk of the country's revenue and morally felt themselves justified in running the country by reason of their financial contribution, their technical proficiency, and their entrepreneurial skill. The bloodshed in independent black countries as scattered as the Congo, the Sudan, Zanzibar, and Nigeria provided Rhodesian publicity officers with an unlimited amount of material for use at home and abroad, all the more so, since the advocates of decolonization had almost inevitably failed to predict the civil strife which they later deplored. Within Rhodesia itself, the townsmen were not, for the most part, functionless *rentiers;* the farmers were not absentee landlords. The settlers did not have to contend with an unemployed and unemployable academic proletariat, for British policymakers had benefited from the example of India, with its huge armies of jobless degree holders; instead the British in Central Africa had created a system of elite education which provided most graduates, black or white, with an almost assured position. In a small-scale society like white Rhodesia, settlers' sons could not easily experience a sense of alienation, of being mere cards in a filing index. And the harsh political environment of Africa proved inhospitable to the emergent youth culture of symbolism, opiates, and insurrectionary histrionics.

The whites finally made a major readjustment concerning African administration in the countryside. In the late 1940s, African nationalists in Zambia and Malawi still defended the chiefs against the apparent threat of "direct rule" as it was practiced south of the Zambezi. In Southern Rhodesia chiefs retained only limited power and often received salaries no higher than those of truck drivers. The postindependence years saw a strange reversal. When the British relinquished their hold on Africa, they abandoned their erstwhile agents, the chiefs, even relatively powerful suzerains like the kings of Barotseland whose special status had still been confirmed in 1953 by the Northern Rhodesia (Barotseland) Order in Council. The newly independent governments of Malawi and Zambia became ardent advocates of direct rule. Modern African administrators in terms somewhat similar to those used by pioneer British officials half a century earlier, said that the power of chiefs was bound to decay, that tribalism formed an obstacle on the road to progress, and that the future must rest with a centrally controlled bureaucracy. The white Rhodesians for their part began to rediscover the chief. To Rhodesian administrators of an older vintage, the new course in fact represented a retreat of white power from the countryside.

The shift began in 1961, when the government found that its authoritarian manner of enforcing the contentious Native Land Husbandry Act would not work. The law was designed to create negotiable land rights, to prevent the excessive fragmentation of land holdings, to expand agricultural production, and to create a new class of independent smallholders. It was designed to change the economic behavior of the rural population, but it completely failed in its purpose. Its implementation evoked strong resistance, along with powerful emotional undercurrents.

Willy-nilly, the government was forced to take a more circumspect approach. The authorities also developed more virgin land; they provided more irrigation works and more roads. African settlers started to move into remoter areas that previously had been little used. The government became increasingly convinced that industrial expansion could not by itself absorb the growing labor force. Experts argued that it was cheaper and less dangerous to develop the countryside than to maintain masses of workmen in the cities, where unemployment was a constant danger.

During this period white Rhodesian planners for the first time turned to the chiefs. But now the European administrators could no longer simply speak as rulers pure and simple, able to impose their will upon the ruled as the occasion seemed to demand. The chiefs insisted on bargaining for various concessions. They received various new privileges, and without their support, UDI would probably have failed to succeed. Admittedly, the chiefs could not speak for the urban population. But only a relatively small proportion of Africans were permanently urbanized. The great majority of Africans still had a dual loyalty to contrasting value systems; they had one foot in the village and one in the town. The power of the chiefs had not therefore disappeared, despite the previous policy of displacing the traditional elite.

Many chiefs were not simply government stooges. Their loyalty was by no means conditional. For all their new privileges, the chiefs still had to balance precariously between the government and their followers. Their ambiguous status reflected the social conditions of their subjects, most of whom remained half peasant, half proletarian. In the past, the chiefs of Central Africa had been far from consistent supporters of the status quo. During the 1950s, for instance, Chitimukulu, paramount of the Bemba, had refused to even meet Welensky, the federal prime minister. The whites therefore faced the possibility that one day Mangwende or some other dignitary might refuse to meet Ian Smith or Smith's successor. For salaries alone could not buy loyalty. And as a Rhodesian chief put the matter in a conversation with a distinguished anthropologist, "If we shall have to choose between the government and our people, we must of course choose the people." [2]

Arms and Men

When Jameson considered his chances of war with Lobengula, he asked for advice from Rhodes. Rhodes laconically cabled back "Read

[2] J. F. Holleman, *Chief, Council and Commissioner: Some Problems of Government in Rhodesia* (Assen, The Netherlands: Royal Van Gorcum Ltd., 1969), p. 370.

Luke 14:31." Jameson opened a Bible and looked up the reference which said, "Or what king, going to make war against another king, sitteth not down first and consulteth whether he be able with ten thousand to meet him that cometh against him with twenty thousand." Ian Smith profited from Jameson's example, for during the brief course of its independent existence, Rhodesia faced potential military threats of several kinds. When the country declared its independence, its peace-time defense force amounted to two high-grade professional infantry battalions—one white, one black—a special air service unit, and supporting services. In case of war the army could be expanded to two brigade groups with support services, mainly manned by white conscripts, equivalent in quality to good British Territorial Army units. The army was supported by a balanced force of five air squadrons, a well-trained police force with its own reservists, and an extensive and reliable intelligence system. Economically, the Rhodesians had no trouble in sustaining this effort. Rhodesian defense expenditure remained small; there was ample room for expansion.[3] In the last resort, the Rhodesians could rely on South African help.

In 1965 the British had no means of immediately countering this establishment, even had such a course been politically feasible, and even if South Africa, by far the strongest military power in Africa, had permitted the British to intervene. At the time of UDI, Great Britain apparently only had available one brigade group (between 3,000 to 3,500 men) to deal with unforeseen emergencies. This force would have been inadequate to seize the country. The British could probably not even have seized the electrical installations at Kariba, without risking their destruction and thereby knocking out the vital Zambian copper industry. Even had the British expanded their forces, they would have faced fantastic logistical problems. A giant military airlift to Rhodesia, even if carried out with United Nations aid, would apparently have tied down the bulk of the Royal Air Force Transport Command; it would also have entailed a huge effort to set up fuel and repair depots en route.

[3] According to the figures provided by David Wood, *The Armed Forces of African States*, Adelphi Paper No. 27 (London: Institute for Strategic Studies, 1966), p. 29, comparative figures amounted to the following:

	Defense expenditure as a percentage of the total budget	As a percentage of the estimated gross national product
UAR	17.4%	8.6%
Rhodesia	6.6	1.9
South Africa	19.9	3.5
Zambia	5.7	2.5
Senegal	11.6	7.6

British intervention would also have raised a ticklish problem of military loyalties. An enterprise designed to topple Smith so as to make Nkomo prime minister would not have proved popular with the British army, a force composed of professional soldiers not distinguished for the fervor of their anticolonial sentiments.

In theory the United Nations might have intervened. But Smith apparently felt that the United States was too strongly committed in Vietnam to risk another Congo; the Soviet Union was unlikely to engage in any adventures far from the periphery of its own empire. The United Nations on its own was militarily helpless. The Organization of African Unity lacked a usable military instrument. And many independent African states suffered from bloody internal dissensions; decolonization in fact had reopened the old rift on the southern frontier of Islam in such countries as the Sudan, Chad, and Nigeria. The independent African states encountered serious financial problems; they lacked a common command structure and a common tactical doctrine for their armies; they were devoid of adequate air transport and air support. There was a general shortage of well-trained staff officers and military technicians. Operations far from home might, moreover, occasion serious disciplinary problems. These weaknesses could not be easily remedied. Even if they had been surmounted, military expansion was apt to have serious political as well as financial consequences. The African states all relied on professional soldiers. But regulars might easily become a new Praetorian class in developing countries without a defined national consciousness. An African government composed of civilians might have to face a *coup d'état* headed by dissatisfied officers. Hence military expansion posed serious difficulties for a state like Zambia.

The Rhodesians also had to reckon with intervention from foreign volunteers or from African partisans. Foreign volunteers however failed to arrive. The Western campus rebels of the 1960s would cheerfully masquerade in the garb of guerrillas, but they did not join the equivalent of the Lincoln Brigade, the Attlee Brigade, or the Thälmann Brigade, which had played a distinguished military role during the Spanish Civil War. When it came to real fighting, Africans could only rely on themselves. Under existing circumstances guerrilla warfare was the only means of combat available to them. Partisan operations however entailed a host of unforeseen military and economic problems. Established governments usually proved reluctant to harbor large bodies of armed men whom they could not control. Zambia offered bases for bushfighters, but there was considerable division within the Zambian ruling party as to the extent of support Zambia should provide. In any case Zambia had to tread softly, lest she provoke reprisals from South Africa.

Partisans moreover encountered many difficulties of a military kind. Rhodesia lacked dense jungles, great swamps, or alpine massifs—natural hideouts of guerrillas. Most of the territory consisted of bush and savanna, usually open to observation from the air. There were pockets of difficult terrain, but these did not make up a contiguous and inaccessible geographical base. The thorough-going nature of white settlements had not left room for huge native areas where guerrillas might assemble in secrecy. White farms were scattered through many parts of the land, and the whites knew their country as well as the Africans; government forces also had the inestimable advantages of the helicopter. Rhodesian towns, too, were comparatively well laid out. They did not resemble the urban jungles of great Algerian cities. Access by road to African townships, as well as to their electricity and water supplies, could be regulated from without; hence, urban guerrillas faced an exceedingly difficult task. The local administrations remained efficient and not much prone to graft—unlike in so many Southeast Asian countries, where incumbent administrations had to face threats from partisan attacks.

African underground leaders also had to cope with other obstacles of a political kind. During the 1960s something like a quarter of a million Africans from outside Rhodesia resided there. The immigrants, who had come to earn higher wages in the country of their choice, were difficult to organize. The government did have to deal with a serious problem of unemployment, but by 1969 jobs again started to increase,[4] thereby relieving the authorities of certain headaches and depriving the guerrillas of valuable recruits.

The partisans who did succeed in making their way across the Zambezi encountered much harsher conditions than they had apparently anticipated. Admittedly, they had idealism, toughness, and stamina. As always, Africans proved skillful and adaptable bushfighters. Their weapons, manufactured in China and the Soviet Union, were of high quality. Their training, received as far afield as China, the Soviet Union, Cuba, Algeria, and Tanzania, seemed satisfactory, though insufficiently coordinated. Yet by 1970 the partisans had failed to make any serious headway. They could not move among the civilian population like fish in the water.

The partisans in fact suffered from severe weaknesses. For one thing they were politically split. The majority supported an alliance formed in 1968 between the Zimbabwe African People's Union and the exiled South African National Congress (ANC). This group took a pro-Soviet

---

[4] "Rhodesia: Sitting Pretty," *Africa Report* (December, 1969), pp. 9–11.

line and was linked in turn to the South African Communist Party, which claimed to form the leading force in the South African liberation struggle.[5] The Soviet Union warmly supported this alliance, while at the same time condemning the Chinese, who spoke of a worldwide struggle between the rich and the poor nations, the world of the cities, and the world of the countryside.[6] But there was also a rival Rhodesian organization known as the Zimbabwe African National Union (ZANU). This was allied to the Pan-Africanist Congress of South Africa (PAC), a militantly black body, which supported Peking in the struggle dividing the Communist world. (In 1968 the Organization of African Unity withdrew its support from PAC, Zambia banned the organization and raided ZANU offices.) The guerrilla leaders thus had to cope with all sorts of political problems which were acerbated by quarrels totally extraneous to African issues. The partisans were also hampered apparently by numerous breaches of security and by the operations of the South African and Rhodesian intelligence networks, which remained well informed concerning developments north of the Zambezi and those within the Communist blocs. The guerrillas could not secure mass support; they also had to deal with all manner of disciplinary problems, especially as some underground fighters claimed to have been induced into military service by coercion or deception. The guerrillas were unable to set up permanent military bases in Rhodesia. By 1968 the security position had sufficiently improved from Salisbury's point of view to enable the government to abolish the mandatory death penalty for the illegal possession of arms.[7]

African Crucible

"Within hardly a century of class domination," wrote Karl Marx in his *Communist Manifesto*, "the bourgeoisie has created more numerous and more colossal means of production than all past generations combined. The conquest of nature; the use of machinery; the application of chemistry to industry and farming; steam navigation; railways; electric

---

[5] "Strengthen the Anti-Imperialist Unity: A Joint Communiqué" [between the South African Communist Party and the East German Socialist Unity Party] *South African Communist*, No. 32 (First Quarter 1968), pp. 73–75.

[6] Vasily Solodovnikov, "The Soviet Union and Africa," *The African Communist*, No. 36 (Fourth Quarter 1968), pp. 74–86.

[7] Rhodesia, *The Minister of Law and Order, the Hon. Mr. Desmond Lardner-Burke Announces Abolition of the Mandatory Death Sentence* (Salisbury: Government Printer, 1968), p. 4.

telegraphs; the reclamation of whole continents; engineering ventures designed to open rivers to shipping; the magic appearance of huge populations—who could have imagined in past centuries that such productive forces might emerge from the collective labors of society?"[8]

The astonishing development of Central Africa during the imperial and the postimperial epoch seemed to justify Marx's assessment. Within eighty years the area had changed beyond recognition. Yet in many respects the prophets of old had failed. Missionaries like Livingstone; revolutionaries like Marx had one thing in common; they believed that the Western bourgeoisie would change the whole world in its own image. To some extent they had been right. But ethnic patterns created in Africa during the course of countless migrations had remained. Much of Africa's precolonial legacy remained, albeit in a greatly altered form.

In certain respects Rhodes had been a better prophet than either Livingstone or Marx. Western Christians had not converted, Western proletarians had not subverted the mass of Africans. Rhodes had created a country that survived despite all predictions to the contrary. From the start Rhodesia had seemed a political archaism. Chartered company governance persisted in Rhodesia at a time when chartered company rule had become no more than a dim historical memory in the rest of the world. Chartered company administration was succeeded by the dominion of a settler oligarchy, which successfully held on to power in an age that rejected most principles in which the colonists believed. Rhodesia was a country that consistently belied the experts. Chartered company government had functioned quite effectively there. In the economic sphere the chartered record had indeed compared favorably with that of the more bureaucratic and less adaptable Colonial Office. Settler rule likewise continued in an age that believed such a form of government not only an immoral but also unworkable expedient. Yet even Rhodes's assumptions had turned topsy-turvy. Rhodes had hoped to find a new Rand in the distant north, where a great British community would be founded on the golden wealth of the interior. The tide of history would inevitably sweep Rhodesia into a greater British South Africa. South Africa would form a cornerstone of an African empire extending from the Cape across Rhodesia, Zambia, and Malawi to distant Cairo; Britain's dominions in Africa would in turn form part of a wider British Commonwealth.

By 1970, there was indeed a Second Rand in Central Africa. But its riches derived from copper, not from gold. The red metal sustained

[8] Translated from Karl Marx and Friedrich Engels, *Manifest der kommunistischen Partei* (Berlin: Verlag Neuer Weg, 1945), pp. 8–9.

not a British but an African state. Decolonization had set off a new scramble for Africa; new competitors had entered the scene, none of whom Rhodes had even considered. Chinese labor had reappeared in a new and more formidable guise. Peking was about to build a railway from the Copper Belt to the Indian Ocean, thereby shifting Zambia's center of gravity to the north. In addition Chinese and Russian functionaries were trying to spread their own political philosophy; they both conducted conventional as well as "guerrilla diplomacy." But by 1970, the principles of Marxism-Leninism, whether in their Soviet or Chinese guise, had apparently proved prescriptions for failure in Southern Africa. Marxist-oriented resistance organizations, with euphonious acronyms for their titles, had failed to make any serious impact on the white south. Africans proved as difficult to convert to the rigid discipline of dialectical materialism and the party *apparat*, as to the discipline enforced by missionary Christianity and the church hierarchies.

The older colonial powers had not been displaced from Africa. In addition, a smaller Western state had begun to make its appearance on the Central African scene, a country whose African career had seemed at an end when Mussolini's empire collapsed. By 1970 Italian manufacturers were supplying high-quality helicopters to the Zambian army; Italian instructors were teaching Zambian pilots how to fly; Fiat executives were preparing to set up a plant, whose production would compete with British-built autos.

From the economic standpoint Zambia, by 1970, had excellent prospects. It did, however, face serious political dissensions and the remoter peril of internal splits. The policy sanctions against Rhodesia had injured Zambia to a greater extent than any other member of the United Nations. The government's endeavor to disengage the country from the south had acerbated existing ethnic tensions. The shift of Zambia's power focus away from the west and the center, formerly the predominant regions, had created much ill feeling; there was talk of sedition among some of the Lozi and the Tonga people, who were least likely to gain from the shift in the country's center of gravity. In Zambia, as in the rest of Africa, industrialization had entailed unforeseen consequences. The level of production had risen. But the benefits of industrialization were apt to worsen ethnic disagreements, as urbanized and educated men from different tribes and different races competed for jobs and similar advantages. Graft could not be eliminated in a country like Zambia where, for the most part, loyalty to the extended family, the neighborhood, or an ethnic community counted for more than loyalty to an impersonal organization such as the civil service, the state, or even the party. Political rhetoric helped to accelerate a revolution of rising expectations—rising expectations all too easily turned into cynicism; cynicism in turn led many to place their trust in their immediate ethnic group rather than in a wider transtribal community.

Malawi—the missionaries' hope of old; the most ancient center of British, especially of Scottish, influence in Central Africa—had likewise confounded all the prophets. Malawi did not turn out to be a Central African Jerusalem destined to evangelize its neighbors, despite the outstanding role played by a whole army of expatriate Malawian intellectuals—teachers, preachers, politicians, and trade unionists—in many parts of Southern Africa. Malawi had been the weakest link in the chain of the Federation of Rhodesia and Nyasaland, a land of rural poverty, and of a many-faceted rural radicalism. But for the time being, the motherland of John Chilembwe turned out to be one of the most conservative states in Africa. By 1970 the country was making territorial claims on Tanzania and on Zambia, and Dr. Banda had established a *modus vivendi* with the Portuguese, the Rhodesians, and the South Africans. All opposition to Banda's personal rule had been suppressed; the Malawians had acquired a sense of national identity that oddly blended African legacies with elements derived from Scottish Calvinism. Banda, one of the most radical of African statesmen in the federation, was now accounted a white man's African by many black nationalists. But his personal rule continued. Malawi's economy, like Zambia's, was progressing at a rate that would have confounded prophets of an earlier generation.

The future of Rhodesia depended on events on the wider Southern African stage. By 1970 the country's position appeared hopeful to the whites. Rhodesia's eastern flank in Mozambique was being defended by the Portuguese, that is to say, by Rhodes's erstwhile enemies, whom he had once wished to despoil of colonial territory. The Portuguese had to cope with guerrillas based on Tanzania; these operations were conducted above all by the Frente de Libertação de Moçambique (FRELIMO), a Marxist pro-Soviet organization allied in turn with ZAPU, the ANC, and the Movimento Popular de Libertação de Angola (MPLA). FRELIMO had the benefit of Russian backing; FRELIMO fighters used weapons of Communist manufacture, including many arms from East Germany. The Portuguese were fighting in areas as scattered as northern Mozambique, parts of Angola, and faraway Guinea. Their military and economic efforts imposed tremendous burdens on the mother country, which was forced to subsidize an extensive colonial structure. Portugal's military center of power had indeed shifted from Europe to Africa. The bulk of the troops engaged in Sub-Saharan Africa were no longer black, as in the past when small forces had sufficed to control the colonies; instead Portugal's colonial armies largely consisted of whites, well over

100,000 men, by far the largest mobilized military force south of the Sahara. Their deployment entailed vast administrative and logistic problems. The Portuguese resolved to hold on to all parts of their African empire regardless of cost and thereby committed themselves to a policy of strategic dispersal. This approach proved particularly costly in Portuguese Guinea. Here much of the terrain particularly favored the guerrillas; the partisans could make good use of neighboring sanctuaries within close vicinity. Under the auspices of the Marxist, pro-Soviet Partido Africano da Independência da Guiné e Cabo Verde (PAIGC), the bushfighters moreover had attained an unusual degree of discipline, civic cohesion, and political unity.

The Portuguese army however enjoyed considerable advantages. It was technologically superior to its opponents. It was also more united. In Angola and Mozambique alike, the African insurgents suffered from numerous internal dissensions which derived from issues connected with social doctrine, strategy, ethnic affiliation, and conflicting personalities. The Portuguese for their part improved their counterrevolutionary tactics. In Angola the army perfected a new program of psycho-social warfare, which, in certain respects, sought to apply Maoist concepts in reverse. The Portuguese began to realize that warfare was politics by other means and that military successes were likely to be stillborn if the military were to operate in isolation. The Portuguese thus tried to create new village communities that could, at the same time, be protected against guerrilla assaults and provided with social services. Soldiers were used to build schools, teach skills, build roads, and carry out engineering projects.

By 1970 FRELIMO had attained some success in the northern portion of Mozambique; but Portuguese power remained little affected as far as the territory as a whole was concerned. Neither had FRELIMO succeeded in the essential task of creating a sense of national unity among the various tribal communities of the region. The resistance movement suffered both from Portuguese infiltration and from what might be called an excess of revolutionary back-seat driving. Too much of its personnel was apparently deployed at headquarters and base camps in independent Africa and elsewhere. Too few were engaged in effective military operations within the sphere of Portuguese influence.

Meanwhile, the Portuguese consolidated their position in the economic field. Planners, for instance, had designed the enormous Cabora Bassa project, a giant scheme designed to supply the country with hydro-electric power, to create a huge lake on the Zambezi, to promote vast irrigation works, to encourage industrial development, and to attract more white immigrants. Portugal derived support from South Africa. Portugal's confidence in her colonial future as yet seemed unshaken. Much, however, depended on Portugal's internal evolution and on the country's future willingness to go on bearing the burden of empire, with its vast military and financial outlay. Without the Portuguese bastion of Mozambique, Rhodesia would end as it started, an exposed white salient on the highveld in the far interior. But as long as the Portuguese stand firm, Rhodesia remains in a strong strategic position, with only a relatively short stretch to guard on the Zambezi.

Seen in strategic terms, Rhodesia, Angola and Mozambique form the outer bastions of a wider system, which ultimately hinges mainly on South Africa. By 1970 neither the British nor the Americans were in a favorable position to exercise serious pressure on South Africa. A friendly South Africa, with its naval facilities and its command over the vital Cape route, remained a strategic necessity for the West, especially in view of the growth of Soviet strength in the eastern Mediterranean, the continued closure of the Suez Canal, and the impressive naval strength which the Soviet Union could now deploy in the Indian Ocean.

The new southern bloc, for its part, now had a solid infrastructure. Angola, Mozambique and Rhodesia alike had made great material progress over the last decade; the economy of the Portuguese colonial empire had changed beyond recognition. Above all, South Africa's economy had displayed great resilience and an extraordinary capacity for expansion. Since 1910 the gross domestic product has roughly doubled every eleven years. South Africa, which contains about 6 percent of Africa's population, has generated something like 24 percent of the total income of the African continent. South Africa is the only economically independent nation in Africa in the sense that the country could largely determine its own destiny. By 1970 secondary industry contributed more to the gross national product than any other form of enterprise. South Africa formed the industrial heart of the continent, able to manufacture highly sophisticated equipment as varied as cars and mining machinery, massive steel cranes, armor plating, and chemicals, as well as computers. South Africa was the world's largest producer of gold. It also turned out a great variety of strategic commodities such as uranium, manganese, and nickel. Above all South Africa had reached the point where the economy was capable of producing sufficient capital to pay for its own expansion. (In 1967, for instance, foreign capital represented only 6.3 percent of the gross domestic investment.) South Africa, in other words, had largely become financially self-sufficient, and was even exporting capital. Economically, South Africa depended little on the superpowers, a point inadequately understood by her American critics, who urged that a financial boycott should be instituted by the United States to bring South Africa to its knees.[9]

From the military standpoint, South Africa had developed into a formidable power by African standards, the only indigenous country on the continent capable of fielding a balanced force. South African manufacturers could now fashion the most diverse weapons, including guided missiles. In all probability, South Africa had acquired the ability to manufacture nuclear arms if required. At the same time South African military expenditure was not sufficiently great to interfere with the country's economic growth; indeed the South Africans spent a much smaller proportion of their gross national product on defense than the British, the Americans, or the Russians.[10] Internally the South African security forces had pretty well shattered all revolutionary cadres. Guerrillas moreover faced almost impossible geographical obstacles. The terrain is not particularly suited to rural partisans, and the urban guerrilla's task was made peculiarly hard by the government's ability to control physical access to the African townships as well as the water and electricity supplies. The government had undertaken vast urban renewal projects. These had not only given a stimulus to the economy and improved housing conditions, they had also done away with many city "jungles," which otherwise might have provided convenient hiding places for city-born partisans.

The South African authorities also enjoyed other advantages. By the standards of Africa, the South African administration was fairly competent and reasonably free from graft. Insurgents could not assume therefore that administrative instability and inefficiency would impede counterrevolutionary operations. The South African intelligence network was effective. Far from being able to infiltrate its men into sensitive posts, the South African opposition was itself penetrated by government agents. African nationalists also faced other obstacles. The black population was ethnically diverse, and the different African proto-nations were

[9] In 1969 foreign capital invested in South Africa amounted to over R 4,000 million. (U.S. $1.00 = R 0.71) Of this only some R 500 million derived from the United States. The Americans were likewise ill-placed to exert commercial pressure on South Africa. In 1966 South Africa's exports were distributed as follows: Africa: R 185.7 million; Europe: R 690.8 million; Asia: R 98.5 million; Oceania (including Australia), Canada, and other countries: R 54.7 million; United States: R 127.3 million.

[10] In 1968 South Africa's defense expenditure amounted to 2.5 percent of the gross national product. The corresponding figures respectively were 9.3 percent for the Soviet Union, 9.2 percent for the United States, and 5.3 percent for Great Britain.

far from united. Many black workers remained migrant laborers. Many of these workers had entered South Africa from outside in order to benefit from the superior wages and better living conditions provided by employers in the republic. The black proletariat thus remained heterogeneous and hard to organize. At the same time, industrialization produced some real benefits for many, many Africans, however unevenly distributed these benefits might be. There was much black discontent. But there was no widespread desire for a revolutionary war.

By 1970 the Republic of South Africa thus seemed further removed from a major armed upheaval than at any time previously in the twentieth century. Indeed South Africa had been nearer to civil war in 1922, when the skilled white workers had taken up arms in Johannesburg, or in 1914 when nationalist Afrikaans-speaking farmers had attempted to start a rebellion in league with Germany. Strategically, as we have seen, the closing of the Suez Canal had restored the Cape to its classical importance in maritime strategy. Even if the Suez Canal were to be reopened, the trend toward the construction of giant vessels too large to pass through the canal was likely to make shippers even more dependent on South Africa's goodwill in the future.

South Africa was therefore in a position to push her influence beyond her borders, both into "black" countries like Botswana, Malawi, and Zambia, and into "white" territories like Rhodesia. The effects on the latter country were ironic. Rhodes had hoped that an English-speaking Rhodesia would one day join South Africa and thereby help to keep the subcontinent within the British imperial orbit. Now Rhodes's old design received an unexpected twist. The Rhodesian settlers were becoming British Afrikaners; UDI was their Great Trek.

British policy during the 1960s had turned out to be utterly ineffective. It had derived from a curious mélange of contradictory motives in which conflicting party loyalties, clashes of personalities, parliamentary considerations, and Commonwealth and United Nations affiliations had all played their part. There had been the illusion of British moral leadership taking the place of a vanished imperial supremacy. There had been outlandish misconceptions concerning the realities of Rhodesian power; these errors were compounded by what Rhodes had called his countrymen's "unctuous rectitude." British humanitarian and anticolonial lobbies had helped to prevent the emergence of a British Central African dominion capable of acting as a counterweight against South Africa. Instead British policy, together with international sanctions, had the unintended effect of solidifying a new southern white bloc under South African leadership. The Rhodesians were forced, willy-nilly, to conduct more and more of their economic, diplomatic, and even cultural affairs through South Africa. In this respect the country reverted to the position that it used to occupy in the early days of the charter, when Rhodes had run his local affairs through the British South Africa Company's offices at the Cape. The Rhodesian settlers came to take pride in defying all they had once honored—Queen and mother country, Union Jack and Commonwealth. At the same time they challenged all the accepted "inevitables" of the postimperial era; the surge of world opinion, the wind of change, the tide of history. These seemingly all-pervading powers would only be challenged by men unusually clever or unusually stupid. White Rhodesia had a plentiful supply of both. The white Rhodesians also had a measure of that toughness which they had bred into their one and only original creation, the Rhodesian Ridgeback, a big farmyard dog distinguished by its willingness to tackle even the African lion. The whites in turn were opposed by black nationalists; by men as determined, and as convinced of the absolute justice inherent in their cause as the Europeans.

By 1970 the "white bastions" seemed fairly safe from armed assaults. But there were indications that these military problems might pale into insignificance before the exigencies of progress. By 1970 the Republic of South Africa contained something like 19,000,000 people (among them some 3,600,000 whites). The three Central African states comprised over 13,000,000 inhabitants. But from the Cape to the Congo the population was rising rapidly. Demographic predictions of course can never be accurate because so many unpredictable factors must enter into the experts' calculations. But by the end of the present century South Africa may well have something like 45,000,000 or 50,000,000 mouths to feed. The population of the three Central African states will certainly amount to 30,000,000 or more.

The peoples of Central and Southern Africa will therefore have to cope with the same difficulties that now beset the industrialized portions of the Northern Hemisphere. They will face new problems of urban organization, of pollution and traffic control, of soil and water conservation. They will have to deal not only with racial dissensions but with all the discontents bred by mass consumer societies. The ancient Bantu kings had often been able to solve internal troubles by organizing migrations or military campaigns. The old-style Boers sought new land whenever they saw smoke rising from some newly built homestead on the distant horizon. But future treks will not avail against the challenges of the multiethnic megalopolis. The experiences of older countries like the United States as yet provide but limited guidance. And whatever their color or conviction, the peoples of Southern Africa as yet must conquer perils that would have taxed alike the courage of Mziligazi, the faith of Chilembwe, and the resolution of Cecil John Rhodes.

Suggested Readings

General Histories

The only paperback history previously published on Central Africa is A. J. Wills, *An Introduction to the History of Central Africa,* 2nd ed. (London: Oxford University Press, 1967). This is based on secondary works and is designed for teachers and students of the history of Central Africa. It is considerably more successful as a work of synthesis than A. J. Hanna, *The Story of the Rhodesias and Nyasaland* (London: Faber & Faber Ltd., 1960). Both works are however already out of date in certain respects. Readers may still consult W. V. Brelsford, editor, *Handbook to the Federation of Rhodesia and Nyasaland* (London: Cassell & Co. Ltd., 1960). This contains a number of general essays, including one by J. Desmond Clark, "Early Man and the Stone Age," pp. 30–42; another by Roger Summers, "The Iron Age Cultures and Early Bantu Movements," pp. 43–56; and by Clyde Mitchell, "The African Peoples," pp. 117–81. There are also essays dealing with geography, geology, and many other questions.

The author of this work wrote *A History of Northern Rhodesia: Early Days to 1953* (New York: Humanities Press, Inc.; London: Chatto & Windus Ltd., 1969); and *A History of Southern Rhodesia: Early Days to 1934* (New York: Humanities Press, Inc.; London: Chatto & Windus Ltd., 1969).

169

The two works concentrate on the impact of European colonization on Africa; they are written from the European point of view and are based on archival sources in Rhodesia and Zambia. Richard Hall, *Zambia* (London: Pall Mall Press Ltd., 1965) and John G. Pike, *Malawi: A Political and Economic History* (New York: Frederick A. Praeger, Inc., 1968) serve for general reference. Richard Gray, *The Two Nations: Aspects of the Development of Race Relations in the Rhodesias and Nyasaland* (London: Oxford University Press, 1960), deals with race relations from the British liberal point of view. The more moderate settlers' case is put forth in L. H. Gann and Peter Duignan, *White Settlers in Tropical Africa* (Harmondsworth, Middlesex: Penguin Books Ltd., 1962). B. Vulindlela Mtshali, *Rhodesia: Background to Conflict* (New York: Hawthorn Books, Inc., 1967) deals with the problems from an African standpoint. The best general reference work on the history of Southern Africa as a whole is the encyclopedic study by Eric Walker, *A History of Southern Africa*, 3rd ed. (London: Longmans, Green & Co., Ltd., 1957). This is written from the point of view of what might be called a British liberal imperialist.

The Ancient Past

The best and most easily accessible account of man's earliest past in Southern Africa is J. Desmond Clark, *The Prehistory of Southern Africa* (Harmondsworth, Middlesex: Penguin Books Ltd., 1959). This also contains a detailed bibliography. Highly recommended for its readability, accuracy, and wealth of illustrations is Brian M. Fagan, *Southern Africa During the Iron Age* (New York: Frederick A. Praeger, Inc., 1965), as well as Brian M. Fagan, editor, *A Short History of Zambia* (Nairobi: Oxford University Press, 1966), a book which ought to be in any university library. There is also an extensive literature concerning the early cultures of Rhodesia. Roger Summers, with contributions by H. B. S. Cooke and others, *Inyanga: Prehistoric Settlements in Southern Rhodesia* (Cambridge: Cambridge University Press, 1958) deserves special notice. So does Roger Summers, *Zimbabwe: A Rhodesian Mystery* (Johannesburg: Thomas

Nelson & Sons, 1965), which summarizes the author's archaeological work in a popular fashion. Students of Bushman art as well as art lovers in general should also consult Roger Summers, *et al.*, editors, *Prehistoric Rock Art of the Federation of Rhodesia and Nyasaland* (London: Chatto & Windus Ltd.; Salisbury: National Publications Trust, Rhodesia and Nyasaland, 1959).

The Portuguese Impact and the Interior

The two standard works on Portuguese colonization in South East Central Africa, both of them based on a great deal of archival research, are Eric Axelson, *South-East Africa, 1488–1530* (London: Longmans, Green & Co., Ltd., 1940), and *The Portuguese in South-East Africa, 1600–1700* (Johannesburg, Witwatersrand University Press, 1960). There is a detailed critique of Portuguese race attitudes in C. R. Boxer's little work, *Race Relations in the Portuguese Colonial Empire, 1415–1825* (Oxford: Clarendon Press, 1963); Boxer argues that the Portuguese had much the same racial prejudices as other European colonizers. The Portuguese case is put forward by A. da Silva Regô, *Portuguese Colonisation in the Sixteenth Century: A Study of the Royal Ordinances* (Johannesburg: Witwatersrand University Press, 1959). Silva Regô, a Portuguese scholar and clergyman, stresses what might be called the element of trusteeship in Portuguese colonial legislation.

For the African side of the story, readers should turn to Terence O. Ranger, editor, *Aspects of Central African History* (London: William Heinemann Ltd., 1968). This contains an article by Edward Alpers, "The Mutapa and Malawi Political Systems," pp. 1–28. Equally useful is a collection of essays by Eric Stokes and Richard Brown, editors, *The Zambezian Past: Studies in Central African History* (Manchester: Manchester University Press, 1966). This contains, among others, an essay by K. K. Robinson, "The Archaeology of the Rozwi," pp. 3–27 and another by D. P. Abrahams, a noted ethnohistorian, "The Roles of 'Chaminuka' and the Mhondoro Cults in Shona Political History."

Southern Backwash and Slave Traders' Frontier

A major composite work, for the first time, tries to present South African history from the Afrocentric and also from an anthropological standpoint is Monica Wilson and Leonard Thompson, editors, *South Africa to 1870,* The Oxford History of South Africa, vol. 1 (Oxford: Clarendon Press, 1969). The history of the Ndebele nation from its origins to the destruction of the Ndebele kingdom is told from an African point of view in Stanley Samkange, *Origins of Rhodesia* (New York: Frederick A. Praeger, Inc., 1969). There are two classical works written by anthropologists having a thorough knowledge of history: J. A. Barnes, *Politics in a Changing Society: A Political History of the Fort Jameson Ngoni* (Cape Town: Oxford University Press, 1954) and J. Clyde Mitchell, *The Yao Village: A Study in the Social Structure of a Nyasaland Tribe* (Manchester: Manchester University Press, 1956). The story of Central Africa's gunpowder frontier remains to be written. The best general works are still the classics by Sir Reginald Coupland, *East Africa and Its Invaders: From the Earliest Times to the Death of Seyyid Said in 1856* (Oxford: Clarendon Press, 1938) and *The Exploitation of East Africa, 1856–1890: The Slave Trade and the Scramble* (London: Faber & Faber Ltd., 1939).

Imperial Advance and Evangelization

There is a great wealth of missionary literature on Central Africa, but there is as yet no single good missionary history. The most original of many fine Livingstone biographies is Michael Gelfand, *Livingstone the Doctor; His Life and Travels: A Study in Medical History* (Oxford: Basil Blackwell & Mott Ltd., 1957), written by a distinguished Rhodesian physician and anthropologist. H. Alan C. Cairns, *Prelude to Imperialism: British Reactions to Central African Society, 1840–1890* (London: Routledge & Kegan Paul Ltd., 1965) is an excellent study of attitudes. Robert Rotberg, *Christian Missionaries and the Creation of Northern Rhodesia, 1880–1924* (Princeton, N.J.: Princeton University Press, 1965) is marred by the author's antimissionary prejudices. The early penetration of Nyasaland is outlined in A. J. Hanna, *The Be-*

ginnings of Nyasaland and North-Eastern Rhodesia, 1859–95
(Oxford: Clarendon Press, 1956), a work written in the tradition of British imperial history. Hanna also compiled *The
Birth of a Plural Society: The Development of Northern
Rhodesia under the British South Africa Company, 1894–
1914* (Manchester: Manchester University Press, 1958). This
study attempted to combine historical methods with those of
the British school of functional sociology. Its political bias
stands revealed in the author's dedication of the work to Sir
Roy Welensky. The history of Southern Rhodesia's conquest
has been assessed from the chartered company's point of view
by Hugh Marshall Hole, *The Making of Rhodesia* (London:
Macmillan & Co. Ltd., 1926; London: Frank Cass & Company Ltd., 1967). Hole was a senior official in the British
South African Company's administration. The title page of
his book has a little inset map of the Cape-to-Cairo route
under British suzerainty, complete with Rhodes's dictum, "All
that red—that's my dream."

Recent works, based on thorough archival study include
Stanford Glass, *The Matabele War* (London: Longmans,
Green & Co., Ltd., 1968), as well as T. O. Ranger, *Revolt in
Southern Rhodesia, 1896–97* (Evanston, Ill.: Northwestern
University Press, 1967), a classic which attempts to tell the
story above all from the African point of view. The best and
most readable Rhodes biography is still Basil Williams, *Cecil
Rhodes* (London: Constable & Co. Ltd., 1938). The most
recent standard work is John Gilbert Lockhart and C. M.
Woodhouse, *Cecil Rhodes: The Colossus of Southern Africa*
(New York: The Macmillan Company, 1963). Philip Mason,
*The Birth of a Dilemma: The Conquest and Settlement of
Rhodesia* (London: Oxford University Press, 1958). This
assesses the development of race relations in the terms of a
liberal imperial official who had once held high office in the
British Indian administration. The standard biography of
Johnston is Roland Oliver, *Sir Harry Johnston and the
Scramble for Africa* (London: Chatto & Windus Ltd., 1957).

Imperial Zenith and Decolonization

In addition to the general works in the first section, readers should consult Claire Palley's massive work, *The Constitu-*

tional History and Law of Southern Rhodesia, 1888–1965 with Special Reference to Imperial Control (Oxford: Clarendon Press, 1966), a magisterial study written from the British imperial and humanitarian standpoint. This is especially valuable for an examination of segregation practices in Rhodesia. The best case study of an African nationalist movement, and probably the best of its kind, is George Shepperson and Thomas Price, *Independent African; John Chilembwe and the Origins, Setting and Significance of the Nyasaland Native Rising of 1915* (Edinburgh: Edinburgh University Press, 1958). It is valuable especially for the information provided on the links between Afro-American and Central African nationalism. Robert Rotberg, *The Rise of Nationalism in Central Africa: The Making of Malawi and Zambia, 1873–1964* (Cambridge, Mass.: Harvard University Press, 1965) is an intensely committed work on the side of African nationalism, and has an excellent bibliography. A. L. Epstein, *Politics in an Urban African Community* (Manchester: Manchester University Press, 1958) is a thorough study of emergent African politics in the Copper Belt. The most recent study on the development of African nationalism during the post-conquest period is Terence O. Ranger, *The African Voice in Southern Rhodesia, 1898–1930* (London: Heinemann, 1970) which gives an eloquent account of an unknown generation of African opinion-makers.

There is a wealth of material concerning the politics of federation and decolonization. Colin Leys, *European Politics in Southern Rhodesia* (Oxford: Clarendon Press, 1959) is a sharp attack on settler politics written by a political scientist. Decolonization and its aftermath in Zambia is discussed in David C. Mulford's *Zambia: The Politics of Independence, 1957–1964* (London: Oxford University Press, 1967). The Rhodesian independence issue is dealt with by Kenneth Young, *Rhodesia and Independence* (New York: James H. Heinemann, Inc., 1967), which takes the white Rhodesian side; and by Frank Clements, *Rhodesia: A Study of the Deterioration of a White Society* (New York: Frederick A. Praeger, Inc., 1969). Mr. Clements is a former mayor of Salisbury and an opponent of Ian Smith.

Written from the African Nationalist standpoint is B. Vulindla Mtshali, *Rhodesia: Background to Conflict* (New York: Hawthorn Books, Inc., 1967); and John Day, *Interna-*

tional Nationalism: The Extra Territorial Relations of Southern Rhodesian Nationalists (London: Routledge & Kegan Paul Ltd., 1967). This gives a succinct account of the various Rhodesian nationalist movements, their internal feuds, and their attempts at military organization. The author, though sympathetic to the African nationalists, stresses their present weaknesses. Nathan M. Shamuyarira, *Crisis in Rhodesia* (London: Andre Deutsch Ltd., 1965) provides an account based on the personal experiences of a former university lecturer, who played an active part in African politics and helped to build up KANU. Donald Smith, *Rhodesia: The Problem* (London: Robert Maxwell, 1969) is a brief study written from the pro-European standpoint, particularly useful for its appendices containing various constitutional documents and a chronology. Other works strongly critical of the present white Establishment are Ndabaningi Sithole, *African Nationalism* (London: Oxford University Press, 1968); and James P. Barber, *Rhodesia: The Road to Rebellion* (London: Oxford University Press, 1967).

An economic history of Central Africa remains to be written. The story of mining in Zambia has been covered by Robert E. Baldwin, *Economic Development and Export Growth: A Study of Northern Rhodesia, 1920–1960* (Berkeley: University of California Press, 1966), whilst the history of farming has been dealt with by John A. Hellen, *Rural Economic Development in Zambia, 1890–1964* (New York: Humanities Press, Inc., 1968).

As regards special studies, there is a trilogy concerning the sociomedical history of Central Africa by Michael Gelfand, a distinguished Rhodesian physician. This comprises *Lakeside Pioneers: Socio-Medical Study of Nyasaland (1875–1920)* (Oxford: Basil Blackwell & Mott Ltd., 1964); *Northern Rhodesia in the Days of the Charter: A Medical and Social Study, 1878–1924* (Oxford: Basil Blackwell & Mott Ltd., 1961); and *Tropical Victory: An Account of the Influence of Medicine on the History of Southern Rhodesia, 1890–1923* (Cape Town: Juta and Company, 1953). A valuable study in the field of social history is Richard Gray, *The Two Nations: Aspects of the Development of Race Relations in the Rhodesias and Nyasaland* (London: Oxford University Press, 1960).

The literature of Central Africa is comparatively rich in biographical and autobiographical works concerning prominent politicians, officials, and administrators. These works differ a great deal from one another in outlook and approach, but inevitably they take the side of the man whom the book is about. They include B. K. Long, *Drummond Chaplin: His Life and Times in Africa* (London: Oxford University Press, 1941). This deals with the life of a distinguished early Rhodesian "Administrator" under the charter. Other biographical works include J. P. R. Wallis, *One Man's Hand: the Story of Sir Charles Coghlan and the Liberation of Southern Rhodesia* (London: Longmans, Green & Co., Ltd., 1950); L. H. Gann and Michael Gelfand, *Huggins of Rhodesia: The Man and His Country* (London: George Allen & Unwin, Ltd., 1964); Sir Roy Welensky, *Welensky's 4,000 Days: The Life and Death of the Federation of Rhodesia and Nyasaland* (London: William Collins Sons & Co. Ltd., 1964); Kenneth D. Kaunda, *Zambia Shall Be Free: An Autobiography* (London: William Heinemann Ltd., 1962); and Sir Robert C. Tredgold, *The Rhodesia That Was My Life* (London: George Allen & Unwin Ltd., 1968).

The anthropological literature concerning Central Africa is so extensive that we cannot refer to it here. J. F. Holleman, *Chief, Council and Commissioner: Some Problems of Government in Rhodesia* (Assen, The Netherlands: Royal van Gorcum, Ltd. on behalf of Afrika-Studiecentrum, 1968) deserves special mention because of its up-to-date sociopolitical implications. It is, in fact, the best study of "native policy" in Rhodesia. An earlier book which still has much value is Elizabeth Colson and Max Gluckman, eds., *Seven Tribes of British Central Africa* (London: Oxford University Press, 1951; Manchester University Press, 1959).

APPENDIX: SOME COMPARATIVE STATISTICAL DATA

	Malawi	Rhodesia	Zambia	United States
Area (in 1,000 square miles)	45	150	291	3,615
Agricultural Land (as a percentage of the area, 1969)	14%	17%	46%	47%
Agricultural Land per Capita (in acres)	1.0	3.2	20.6	5
Population (1969, in millions)	4.4	5.1	4.2	203.2
Annual Population Growth Rate (in percent)	2.5%	3.2%	3.1%	1.1%
Persons per Square Mile	96	34	14	56
Urban Population (in percent)	5%	18%	21%	70%
Percentage of Labor Force in Agriculture	81%	73%	81%	5%
GNP per Capita (1967 prices; data, unadjusted for differences in purchasing power between different countries. In U. S. dollars.)	52	225	297	3,966
Infant Mortality (per 1,000 live birth)	137	83	194	22
Literacy Rate (in percent)	15%	25–30%	15–20%	98%
Electricity Production per Capita (1968, KWH/year)	23	1,130	839[1]	7,100

SOURCE: Statistics and Reports Division, Office of Program and Policy Coordination. Agency for International Development. Africa: Economic Growth Trends. Washington, D.C., 1970.

[1] Includes imports from the Congo.

Index